Purpose and Work

Purpose and Work

How purpose supports motivation, productivity and performance at work

Jessica Zwaan

Publisher's note

Every possible effort has been made to ensure that the information contained in this book is accurate at the time of going to press, and the publishers and author cannot accept responsibility for any errors or omissions, however caused. No responsibility for loss or damage occasioned to any person acting, or refraining from action, as a result of the material in this publication can be accepted by the editor, the publisher or the author.

First published in Great Britain and the United States in 2026 by Kogan Page Limited

All rights reserved. No part of this publication may be reproduced, stored in a retrieval system or transmitted in any form or by any means – including electronic, mechanical, photocopying, recording or by any artificial intelligence (AI) or machine learning system – without the prior written permission of the publisher. Unauthorized use, including the use of text or images to train AI models, is strictly prohibited and may result in legal action.

Kogan Page

Kogan Page Ltd, 2nd Floor, 45 Gee Street, London EC1V 3RS, United Kingdom
Kogan Page Inc, 8 W 38th Street, Suite 902, New York, NY 10018, USA
www.koganpage.com

EU Representative (GPSR)

eucomply OÜ, Pärnu mnt 139b -14 11317, Tallinn, Estonia
www.eucompliancepartner.com

Kogan Page books are printed on paper from sustainable forests.

© Jessica Zwaan, 2026

The moral rights of the author have been asserted in accordance with the Copyright, Designs and Patents Act 1988.

ISBNs

Hardback	978 1 3986 2192 3
Paperback	978 1 3986 2194 7
Ebook	978 1 3986 2195 4

British Library Cataloguing-in-Publication Data

A CIP record for this book is available from the British Library.

Library of Congress Control Number

2025047442

Typeset by Integra Software Services, Pondicherry
Printed and bound by CPI Group (UK) Ltd, Croydon CR0 4YY

To Abby, my sister, who has gifted me with big lessons in purpose, curiosity and kindness (to myself and to others). Always with openness, always with love.
And to Lottie, I cannot wait to see what meaning you discover for yourself in this magnificent world.

CONTENTS

List of figures xi
About the author xii
Foreword by Dart Lindsley xiii
Preface xviii
Acknowledgements xxiii
List of contributors xxiv

PART ONE
Seeking purpose

1 **Our pursuit of meaning** 3
   When purpose met product 4
   The death of work, the birth of purpose 7
   The boulder up the hill 12
   Notes and further reading 14

2 **When work became a grind** 17
   Disillusionment for your viewing pleasure 18
   Founder mode 19
   The new economy of work 21
   Understanding the three economies of work 22
   Work as a 'good' 24
   Why does it matter which economy you're in? 32
   Which economy do you exist within? 35
   For us, this is urgent 40
   Notes and further reading 42

3 **Emptiness and achievement** 45
   'Wherever you go, there you are' 46
   The high achievement paradox 49
   PERMA and the limitations of work-based achievements 51
   The work orientation framework 57
   Beyond achievement: Aligning work orientation with wellbeing 62
   Notes and further reading 63

PART TWO
Career crossroads

4 Allowing for the contemplation of change 67
   Living in the present tense of purpose 69
   Viewing purpose from the present tense 72
   The false urgency of early purpose 72
   Purpose as a lifetime portfolio 74
   Allowing for new relationships with purpose frees us all 85
   Notes and further reading 87

5 The risks of leaping 88
   Recognizing the signs of career crossroads 90
   Creating systems to spot career crossroads signals 92
   Creating a culture of career transparency 94
   Beyond the one-dimensional career narrative 96
   Designing roles with purpose variability 102
   The organizational mindset shift 105
   Measuring success beyond retention 107
   The future of work as a purpose ecosystem 109
   Notes and further reading 110

PART THREE
Walking away

6 Identity and life outside work 115
   The high cost of work-as-identity 117
   Building identity frameworks across work economies 124
   Practical implementation across economies 127
   The business case for identity diversification 128
   Notes and further reading 129

7 Quiet quitting 131
   The anatomy of quiet quitting 133
   The specificity problem 134

The purpose paradox 137
Purpose-washing and its many discontents 138
Cultural recalibration or crisis? 142
These dang lazy kids 143
Work as product, employee as customer 146
A future filled with *Feierabend*! 147
Notes and further reading 148

PART FOUR
Building with purpose

8 Transforming corporate cultures 153
Companies that cracked the code 155
Work as vehicle, not a destination 156
The purpose and profit paradox 161
The science of purpose at work: What actually drives performance 162
Where most discussions miss the mark 163
The Kerr test: Are you measuring what you actually want? 165
The three-economy solution: Purpose without pretence 166
Notes and further reading 166

9 Crafting the employee experience 168
All is not lost 171
The reality-ambition gap: A framework for authentic company messaging 175
Bridging the purpose gap: When reality and aspiration have drifted 181
The purpose reconciliation process 182
When rationalization is needed 182
The courage to rebuild 184
The power of rightsizing purpose 185
Notes and further reading 185

10 Aligning values and actions 187
The values delusion: Why traditional approaches fail 188
From values to operating principles 191

Building decision-making filters that actually work 194
The implementation playbook: Making it stick 196
A call to action: Audit your own values vs operating principles 198
From poster to practice 201
Notes and further reading 201

PART FIVE
Working authentically

11 The journey is the reward 205

Designing spaces for purpose co-creation 208
Narrative spaces 211
Purpose rituals 212
Decision-making frameworks 213
Storytelling as shared meaning-making 213
Leadership's new role: Facilitators, not dictators of purpose 215
Purpose as ongoing dialogue: Building feedback loops 216
Measuring what matters: Beyond engagement surveys 218
The skill ecosystem mapping approach 219
Moving from static measurement to dynamic talent ecosystems 220
A change in our methods 221
Notes and further reading 222

Conclusion: Imagining Sisyphus fulfilled and closing thoughts 223

Index 229

LIST OF FIGURES

FIGURES

Figure 2.1	Spectrum of work from commodity to transformation	23
Figure 2.2	Core, augmented, actual product	25
Figure 5.1	T-shaped people and roles	103
Figure 9.1	Purpose triangle	173
Figure 9.2	Reality-ambition gap	175
Figure 9.3	Reality-ambition gap (large gap)	177
Figure 9.4	Reality-ambition gap (small gap)	178

ABOUT THE AUTHOR

Jessica Zwaan is a start-up and technology executive with a colourful background in operations, people and talent spanning across three continents.

She has served as Chief Operating Officer of Talentful, a global RPO for some of the most admired technology businesses across the world; Chief Operating Officer at Whereby, a fully remote video meetings company, and in executive People roles at various businesses in Europe.

For years she has worked as Chief People and Operations adviser for start-ups across Europe, helping companies unpick their most challenging people and operational work.

She has a first-class honours law degree from University of Law in London, focusing her dissertation on the legal implications of remote working cross-border. She is a diploma-member of CIPD and has a Bachelor of Communications Journalism from the University of Queensland, Australia.

Jessica can often be heard on podcasts talking about transformative approaches to operations, people and talent. She loves a good yarn about scaling leadership as much as one about your favourite fiction title. Outside of work, she is a cyclist, vegan foodie, enthusiastic dancer and terrible (but very passionate) crafter.

FOREWORD

I first encountered Jessica Zwaan as a guest on my podcast, *Work for Humans*. Most of my discussions feature experts from far-flung fields – architecture, political science, experience design – requiring me as their host to bridge their discipline to the core topic of designing better work. Reading Jessica's book, *Built for People*, I knew this interview would be different. I had found a kindred intellect. The conversation would not be about bridging differences, but about exploring the subtle variations in our shared core belief: employees are customers, and work is a product. This was an exciting discovery, one that revealed we had reached similar conclusions about what ails the modern workplace and how to build it better.

It is perhaps unsurprising that our careers led to similar conclusions. Most business roles focus on optimizing a small, singular piece of the company. In contrast, both Jessica and I spent our careers responsible for improving how organizations perform as a whole.

As a COO for a series of successful startups, Jessica's roles had required her to make strategic organizational design and investment decisions for the entire company—a problem that cannot be solved in fragments. My own experience involved a decade leading business architecture for Human Resources at Cisco Systems, where I coordinated investments in operational capabilities across the business to support new product lines and routes to market. Our respective roles demanded a systems view of business.

Since that first meeting, I have had the privilege of observing Jessica's intellectual leadership in the global community dedicated to applying a product approach to people functions (PX). I got the first glimpse when I saw Jessica organize and lead a 24-hour live-streamed charity fundraiser that assembled leading PX practitioners around the globe. We put on a good show for listeners, but it was an even greater contribution to the PX community. Many of us met each other for the first time during that event. For the first time PX felt like a movement. More recently I attended a summit for pioneering CEOs, CHROs and work design experts from across the globe. Many of the leaders I met there cited *Built for People* as a career altering introduction to designing work as a product. I noted how this gathering of leaders and experts oriented toward Jessica like iron filings toward a magnet.

As Jessica so astutely articulated in *Built for People* all companies manage three products: the core service or item sold to the traditional customer, the financial instrument for shareholders, and the product sold to the third customer – employees. That product is work, and employees are subscribers to it.

Built for People laid the work-as-product foundation, but begged the question: What do customers really want from that product? Popular books on employee motivation often start with a list of motivators. These lists vary, but nearly always include purpose or something similar.

In *Work Rules!* Lazlo Bock writes that employees want trust, freedom, authority and meaningful work; in *The Culture Code,* Coyle names safety, vulnerability, and purpose; in *Build It,* Elliot and Corey list recognition, learning, and again, purpose; in *Start with Why* Simon Sinek focuses entirely on purpose, and in *The Truth About Employee Engagement,* Lencioni focuses on what causes misery at work: anonymity, immeasurement, and the inverse of purpose, irrelevance. Daniel Pink's *Drive,* which spent 152 weeks on the NYT bestseller list, did more than any other to establish purpose as a thing everyone one wants from work. Pink describes purpose as the ability to give back to society through work.[1]

This advice seems plausible, but those of us responsible for building purpose into work face a serious challenge. What does 'purpose' even mean? Is one person's purpose the same as another's? Is Pink right that world-changing work the only work worth doing? What if my company doesn't do something world-changing?

In her book *Today was Fun,* Bree Groff recounts the story of how, while visiting NASA, President John F Kennedy asked a janitor what he did there. The man said 'Well, Mr President, I'm helping put a man on the moon.' Groff used to tell this story to highlight the importance of purpose to her consulting clients, but one day she saw her mistake. 'When you value world-changing scale as the ultimate awe-worthy goal, you simultaneously devalue human-scaled, one-on-one impact. The janitor could have responded, 'I'm taking care of this floor, in this building, in this corner of the world because it's important. I'm making life a bit cleaner and easier and happier for Anne in engineering and Joe in communications. Isn't that enough?'

The sharp-witted satirists behind the series *Silicon Valley* skewered overblown purpose when a series of founders seeking venture capital pitched the most mundane products on the planet with claims like, 'We are making the world a better place through paxos algorithms' or 'We are making the world a better place through software defined data centers for cloud computing.'

One CEO stood on stage and declared, 'I don't want to live in a world where someone else is making the world a better place than we are.'

When did purpose become the butt of jokes? The fatal flaw lies deep in the history of management.

Scientific Management, pioneered by Frederick Taylor in the early twentieth century, treated workers as machines whose output could be optimized by studying physical movements. It considered satisfaction with work a valuable outcome of efficiency, but ignored the possibility that finding work rewarding might be necessary to achieve that efficiency. It assumed that pay is the only motivator. This mechanistic view was born from an age of engineering optimism that believed all problems, including human ones, would yield to rigorous scientific analysis.

The Human Relations movement, stemming from Elton Mayo's Hawthorne Studies, challenged this by showing that productivity correlated more strongly with workers' feelings, social relationships, and the attention they received than with pay or physical conditions. The focus shifted from external motivators to internal states like attitude and morale.

This is an interesting case of two intellectual traditions setting themselves in such strong opposition to each other that they fail to notice the false assumptions upon which both are based. Despite their apparent differences, both movements share two fundamental beliefs that impede a genuine understanding of purpose.

1. The objective problem: maximizing output

Both sides framed the core objective as engineering maximum worker output. This is not a design question; it's an extraction question. A wise product designer does not ask, 'how do I build this to get the most money out of customers' pockets?' The better path to revenue is asking, 'What problem is my customer trying to solve with my product?'

As Harvard professor Kim Clark noted in his book *Leading Through*, if a company claims to be employee-centered but prioritizes profitability and shareholder value as its true purpose, employees will see that hypocrisy. When purpose is transparently used to extract value from the workforce, it inevitably comes across as cynical.

2. The nomothetic problem: seeking a general formula

Both movements assumed that within their data lay a generalizable formula – a scientific key to unlocking predictable performance across the entire workforce. This is the nomothetic practice of psychology, which seeks general laws to predict behavior.

In motivation research, dozens of diverse interview responses are often grouped into high-level concepts like 'purpose'. However, when 10 different people surveyed on purpose have 10 different personal definitions – everything from leaving a legacy for their children, meeting new people, solving puzzles, inventing new things, to simply structuring their day or getting out of the house – the resulting data is not useful for design. The word 'purpose' is far too high-level to serve as a design criterion for building purposeful work. Designers who try to build a generic purpose will always miss the mark because there are as many marks as there are people.

The path to flourishing

The ancient Greek concept of telos offers a powerful alternative. The telos of a thing is its 'final cause' – that for the sake of which something exists. The telos of a knife is to cut; the telos of a doctor is to heal the sick.

Aristotle argued that the highest telos for human beings is eudaimonia (often translated as 'human flourishing'). This is the ultimate good to which all other actions are subordinate. The act of making money, for instance, is subordinate to the higher telos of using that wealth to live a virtuous life and achieve eudaimonia.

Jessica Zwaan's book offers a way out of the current confusion by fundamentally shifting the question. She does not ask, 'How do we make employees more productive?' but rather, 'What job is work doing for different people and at different points in their lives?'

This shift – from grabbing for more extraction to true understanding – transforms everything. It acknowledges that people seek different things from work: some view it as service (a means to support life outside work), others as experience (a vehicle for growth and challenge), and still others as transformation (a calling that shapes who they become).

The mandate is not to manufacture a one-size-fits-all corporate purpose and impose it on the workforce. The mandate is to build workplaces that are honest enough to acknowledge what they actually are, and humble enough to let people decide what role work will play in their personal pursuit of eudaimonia.

As you read this book, I challenge you to ask yourself: what is the telos of your organization? Not the mission statement on the wall, but the actual 'that for the sake of which' you exist. Are you creating conditions where your people can flourish, or are you merely optimizing them for output?

Jessica has created a rare thing: a practical framework that honors both business realities and human dignity. She shows us how to build work that serves eudaimonia rather than demanding eudaimonia serve work. The meaning for the janitor at NASA was his to discover, not ours to impose. This book is your guide to creating the conditions for that discovery.

Dart Lindsley

Note

1 Hewlett, S (2009) 'Me' generation becomes the 'We' generation, 18 June, *Financial Times*

PREFACE

When I was writing *Built for People,* I have to be honest, I didn't really know what I was getting myself into. 'Writing a book is like writing 10 blogs' was something that crossed my mind quite a few times in the early days (*very foolish*). It turns out, perhaps unsurprisingly, that writing a book is a *lot* more difficult than writing 10 blogs; or, honestly, maybe even more challenging than writing 100 blogs. While I was writing *Built for People* there were many chapters, ideas, tangents, interviews, thoughts and paragraphs that were sent to the proverbial scrapheap, very likely never to be seen again. However, one idea that kept swirling around my head was the idea of the relationship with purpose and the employment 'products' we're building, particularly in modern capitalism, and the strange times we found ourselves in at the time of *Built for People*'s publication in 2023.

The years surrounding 2021 exposed a profound tension between capitalism and purpose that became impossible to ignore. As the pandemic forced a global reckoning with work, we witnessed a striking dissonance: companies proclaimed their commitment to purpose and employee wellbeing while simultaneously conducting mass lay-offs via video calls. Industry giants spoke eloquently about their world-changing missions in the same breath as they announced record profits amid widespread hurt and anguish. Many of us in Management, HR and People Operations found ourselves in the uncomfortable position of crafting purpose statements by morning and processing terminations by afternoon. This era laid bare a fundamental contradiction at the heart of our modern workplace narrative – the expectation that profit-driven entities could authentically prioritize purpose when economic pressures mounted. As millions reassessed their relationship with work during the Great Resignation, it became clear that the corporate purpose playbook wasn't just failing; it was actively breeding cynicism. Employees weren't rejecting purpose itself; they were rejecting the inauthenticity of company purpose as a corporate performance.

I was reminded of Studs Terkel's profound observation from his groundbreaking oral history, *Working*:

> Work is about a search for daily meaning as well as daily bread, for recognition as well as cash, for astonishment rather than torpor.[1]

Terkel captured this truth in 1974, yet half a century later, we're still struggling to reconcile this fundamental human need with the realities of modern capitalism. The pandemic didn't create this tension, it merely accelerated and exposed what was already there, forcing us to confront questions we'd been avoiding about the true nature of meaning in work.

My journey into these questions wasn't purely academic. Growing up in rural Queensland, Australia, my father drove trucks across Australia's vast landscapes, and my mother gradually climbed from secretarial work to professional roles in the mining industry. For them, and for many of the communities I've been part of, work wasn't just about pay checks, it was about what it could do for our family, contribution, and their place in the world. Yet somewhere along the way, as work became more abstract, more digital, more disconnected from tangible outcomes, I felt I had witnessed a loss of something essential about this relationship. It's hard for me to reconcile this personal evolution at times, as I feel incredibly privileged to live a life in the city I live in, doing work that I find incredibly intellectually challenging, while remembering where I came from and the world of work that I grew up understanding. There is a dignity in working close to the land, close to your customers, and close to your community; but as the world has evolved and globalized, I've found myself asking questions my parents perhaps never asked themselves. I'm not sure if my parents would have found the same kinds of dissatisfaction those I interviewed for this book have sometimes felt had my parents lived similar lives, or even if my folks asked themselves the same kinds of questions in silence but never out loud.

These nagging thoughts eventually became this book, or at least, the ideas behind this book. There was still so much more work to do. As I spoke with more leaders, employees and organizations about building better workplaces, I kept encountering the same paradox: companies investing heavily in purpose initiatives that employees viewed with increasing cynicism. Something wasn't adding up. The more organizations pushed purpose from the top down, the more purpose seemed to evaporate from the bottom up.

The research process itself has been transformative. I've had conversations with people across industries and roles, from C-suite executives to frontline workers, from people who'd found deep fulfilment in their careers to those who'd walked away entirely. What struck me was the universality of the hunger for meaning, regardless of position or pay grade. The paths to finding this commitment varied wildly, often contradicting the neat narratives presented in leadership books and corporate purpose statements I'd 'grown up' with in the professional sense. There were many times I left an interview with more questions than answers, and many more times I found myself quite tired of hearing my own internal narrative as I attempted to unpick their answers, as much for you as a reader as for myself as an author and practitioner. When I began interviewing people about their relationship with purpose at work, I expected to find clear patterns (foolish, yet again – you'd think I would learn!) – certain industries or roles that naturally provided more meaning, or specific purpose initiatives that consistently succeeded. Instead, I discovered something far more complex and personal. For some, purpose came through deep connection with colleagues; for others, through mastery of a craft; for still others, through alignment with organizational mission. There was no one-size-fits-all approach, no magic purpose statement or framework that could transform work for everyone.

What began as an exploration of a relatively 'simple' theme (foolish, foolish!) soon revealed itself as a much deeper question about our fundamental relationship with work. I discovered that the way we've been thinking about purpose – as something companies can manufacture and deliver to employees – was fundamentally flawed. This realization led me down unexpected paths, from the history of how our relationship with work has evolved over centuries to cutting-edge research on meaning-making in the modern workplace.

The timing of this research and writing coincided with another profound shift in how we think about work: the emergence of sophisticated AI systems capable of performing increasingly complex knowledge, creative and analytical work. As these technologies force us to reconsider what makes human work unique and valuable, the question of purpose takes on new urgency. If machines can write code, analyse data, and even generate creative content, what distinctive value do humans bring? This technological revolution offers both challenge and opportunity – pushing us to dig deeper into what truly makes work meaningful beyond mere productivity or output.

As with my first book (and one of the most joyful and enlightening parts of the author's journey), writing this book has reshaped my own thinking about purpose at work, and without sounding too grandiose, has changed some of my thinking about the path of my own life. Where I once saw purpose as a product to be optimized, I now understand it as a collective journey to be undertaken. Where I once focused primarily on how companies could articulate purpose better, I now see the critical importance of creating spaces where purpose can be discovered collectively.

This shift in perspective hasn't made me any less passionate about building great workplace experiences. If anything, it's deepened my conviction that the employee experience matters enormously. But it's changed how I think about that experience; less as something designed for employees and more as something created with them.

In many ways, this book is the natural evolution of the ideas I explored in *Built for People*. It takes the product mindset I advocated there and extends it to address one of the most complex 'problem-statements' in the modern workplace: how can we feel and develop authentic purpose in a world increasingly sceptical of corporate purpose-washing.

The structure of this book reflects this journey. We begin by exploring how our relationship with work has evolved historically, examining the forces that shaped our current expectations about purpose. We then dive into the modern workplace, revealing both the promise and pitfalls of corporate purpose initiatives. Next, we explore the crossroads many of us face in our careers, as we reconsider and sometimes reinvent our relationship with work. Finally, we move towards practical approaches for creating environments where authentic purpose can flourish – not through prescription, but through co-creation.

Wendell Berry reminds us that

> The world doesn't stop because you are in love or in mourning or in need of time to think.

The field still needs tending, the community still needs feeding.[2] Meaning in work is found when it serves the life of the world. Throughout this exploration, I've been continually drawn back to this essential truth: purpose emerges most naturally when we connect our daily efforts to the lives they touch and the communities they serve. In our increasingly complex and abstract economy, finding these connections requires new approaches, new structures, and new conversations. Authenticity is a word that has appeared over and over. This desire for authentic purpose reflects a fundamental human need to align our external actions with our internal values – to feel that what we do reflects who we are and why we are here on this earth. Yet authenticity in the workplace is extraordinarily difficult to achieve, particularly because of the inherent power dynamics that structure our professional relationships. For leaders, the challenge is uniquely complex. They're caught in a paradox: expected to be vulnerable and authentic while simultaneously maintaining the authority and certainty their roles demand. Several executives I interviewed described feeling trapped in a performance, worried that showing genuine doubt or uncertainty might undermine their effectiveness or even their position. I myself have felt the pull of authenticity and career, something I know is felt more acutely in folks from marginalized communities or those who don't see themselves frequently represented. This creates a particular kind of organizational doublespeak, where authenticity is celebrated in corporate values statements but often subtly punished in practice. Employees quickly learn to perform a carefully calibrated version of 'authenticity' that doesn't threaten existing power structures. Most fundamentally, it means recognizing that authentic purpose can only flourish in environments where power is used to amplify voices rather than direct them.

My hope is that this book offers both a critical perspective on how we've approached purpose in the past and a practical path forward for creating workplaces where meaning can flourish authentically. Not by manufacturing purpose, but by creating the conditions where it can emerge naturally through connection, contribution and collective meaning-making.

While speaking on his podcast, *Work for Humans*, my friend (and author of the Foreword to this book) Dart Lindsley, asked me, 'What job does your job do for you?' a question which, at the time and despite all of my big talk about the productizing work, had stumped me… and even now after writing an entire *second* book with this topic front of mind, I find it complex to get a succinct answer for myself. In writing this I wanted to explore my own relationship with purpose, work and the job my job does for me, while also giving some meaningful frameworks for you to think about and use to break away from the dissonance and longing we can feel when relating our own personal sense of purpose and fulfilment to work.

In short, the job my job does for me is to connect me to wonderful new people, encourages me to explore new ideas, and offers a life yielding an abundance of joy, which may have otherwise remained unreachable to someone of my background. While you read this book, I'd love you to not only be thinking about how these principles, frameworks and real-world examples apply to your role as a manager, a leader, or a people-professional; but also that you take some time to ask yourself, '*What job is my job doing for me?*'

Notes

1 Terkel, S (1974) *Working: People talk about what they do all day and how they feel about what they do*, Pantheon Books, New York, p. 13
2 Berry, W (2000) *Jayber Crow*. Counterpoint, Washington, DC, p. 133

ACKNOWLEDGEMENTS

A list too long to possibly encompass all of the gratitude I want to share!

I would like to send a thank you to everyone who read, contributed, brainstormed, deliberated, argued, or inspired the work in this book. There are too many people to list (a thing I have to say because I will inevitably miss someone), but I would like to thank Dart Lindsley by name. A person who has been an incredible inspiration for me ever since I had the pleasure of meeting him.

Abbie Pugh for her incredible, vibrant brain which never ceased to describe a new thread I was excited to explore. Chris Abbass for allowing me the space and time to write this book while working in his team.

Abby Hayes, Mum and Dad, Kevin Hanna, Emory Sullivan, who love me more than I can understand, but am grateful for every day.

The team at Kogan Page: Lucy and Joe. It's been a joy and a privilege to work with you and the team again.

My final acknowledgement is for my aunty, Dr Jeanne McConachie, who has been a source of inspiration to me as I move through every stage of my life – I hope I make you proud.

LIST OF CONTRIBUTORS

Dart Lindsley, Foreword
Huw Slater, Interview
Emory Sullivan, Interview
Liz Hagearty, Interview
Chris Abbass, Interview
Ben Gallacher, Interview
Sophie Johnson, Interview
Simon Sparks, Interview
Genevieve Nathwani, Interview
Abbie Pugh, Interview
Howard Wu, Interview
Andy Whitlock, Interview
Ben Gately, Interview
Melanie Naranjo, Interview
Olivia Johnson, Interview

PART ONE

Seeking purpose

1

Our pursuit of meaning

> I think most of us are looking for a calling, not a job. Most of us... have jobs that are too small for our spirit.[1]

When steelworker Mike Lefevre spoke these words to Studs Terkel for his 1974 landmark oral history *Working*, he couldn't have known how prophetic they would become.

In the decades since, we've built an entire industry around making jobs feel bigger than they are – not always by actually expanding their scope or meaning (and in fact many of our jobs have become smaller and more optimized) but by wrapping jobs in layers of carefully crafted purpose like fondant on a cake. I've been one of these people doing the wrapping. I've spent hours refining an employee value proposition centred around reaching a company's lofty mission, I've interviewed candidates to eke out their alignment with our shared purpose, and now I find myself wondering if it was time well spent.

I was born in a small rural town in Central Queensland, Australia, the kind of place where life is measured by how hard you work while on shift and, contradictorily, also by how many hours you can spend off the clock fishing, surfing or hosting barbecues. My mother was one of 13 children, my father one of 10, and they raised us with the understanding that nothing comes easy and nothing is given. My parents didn't grow up having much; they were both from low-income working-class families, two of many in communities built on fishing, mining and agriculture. My father drove trucks, criss-crossing the country's wide, empty landscapes, while my mother spent her days behind a desk in the mining industry, grinding for years to move from secretarial work to more professional roles as the decades rolled on. The idea that one may grow up having a spectrum (or even more than a handful) of choices in work and life was a luxury, and one that I was consistently reminded to aim for. So, I did. I was the first in my family to go to university, a first-generation tertiary student navigating a world my parents never imagined for themselves. Now, with two degrees, more than a decade living internationally, and a published book under my belt (two now, I suppose!), I proudly write this from New York City, far from those dusty roads of the Central Queensland I still love, and all the while I still feel the pull of my history defining my relationship with work – what it gives, and what it takes.

When purpose met product

The workplace today has become a modern altar of contrived significance, where well-meaning professionals in People Operations teams (we shan't call it Human Resources anymore – too dehumanizing!) shepherd us through onboarding, training and all-hands meetings that preach our mission statements and company purposes. Throughout the research for this book, I've seen first-hand how we've succeeded and failed. The folks I have interviewed for this work have been told to be authentic, but only in prescribed ways. To bring their whole selves to work, but only the parts that fit neatly into corporate culture. To find purpose in our labour, but only if that purpose aligns with quarterly targets. They have reconsidered careers, left long-term professions, and held deep regrets about the choices they've made. Together their stories can tell us something about the way we've used purpose to incentivize work, and where we've missed the forest through the trees.

Over the years I've been a passionate advocate of using the language given to us by Marketing and Product. Like many in HR, I fell hard for Simon Sinek's prolific advice about 'starting with "why"' – it seemed to offer a neat solution to the messy problem of employee motivation.[2] We took ancient wisdom about meaningful work and purpose, repackaged it in contemporary corporate language, and transformed it into marketable modules and frameworks that could be measured in engagement surveys and quarterly reports.

What emerged was an entire industry dedicated to 'manufacturing meaning'. We spent millions on consultants who taught us to craft purpose statements, on programmes that promised to align personal values with company missions, and on engagement initiatives that turned meaning into metrics. We built elaborate frameworks to better communicate and motivate our employees through our company purpose, because we'd been told – and had come to believe – that purpose wasn't just nice to have, but what people fundamentally needed to feel value in their work. Looking back now, I wonder if we were solving, in part at least, our own need to feel purposeful in HR, rather than meeting employees where they actually were.

This is the story of how we got here – how we transformed from a society that understood work as a means of survival into one that demands our jobs be the primary source of our life's meaning. It's about Silicon Valley's ping-pong tables and meditation rooms, about how our office became the modern equivalent of our community, and how 'workplace culture' became a commodity to be bought, sold and optimized.

But more than that, it's about what we've lost sight of in this transformation, and what we might yet recover if we're brave enough to look beyond the 'purpose industrial complex' that has defined our relationship with work in the 2010s and 2020s. Mike Lefevre was right – for many of us our jobs are too small for our spirits. But perhaps the solution isn't to inflate our jobs with artificial purpose, but to finally admit that work doesn't have to be everything, and as business owners and leaders, we can create a new type of relationship with purpose at work that genuinely brings the work-life connection we crave.

In my first book, *Built for People*, I analogized work to a product; one which is bought and sold on the free market of employee experience. I still believe strongly in this methodology, but I want to examine some of the more controversial elements of this approach that I didn't share in *Built for People*. Work may well be a product, but not all products sell purpose and meaning. Some are for utility, some are for experience, and, of course, some can transform your life. But not all. With that having been said, on the free market of anything, if there are gains to be made, we will find new ways to market our product, where perhaps it's not truthful, viable or necessary.

And there *are* gains. Research proves that teams who feel engaged share a sense of purpose in their work. Survey data from Gallup, McKinsey and Deloitte suggests that employees who report feeling a sense of purpose at work also tend to report higher levels of engagement.[3,4,5] However, the relationship between purpose and engagement is complex and likely bidirectional – engaged employees may be more likely to find purpose in their work, and those who find purpose may become more engaged. Although I always understood that purpose was important, I don't think I had been clear on how precisely to encourage, communicate, or leverage it at scale. This is a particularly difficult challenge in workplaces where the connection to purpose can feel abstract or tenuous – *how can we possibly align an individual's purpose, a life's work, with revolutionizing banking APIs or cloud DevOps?!*

> Gallup's Q[12] Meta-Analysis (2020) found that 'mission and purpose' is one of the 12 key elements that correlates with higher employee engagement. However, the causation direction isn't clear – do engaged employees find more purpose, or does purpose drive engagement? In McKinsey Quarterly (2020) 'Help your employees find purpose – or watch them leave', 70 per cent of employees said their sense of purpose is largely defined by work. Deloitte's 2020 'Global Human Capital Trends' survey found that 79 per cent of organizations that had a clear purpose reported strong engagement during Covid-19.

I write this book acutely aware of my limitations. Despite my best efforts, my research and findings are inevitably shaped by Western and colonial perspectives. Much of the available research itself carries this inherent bias. I acknowledge that for billions of people throughout history and today, work was never – and may never be – a matter of choice, purpose, inspiration, or community. The dark legacy of slavery, poverty and forced labour continues to shape lives and communities globally, but is not covered in this work you're reading today.

> For decades, studies – which supposedly revealed universal truths about human nature – drew their data almost exclusively from American college students. The researchers dubbed this sample population 'WEIRD' – Western, educated, industrialized, rich and democratic. The nomenclature wasn't just clever; the implicit assumption had been that either humans don't meaningfully vary across populations (they do), or that these standard subjects were somehow representative of our entire species (they weren't).[6]

Through this work, I've encountered many cultures that maintain a far more harmonious relationship with purpose and labour than the Western paradigm I was raised in. I include these perspectives where I feel qualified to do so, but I know there are many voices and experiences I cannot adequately represent. I write from a position of immense privilege. This privilege grants me the opportunity to examine how our relationship with work has evolved, but it also limits my view. There are countless stories and perspectives that remain beyond my reach, and I would be remiss not to acknowledge these blind spots before I begin with our long history of work and purpose.

The death of work, the birth of purpose

For centuries, work in the West was a communal act, rooted in survival and shared ambition. People tilled fields, built homes and raised children in muddled, indistinguishable segments of their time in order to sustain themselves, their families and society around them. Labour was life, woven into the fabric of daily existence, and meaning came from knowing your efforts supported the family and your community. Aristotle wrote in *Politics* (c. 350 BCE) that 'The end of labour is to gain leisure'.[7] He wasn't suggesting idleness, but rather that work should serve the whole of life and community, not dominate it.

As societies grew and industrialized, our connections with work and community began to fray. The rise of factories and wage labour distanced workers from the fruits of their efforts. Jobs became commodities, and people found themselves exchanging time for a pay cheque, often without a deeper sense of connection to purpose. The work was repetitive, the rewards abstract, and the sense of meaning evaporated as production lines replaced community-driven labour.[8]

The Industrial Revolution started around 1750 when some extremely clever people invented machines that could do the work of 10 people. Then, by the 1780s, the British countryside was getting a forced makeover through the enclosure movement[9] – imagine your MP (Member of Parliament) suddenly deciding your communal grazing land would look much better as private property, *thank you very much*. Peasants, along with their sheep and their centuries-old ways of life, were essentially forced to trek to the cities and mines in search of – purely metaphorically as you can imagine – greener pastures. Perhaps most powerfully, there's the anonymous folk poem that appeared in many villages during the Parliamentary Enclosure period (c. 1780s):

> *The law locks up the man or woman*
> *Who steals the goose from off the common*
> *But leaves the greater villain loose*
> *Who steals the common from the goose*[10]

The mid-1800s brought integrated factories where workers became as interchangeable as the parts that they were manufacturing, and by the 1870s Frederick Taylor was timing people with stopwatches to make sure they didn't waste precious seconds scratching their nose or, heaven forbid, thinking (an archetype we probably can all identify in our own careers). Taylor presented that the worker's conscious 'restriction of output' or 'soldiering' has always been the original sin of the working class.[11] 'Soldiering' in this instance refers to workers deliberately working at a slower pace than they're capable of; considered a form of passive resistance against management that emerged during the Industrial Revolution.

Friedrich Engels, who lived in Manchester from 1842 to 1844, provided this eyewitness account: 'I have seen hundreds of workers in Manchester trudging through black mud a foot deep, while a thick cloud of coal smoke hung over the city like an umbrella. These people have left their hearths in the countryside not from choice, but from necessity… The machines which were supposed to be a blessing have become their curse.'[12]

These voices remind us that the shift from agricultural to industrial work wasn't just an economic transition – it was a fundamental reimagining of how humans related to their labour, their communities, and their sense of purpose.

The *coup de grâce* came in 1913 when Henry Ford's assembly line turned human beings into components of a great mechanical beast, each person performing the same tiny task over and over to maximize the efficiency of the industrial output. The village cobbler who once crafted an entire shoe over the course of a few days now spent 12 hours a day attaching the same eyelet to the same boot, never seeing the finished product or, quite possibly, the sun.

In the 20th century, William H Whyte's *The Organization Man* (1956) captured how corporate culture became all-encompassing: 'The organization man is the most conspicuous example, but he is only one, for the collectivization so visible in the corporation has affected almost every field of work.'[13] The idea of 'job for life' emerged – people would say 'I'm a Ford man', or 'I'm a BP man', their entire identity wrapped in corporate belonging. These weren't just jobs; they were markers of social status, moral character, and community standing. Your company didn't just employ you – it was something that *defined* you. You may have lived in a company town, or you may have retired with 50 years' service to the same business; these were the behaviours of the workplace rooted in the times of the organization man.

My parents were, in many ways, these kinds of people. Both of them taught me that your job was a long-term commitment, and that what you were at work was as important in many ways as your character. My father's identity as a truck driver wasn't just about operating heavy vehicles across Australia's vast distances – it was about being reliable, trustworthy, someone who could be counted on to deliver. My mother's gradual climb from secretary to professional roles in the mining industry wasn't just career progression – it was her testament to hard work, perseverance and the virtue of staying loyal. Their generation saw job-hopping as somewhere between inappropriate and dangerous; changing companies was like changing families, communities or towns. Folks who moved often were considered to be running from something, unreliable, or aimless.

This wasn't just about economic security – though that was certainly part of it. It was about belonging to something larger than yourself, about having your place in the world defined by your contribution to a particular organization. The company picnics, the long-service awards, the family days – these weren't just perks, they were rituals that reinforced the powerful bond between worker and workplace. It was rooted in the belief that loyalty would be rewarded with security – a kind of unspoken corporate covenant.

In the 70s, Terkel documented the fracturing of this identity: *'Work is about a search for daily meaning as well as daily bread, for recognition as well as cash, for astonishment rather than torpor; in short, for a sort of life rather than a Monday through Friday sort of dying.'*[14]

Just under a decade later, in 1983, Arlie Hochschildz introduced in *The Managed Heart* how emotional labour became part of work identity – we weren't just selling our time and skills, but our personalities and feelings.[15] Somewhere along the line, companies realized they could package and sell raw human emotional labour: flight attendants and nurses were being industrially trained to perform warmth on demand, and lawyers to perform ruthlessness. By the 1980s, the majority of the workforce was performing this orchestrated emotional performance, with companies industrializing owning and managing their workers' feelings through specific training and behavioural performance metrics. Hochschildz argues that people became separated from their own emotional truth – their expressions and feelings were now company assets rather than authentic human responses – creating a profound disconnection from ourselves that we're still grappling with today. Personally, I don't take such a strong position, I believe that some folks find labour of the emotional, intellectual, physical, creative kind (or a mix of the four) more appealing, and – whether we like it or not – we must find a way to maximize the relationship between our preferences, our passions, and what is profitable. Either way, I do agree with much of his writing on the capitalizing of emotional labour, which was written before even my birth, let alone my entering the workforce.

Then, more clever people invented a new machine to do the work of one hundred people: the computer. Depending on who you believe, military, science or capital inspired the next great frontier of human progress.[16] Throughout it all, our need for meaning in work never faded and, with the invention of start-ups fuelled by Daniel Pink's *Drive*, the 21st century brought a renewed search for fulfilment, as capitalism and consumption gained momentum on Wall Street and online dotcom. Companies like Google and Facebook began to present their company purpose front and centre to our employee value proposition: harmonizing together from Silicon Valley, a choir of soon-to-be-tech giants sang, 'together we're going to change the world'.[17]

In Fred Turner's *From Counterculture to Cyberculture* he posits:

> The Bay Area's computing industry [having] long embraced a rhetoric of democratic empowerment and collaborative work inherited from both the region's Cold War research culture and its counter-cultural past.

Silicon Valley didn't just create technology; it created a new mythology of work – one where 'changing the world' and making money weren't just compatible, but synonymous. This wasn't the old corporate bargain of trading time for security; this was a promise of personal transformation alongside professional success.

It worked. We bought it. For my entire professional life the messages on mission and purpose as being central to employee engagement were clear and resonant. Josh Bersin published that purpose-driven companies have a whopping 40 per cent higher level of workforce retention than their competitors.[18] SHRM reported that 73 per cent of employees who say they work at a 'purpose-driven' company are engaged, compared to just 23 per cent at companies that aren't.[19] McKinsey told us that employees who live their purpose at work are four times more likely to report higher engagement levels.[20] The statistics seemed to pile up, all pointing to the same conclusion: purpose wasn't just good for the soul, it was good for business.

HR departments worldwide embraced this new perspective with almost religious fervour. We built elaborate purpose frameworks, created mission-aligned value propositions and developed interview questions designed to probe candidates' purpose-alignment. The tech industry's purpose-driven approach became a template for other sectors, spreading from Silicon Valley start-ups to traditional corporations eager to attract and retain talent in an increasingly competitive market. What started as a counter-cultural movement had become the new corporate orthodoxy.

The year 2020 changed something for many of us. As billions of us sat isolated in our homes, watching our computer screens become portals to an increasingly uncertain and dangerous world, the corporate narratives about purpose began to ring hollow. The pandemic stripped away the carefully constructed office cultures, the free snacks and the happy hour drinks, leaving us alone with our spreadsheets, our thoughts, our children, our hobbies. Companies that had trumpeted their world-changing missions found themselves struggling to justify why their employees should risk their health for quarterly targets. The grand narratives of Silicon Valley purpose began to compete with more immediate questions of wellbeing, family and what really matters when the world seems to be falling apart. As Annie Auerbach highlighted in *Flex* (2021), the pandemic didn't change everything – it just crystallized what was already changing.[21] What emerged was a workforce more willing to question whether corporate purpose could truly fill the meaning-shaped hole in our modern working lives.

People sought purpose beyond the nine to five – whether through creative industries, entrepreneurship or professions that promised to make a difference. The pandemic had forced us to confront our mortality and reassess our values, leading to what LinkedIn feeds breathlessly dubbed 'The Great Reflection' (or Resignation). Millions of workers, armed with savings from lockdown and a renewed sense of life's brevity, began voting with their feet. They left stable corporate jobs to become pottery artists, life coaches, sustainable fashion designers and start-up founders. The promise of purpose became more alluring than the guarantee of a pension that may never eventuate.

Paradoxically, we in management dug our heels into work-purpose even deeper, despite its increasingly apparent failings and hypocrisies. Companies responded to mass exits by doubling down on their mission statements, rolling out wellness programmes, and promising even grander visions of workplace meaning. CEOs penned LinkedIn posts about authentic leadership and mission-centric workplaces. The corporate world seemed to believe that if the medicine wasn't working, the solution was a larger dose. Even as evidence mounted that workers were leaving for their families and flexibility rather than more company purpose, organizations continued to prescribe meaning as the cure for all workplace ills. It was as if, having built our professional culture around the promise of purpose, we couldn't admit that perhaps we'd been selling a solution to the wrong problem.

Then, when I least expected it, I got a text that a group of new, very, very clever people had invented a machine that does the work of *thousands, maybe even millions*, of people and its name was ChatGPT. Large language models burst into our collective consciousness with exponential growth and intelligence, forcing us to confront questions about purpose and work that we'd been dodging for decades. This isn't just another piece of workplace software. It's becoming an existential awakening in corporate form.

The timing was uncanny. Just as we were questioning our relationship with corporate purpose, artificial intelligence arrived to question our relationship with work itself, let alone our relationship with intelligence and creation. We'd spent centuries moving from manual labour to knowledge work, carefully constructing our professional identities around our ability to think, write, analyse and create. Now, algorithms could generate marketing copy, write code, analyse data and even engage in creative work – all those tasks we'd convinced ourselves were uniquely human.

The irony wasn't lost on those of us in People and HR roles. We'd spent years helping organizations craft purpose statements and mission declarations, only to find ourselves grappling with an innovation that threatened to redefine the very nature of human work. As Kai-Fu Lee observed in *AI 2041*, the question isn't just what jobs AI will take, but what purpose we'll create for ourselves when traditional work is transformed.[22]

Today, the challenge remains to me to be worryingly similar to what it was in 1750: how to reclaim meaning in a world where work is often seen as a transaction rather than a deeply human, community-driven endeavour. The hunger for significance in what we do today speaks to a truth that has endured across time – the human desire to contribute, to be part of something larger than ourselves, has not and will not change.

The boulder up the hill

The myth of Sisyphus offers perhaps the most enduring metaphor for modern work ever conceived. For those unfamiliar with the Greek myth, Sisyphus was condemned by the gods to spend eternity rolling a boulder up a mountain, only to watch it roll back down each time he neared the summit. This punishment was specifically designed by the gods to be futile – the ultimate form of meaningless labour.

Albert Camus famously reimagined Sisyphus as the archetypal modern worker in his 1942 essay *The Myth of Sisyphus*, where he famously declared, 'One must imagine Sisyphus happy.'[23] This wasn't mere philosophical wishful thinking, Camus was grappling with how humans find ways to endure and even find satisfaction in repetitive labour. The assembly line worker, the data entry clerk, the customer service representative – all modern Sisyphuses, pushing their own boulders up their own mountains, hour after hour, day after day, year after year.

What's particularly fascinating is how contemporary work has managed to make Sisyphus's condition even more absurd. At least Sisyphus could see his boulder and mountain; they were tangible, physical things. Today's knowledge workers push invisible boulders up metaphorical mountains, creating PowerPoint decks that will be forgotten, sending emails that will never be read, generating reports that disappear into digital archives. We've somehow managed to make Sisyphus's labour more abstract while keeping it just as endless. The gods, one imagines, would be impressed by our innovation in futility.

I am fascinated by work. I grew up in a world where work was one very discrete and rigid thing; choiceless, narrow, geographic, hereditary. Throughout my life I've discovered it could be anything but; it is a thriving marketplace from which the privileged can shop and derive any kind of reward. I am also fascinated by problems, and purpose at work feels like one of the biggest ones to crack before we can truly understand how to change it for the better. It may feel this book takes a more cynical lens to work, but that is only because I've tried hard to shape a question that is challenging to face head on; can we finally conquer, or should we ignore, the role of purpose in work?

After spending years helping build positive workplace cultures and arguing that work should be treated as a carefully crafted product, it might appear contradictory to now question the very foundations of how we've constructed modern work. But here's the thing: after watching the tech industry's purpose-driven facade crack under the pressure of a pandemic, after seeing AI make us question what 'knowledge work' even means, and after witnessing thousands of purpose-aligned employees being laid off via email, I couldn't ignore the Sisyphean nature of what we've built. This isn't a repudiation of *Built for People* – I still believe in creating better workplaces. But it's time for some honest conversations about what we in leadership, HR and People Operations can actually do to solve what might be the biggest product challenge we've ever faced: how to design work that meets people's real needs, not just their aspirational ones.

If *Built for People* was about how to design better work environments, this book is about fundamentally rethinking what we're designing them for. Maybe we don't need to build more purpose-washing or hollow wellness programmes to feed our desire for significance and contribution. Maybe what we need is to understand that for some people, work is just work – and that's okay. For others, it's a calling – and that's okay too. Our job isn't to force everyone into the same purpose-driven mould, but to create flexible systems that allow for different relationships with work. This book is about how HR teams can move from being purpose evangelists to becoming architects of choice, creating workplaces that accommodate both the Sisyphuses who've found happiness in their boulder-pushing and those who would rather find their meaning on another hill.

Notes and further reading

1 Terkel, S (1974) *Working: People talk about what they do all day and how they feel about what they do*, Pantheon Books, New York, p. 448
2 Sinek, S (2009) *Start with Why: How great leaders inspire everyone to take action*, Portfolio, New York
3 Gallup (2020) Q^{12} meta-analysis of employee engagement and team performance. Gallup Internal Report (summary findings published 2020). (Note: This includes 'mission or purpose of my company makes me feel my job is important' as one of the 12 elements)
4 McKinsey & Company (2021) Help your employees find purpose – or watch them leave, McKinsey Quarterly, 5 April. (Draws on an August 2020 survey of 1,021 US workers; notes that about 70 per cent of employees say their sense of purpose is largely defined by work)
5 Deloitte (2020) 2020 Global Human Capital Trends: The social enterprise at work. (Highlights integration of purpose into organizational DNA – 'purpose, potential and perspective' are core attributes – and emphasizes embedding meaning, belonging and wellbeing into daily work)
6 Henrich, J, Heine, S J and Norenzayan, A (2010) The weirdest people in the world?, *Behavioral and Brain Sciences*, 33(2–3), 61–83. doi:10.1017/S0140525X0999152X (archived at https://perma.cc/S5EV-HGSX)
7 Aristotle (c. 350 BCE) *Politics*. Translated by B Jowett. https://classics.mit.edu/Aristotle/politics.html (archived at https://perma.cc/GH62-TCTG)
8 Adam Smith in *The Wealth of Nations* (1776) observed this transformation, noting how division of labour, while efficient, could lead to workers becoming 'as stupid and ignorant as it is possible for a human creature to become' because their work was reduced to a few simple operations. Smith, A (1776) *An Inquiry into the Nature and Causes of the Wealth of Nations,* Book V, Chapter 1, Part III, Article 2, Strahan, W and Cadell, T, London

9   Staff (2024) Enclosure (Inclosure). Practical Law UK Glossary w-022-3305. Thomson Reuters Practical Law
10 McKie, D (2006) *Riding Route 94: An accidental journey through the story of Britain*, Atlantic Books, London
11 Taylor, F W (1911) *The Principles of Scientific Management*, Harper, New York
12 Coney, B (2020) In working-class Manchester, Friedrich Engels became a revolutionary, *Jacobin*, 28 November. (Quotes Engels observing: 'I have seen hundreds of workers in Manchester trudging through black mud a foot deep, while a thick cloud of coal smoke hung over the city like an umbrella. These people have left their hearths in the countryside not from choice, but from necessity… The machines which were supposed to be a blessing have become their curse.')
13 Whyte, W H (1956) *The Organization Man*, Simon & Schuster, New York, p. 7
14 Terkel, S (1974) *Working: People talk about what they do all day and how they feel about what they do.* Pantheon Books, New York, p. xiii
15 Hochschild, A R (1983) *The Managed Heart: Commercialization of human feeling*, University of California Press, Berkley
16 To be fair to the computer, the clearest scholarly work its origins come from are Paul Ceruzzi's *A History of Modern Computing* and Martin Campbell-Kelly's *Computer: A history of the information machine*. Both of these sources serve to challenge the simplification of 'military, science, or capital' as I've presented it here. Ceruzzi, P E (2003) *A History of Modern Computing*, 2nd edn. MIT Press, Cambridge, MA
    More accurately and with more detail: Janet Abbate's *Inventing the Internet* (1999) documents how the narrative of military origins has been somewhat overstated. While ENIAC and Colossus were important military projects, parallel developments were happening in academia and research labs. Campbell-Kelly, M and Aspray, W (2004) *Computer: A history of the information machine.* 2nd edn., Westview Press, Boulder, CO
    David Alan Grier's *When Computers Were Human* (2005) reveals that many early computing developments came from the need to process mathematical tables for navigation, engineering, and science – showing how the scientific need predated military applications. Abbate, J (1999) *Inventing the Internet*, MIT Press, Cambridge, MA
17 Fred Turner's *From Counterculture to Cyberculture* (2006) traces how Silicon Valley's corporate culture emerged from 1960s counter-cultural ideals about changing the world, specifically documenting how tech companies adopted this language of purpose and mission. Turner, F (2006) *From Counterculture to Cyberculture; Stewart Brand, the Whole Earth Network, and the Rise of Digital Utopianism*, University of Chicago Press, Chicago

18 Though I should add that this statistic should be treated with appropriate scepticism as the methodology isn't fully clear. Bersin, J (2016) *Purpose-driven companies evolve faster and have higher retention*, Josh Bersin, 16 January. https://joshbersin.com/2016/01/purpose-driven-companies-evolve-faster-and-have-higher-retention (archived at https://perma.cc/CW4H-NQVR)

19 SHRM (2017) Employees are just not that into their jobs, *Society for Human Resource Management*, 4 April. www.shrm.org/resourcesandtools/hr-topics/employee-relations/pages/employees-are-just-not-that-into-their-jobs.aspx (archived at https://perma.cc/6HE7-4SXS)

20 McKinsey & Company (2021) Help your employees find purpose – or watch them leave, McKinsey Quarterly, 5 April. www.mckinsey.com/capabilities/people-and-organizational-performance/our-insights/help-your-employees-find-purpose-or-watch-them-leave (archived at https://perma.cc/Y9PE-PHJK)

21 Auerbach, A (2021) *Flex: Reinventing work for a smarter, happier life*, HarperCollins, London

22 Lee, K-F and Qiufan, C (2021) *AI 2041: Ten visions for our future*. Currency, New York

23 Camus, A (1942) *The Myth of Sisyphus*. Translated by J O'Brien. Vintage International, New York, p. 123

2

When work became a grind

Your phone buzzes. You look away from Slack for just a moment. Another TikTok notification. This time it's a twenty-something in business casual dress, dramatically lip-syncing about their soul-crushing corporate job while pretending to answer emails. The hashtag: #corporatetok. Eight million views. In the comments, thousands of young professionals share their own tales of workplace ennui. Scroll further and you find countless memes about 'living for the weekend', a few jokes about crying in bathroom stalls, and a self-recorded rant about the now-ubiquitous phrase 'quiet quitting' (which we will explore with a little sass included – *why not?!* – in Chapter 7).

A senior professional in the tech industry who I interviewed for this book shared with me, while also asking for anonymity, that they find themselves, 'scrolling these spaces to regain a sense of perspective' as they try to grapple with how to manage their younger-generation teams. It reminds me of a parent trying to feed their children vegetables after years of watching cartoons telling them that broccoli is disgusting.

Together we've developed an entire cultural language around the meaninglessness of work, a shared vocabulary of despair that often seems to be equal parts comedy as it is a cry for help. The modern worker is expected to participate in this theatre of cynicism, where admitting you find purpose in your job is almost suspicious, and confessing you actually like what you do feels somehow naive on one end, and near to bootlicking on the other. Yet this collective performance of purposelessness isn't just harmless venting – it's a self-fulfilling prophecy that shapes how we experience, design and value work itself. As we mindlessly share that next 'corporate burnout' meme, it makes me pause to consider if we are documenting a broken system, or are helping to break it.

Disillusionment for your viewing pleasure

The image of soul-crushing corporate work has been a cultural touchstone for generations. From Charlie Chaplin's *Modern Times* (1936) showing workers literally consumed by machinery,[1] to the cubicle dystopia of *The Apartment* (1960),[2] pop culture has long portrayed work as a dehumanizing grind. But perhaps nothing captured corporate ennui quite like *Office Space* (1999), where Peter Gibbons memorably declares, 'We don't have a lot of time on this earth [...] Human beings were not meant to sit in little cubicles staring at computer screens all day.'[3] The film became a cultural watershed, giving voice to a generation's frustration with quarterly reports and middle-management absurdity.

The 2000s brought us *The Office* (both UK and US versions), which turned workplace tedium into must-watch television, satirically pinching us all where it hurt.[4] Dunder Mifflin sells paper, they don't manufacture paper, they are essentially middlemen in the economic value chain, of which – when presented to us plainly – it is impossible not to see the futility. *Sysiphus rolls the boulder back up the hill*. These aren't just comedies – they are documentaries of despair, breaking the fourth wall and stepping into our zeitgeist. We enjoy them because we see ourselves in them, as workers trapped in systems whose underlying absurdity becomes crystal clear (and a little painful) when viewed through the lens of satire.

The artistry of these workplace comedies lies in their ability to hold up a mirror to our own experiences while highlighting the often Kafkaesque nature of modern corporate culture. When Peter Gibbons in *Office Space* mindlessly repeats 'I have eight different bosses', or when Jim Halpert stares knowingly at the camera after another of Dwight's bureaucratic tirades, we laugh because we intimately understand these moments. We've lived them. The comedy stems not just from clever writing or performances, but from the profound recognition of our own participation in systems that, when examined closely, seem to exist at times only to perpetuate themselves.

This resonance goes beyond simple workplace frustrations. These shows tap into a deeper existential question about meaning in modern capitalism. Watching Michael Scott desperately try to imbue importance into selling paper, we're confronted with the artificial constructs that govern our own professional lives. The middle management enthusiastically announcing a failure as a success, arbitrary meetings, corporate buzzwords – all of these become subjects of mockery because they represent the layers of abstraction that separate us from meaningful work.

And yet, these shows also capture something profoundly human in our response to this absurdity. The friendships formed, the small acts of rebellion, the moments of genuine connection – these emerge as ways we cope with and find meaning despite the system's futility. It's where we can see the purpose lie within the character's lives, and I am a genuine believer that life and truth is found in art, so I was inclined to believe that, when entering my research for this book, that I would find a kernel of truth in this abstraction.

Social media transformed this narrative from entertainment to shared experience. Sites like *Corporate Bro* on Instagram (2.5 million followers)[5] and Reddit's /r/antiwork (2.7 million members)[6] turned corporate disillusionment into memes, while TikTok's #corporatetok garnered billions of views by turning workplace despair into bite-sized content. The popularity of phrases like Sunday scaries, bare minimum Mondays, and quiet quitting suggests we've developed an entire community lexicon around work-related dread. Together, these communities have forged a community meta-analysis of the contradictions, absurdity and cynicism I found in my research when I began to explore the idea of purpose at work in modern times.

Founder mode

Perhaps no surprises here given the platform's changes over the recent years, but there's been a notable shift in 'tech-founder Twitter' discourse from 2020 to 2024, moving from celebrating company culture and purpose, to being increasingly sceptical of corporate attempts to provide meaning through work, or increasingly traditional, even draconian, in their descriptions of their employees' commitment to work.

Ed Zitron (on X, formerly Twitter, as @edzitron) is a media relations firm founder and writer for publications including *VICE* and *Business Insider*. He's become particularly known for his sharp criticism of corporate culture through his newsletter 'Where's Your Ed At' and his social media presence. His acerbic commentary on corporate culture has drawn a massive following of almost 100,000 at the time of writing, regularly dissecting the gap between companies' lofty mission statements and their actual behaviour.[7] Every time a tech CEO talks about 'mission' and 'purpose', he encourages us to check if they're about to announce lay-offs.

His key arguments frequently focus on return to office (RTO) mandates, corporate communications and technology company culture. He frequently dissects corporate memos about 'culture' and 'collaboration', arguing they're really about justifying real estate investments and maintaining control over employees.[8] He's particularly pointed about how companies talk about 'culture' when they mean 'surveillance'. He deconstructs company-wide emails and LinkedIn posts, showing how language about 'purpose' and 'mission' often precedes or disguises lay-offs or benefit reductions.

A key example of his analysis was during the 2023 tech lay-offs, where he highlighted how companies that had previously touted their family-like culture and world-changing missions reverted to pure business language when conducting mass redundancies.[9]

This growing scepticism isn't just another tech industry trend – it's a warning signal that HR and leaders ignore at their peril. When sophisticated observers like Zitron can predict lay-offs simply by tracking when companies amp up their purpose rhetoric, we've reached a crisis point in how we think about meaning at work. The corporate purpose playbook isn't just failing; it's actively backfiring, breeding cynicism instead of engagement.

For those of us in HR and People Operations, this presents an existential challenge. We've spent the last decade building elaborate frameworks around purpose and meaning, creating employee value propositions that promised transformation, and positioning work as the primary source of fulfilment in people's lives. Now we're watching that carefully constructed edifice crumble, exposed by a combination of economic reality, generational shift and growing awareness that we may have oversold work's capacity to provide meaning. In short, our customers are turning on us, and the writing is on the wall unless we change tactics.

The stakes couldn't be higher. As AI transforms knowledge work and younger generations enter the workforce with fundamentally different expectations about the role of work in their lives, we need a new way to think about purpose and meaning. The old model – where companies try to be a primary source of purpose for their employees no matter the truth behind it – is not just unsustainable; it's becoming actively harmful. It sets up false expectations, creates brittle cultural structures that shatter under pressure, and ultimately leads to the kind of disillusionment we're seeing play out across tech X and beyond.

What we need isn't another purpose framework or engagement initiative. We need a fundamental reimagining of how we think about meaning at work. The alternative is watching our credibility as HR professionals continue to be eroded. Each time a company talks about purpose while conducting lay-offs, each time 'culture' becomes code for control, we lose more of our ability to engage meaningfully with employees. We risk becoming what some already accuse us of being: corporate storytellers spinning tales about meaning while the real business happens elsewhere.

The path forward requires both courage and humility. Courage to admit that our current approach to purpose isn't working, and humility to recognize that meaning can't be manufactured or mandated from above. In the chapters that follow, we'll explore what this new approach might look like, drawing on examples from human beings and organizations that have found more authentic ways to think about purpose at work.

The new economy of work

In 1999, Joe Pine and James Gilmore introduced the concept of the *experience economy* in their groundbreaking *Harvard Business Review* article.[10] They argued that businesses had moved beyond selling mere commodities, products, or services, to selling experiences. A cup of coffee that cost pennies to make at home could command several dollars at a café because customers weren't just buying coffee, they were buying an *experience*.

What Pine and Gilmore identified in consumer behaviour has profound implications for how we think about purpose at work. Just as consumers engage with businesses at different economic levels – from purely transactional to deeply transformational – I argue that employees engage with their work along a similar spectrum.

My mind goes back to the time I was a guest on Dart Lindsley's fantastic podcast, *Work For Humans*.[11] On his podcast, Dart asked me the question, 'What job does your job do for you?' It's a question that strikes at the core of purpose and work. If work is a product (and I believe it is, duh) and should be built like a product (which, of course, I advocate it should), then work is doing a *job* for us – there is some *purpose* behind this relationship, which could be anything from a pay cheque to personal fulfilment, to a life's work. This isn't a new thought, like many things I speak about, I'm bringing both organizational and economic research together, with practical observations and real-life research, to give a new view of the world we work within.

As Joe Pine said on *Work For Humans*, 'We need meaning out of work... our lives are so much richer and we flourish so much as human beings [when we get meaning out of work]'.[12] But the *job* our job is doing for us, is not the same for everyone; yet most companies make the mistake of treating purpose as one-size-fits-all, typically aiming for transformation when their fundamental business model might call for something quite different.

Understanding the three economies of work

The evolution of economic value has followed a telling trajectory: from extracting commodities, to manufacturing goods, to delivering services, and finally to staging experiences. But there's a fifth stage emerging, what is called the 'transformation economy', where businesses don't just sell products or experiences, but lasting personal change. An example is the health app Noom. Unlike traditional diet apps, Noom focuses on psychological transformation of eating habits and relationship with food through cognitive behavioural therapy principles. You are buying Noom because you want to be changed as a consumer, you want the product to transform something *within you*.

I often use an example of coffee when explaining the transformation economy. It is the idea that the further from a commodity you get, the more valuable a product becomes.

Starting with the commodity, Arabica coffee trades between roughly $2.76 and $3.02 per kilogram, while Robusta coffee from Vietnam averages around $2.40 per kilogram.[13] Not much by way of cost to differentiate them. Then the coffee is shipped to a warehouse somewhere in East London or Brooklyn where a tattooed man in a very small beanie roasts it, grinds it, and attaches a thoughtfully designed, aesthetic sticker on the package. Now, this same coffee joins part of the goods economy and is worth double the commodity it once was.

Next up, as you walk past your local Pret or Starbucks and grab a cup (around 10 to 15 grams of the aforementioned commodity) of take-away coffee for £3 or £4, you are engaging in the service economy. You pay a premium for the product because it comes with a service, but it's nothing compared to the price of the coffee at your local artisanal coffee house, with its curated music, free Wi-Fi and ultra-cool clientele, where coffee joins the experiential economy, commanding double the price again. Here, with your laptop and latte, you are paying for the *experience* as much as the commodity itself; Joe Pine describes the 'memory as the core part of the experience'.[14]

Then the transformation economy takes us further still – to coffee as a gateway to personal change, a gateway to you achieving your goals and aspirations. In Joe Pine's words, 'you use experiences as the raw material to guide people to change' where 'people are coming to you with an aspiration'. Think of a trip to a barista course that promises not just knowledge but identity transformation, a coffee masterclass that sells the journey from consumer to connoisseur. Here, you're not buying coffee at all – you're buying who you'll become through your relationship with, and purchasing into, the product. The same bean that began as a commodity becomes a vehicle for personal metamorphosis, its value multiplying exponentially with each step away from its original form. This isn't just about coffee, it's about how value creation has evolved from the tangible to the transformational, from selling things to selling *becoming*.

This transformation economy didn't emerge overnight. We can trace its roots through the evolution of the fitness industry, where Jane Fonda's workout videos of the 1980s gradually evolved into SoulCycle's promise of spiritual enlightenment through spinning. Or consider how Pilates transformed from a simple exercise regime to a more than $170 billion industry selling everything from lifestyle adapting applications to luxury retreats promising total life transformation.[15] Even education followed this path – from the correspondence courses of the early 1900s selling practical skills to today's executive MBAs promising not just knowledge but complete professional reinvention. By the time tech companies started selling us phones and apps in the 2010s, they weren't marketing devices or software – they were selling us better versions of ourselves. 'Think Different' wasn't just Apple's slogan;[16] it was a preview of how products would increasingly be sold not for what they are, but for who they could help us become.

In *Built for People* I argued that work is a product, but I entirely scrapped a chapter where I dove deeper into what kind of product work may be for its consumers. At the time of writing that book, I had a hunch (but little research to back it up at the time) that work could, and perhaps tech work did, form a part of the transformation economy, or at the very least was analogous enough that we could adapt some of the key principles about how to expand on the value of work for our employees.

This idea of work existing along the same economic (purpose) spectrum as the transformation economy nicely mirrors Amy Wrzesniewski's groundbreaking research on how people relate to their work.[17] Her studies revealed three distinct orientations: those who see work as simply a job (service), those who view it as a career (experience) and those who experience it as a calling (transformation), but this is not the full story as I see it. Through the

FIGURE 2.1 Spectrum of work from commodity to transformation

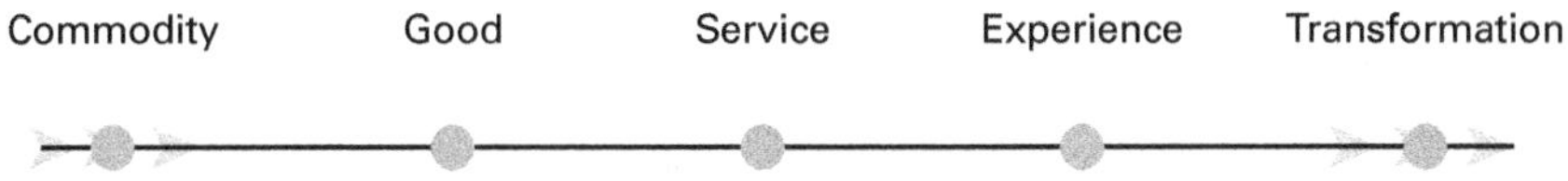

Commodity   Good   Service   Experience   Transformation

development of this book I believe that we aren't just individually attempting to align to these consumer orientations, but the companies we are building also align in a similar way, and this structure can be used to better serve the needs of the team you seek to attract, engage and retain.

> No workplace will ever perfectly, or always, fit into one single economic box, and we should be aware that we may have some roles, some of the time, or some programmes that may move from the goods economy to the transformation economy. At times, an employer may straddle both, or may be able to deliver transformational outcomes through highly refined experiential applications (such as corporate travel or secondment programmes, but we'll get to that!). For the purpose of this book, I want you to think deeply about where it is most likely your workplace or company will centre, rather than presuming this is where you belong. Consider it as being the zone where you begin the work; where the balance between your team's desires (be they a job, a career, or a calling) and your workplace's economic reality (service, experiential and transformational) interlace most consistently.

Work as a 'good'

In *Built for People* I talk about work as a product which has a core, actual and augmented product; a framework developed by Philip Kotler, often called the 'father of modern marketing'.[18] Within this framework I talk about the core 'product' of work being the exchange of labour for income. When thinking about work along the economic spectrum mentioned previously, thinking about work within the 'goods economy' is as close to this core product in Kotler's framework as possible; an income, statutory benefits and legal protections, and no 'service' applied to the delivery of this income. For the sake of practicality, I won't spend any time talking about work within this frame. I presume all of you wonderful readers, as clever and diligent as you are, are looking to elevate and explore what is beyond the statutory minimum of work, and are ready to engage with economies beyond the replicable 'good' of a *job*.

Work in the service economy

In the service economy, we find what my parents would likely categorize as 'proper jobs'. These are the banks, retail, logistics, insurance companies and corporate behemoths where work is exactly what it says on the tin: you

FIGURE 2.2 Core, augmented, actual product

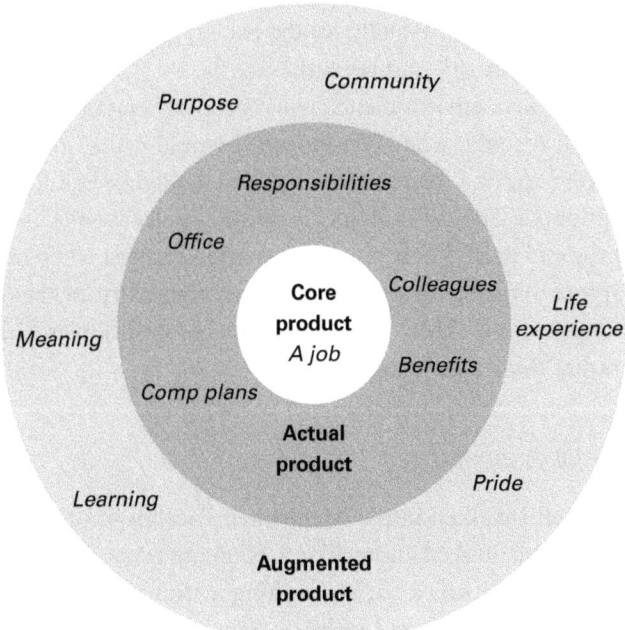

show up, you do your bit, you get paid. Walk into any franchise hospitality or logistics warehouse, and you'll find people who have a refreshingly clear-eyed view of the transaction. When they do, these workplaces succeed in their connection to their employees, perhaps not for the reasons you'd predict, but precisely because they don't necessarily try to dress mutton up as lamb – they know what job their job is doing for them, and more importantly, they know what it is not.

The kinds of workplaces we typically find in this economy are traditional manufacturing, hospitality, banks, insurance companies and smaller middle-economic entities such as, very likely, paper sales. Services overall account for about 79 per cent of US employment, and include major 'tactical' sectors such as financial services (creating millions of jobs) and leisure/hospitality (about 10 per cent).[19,20] These organizations typically successfully position work as a relatively straightforward exchange: time and skills for compensation and benefits (the 'service' beyond the 'good'). Companies like Walmart, Amazon (warehouses) and traditional manufacturing firms exemplify this approach as their primary operating mode.

Navigating to Walmart's careers page at the time of writing, the top headline reads, 'Walmart raises pay for store managers. Walmart store managers are the best leaders in retail, and we're investing in them – simplifying their pay structure and redesigning their bonus programme, giving them the opportunity to earn an annual bonus up to 200 per cent of their base salary.'[21] The focus is unabashedly on the exchange: a clear, uncomplicated relationship between work and reward.

Employees in these environments, when properly engaged, may typically view their work through what Wrzesniewski would call a 'job' orientation. They're looking for fair compensation, clear boundaries and predictable advancement paths. The psychological contract is clear: work is a means to an end, not the end itself. These workplaces often succeed when not overselling their purpose to their consumers; they focus on stability, clear expectations and fair compensation. Their employee value proposition is built around reliability rather than transformation.

The experiential economy

I remember when I walked into a Meta (then Facebook) office for the first time. The reception looked more like a contemporary art gallery than a corporate lobby. There was a barista crafting artisanal coffee in one corner, while graphic designers created pithy posters to paste on the walls: 'they tried to bury us but they didn't know we were seeds' stuck bizarrely close to, 'HACK THINGS' in all capitals. I remember distinctly noticing that every detail, including the semi-industrial 'barely finished' interior, which, it turns out, seems to be replicated worldwide in Meta offices, has been choreographed to make you feel like you've stepped into something special – not just another workplace, but an *experience*.

This isn't accidental. Just as upscale restaurants learned that ambiance could justify charging $35 for $7 worth of pasta, tech companies discovered that transforming the workplace into an experience could attract and retain talent more effectively than mere compensation. Most modern knowledge-work companies, particularly in tech, operate in this space. Companies like Spotify, Airbnb and X have historically competed by creating distinctive workplace experiences, be that offsite experiences with live music, incredible on-site catering, expensive swag and perks, or their investment in time 'off keys' learning and spending time with colleagues.

The experience economy is, at this point, my career's natural habitat and *probably* yours if you're reading this book. This is where most tech companies live, selling work like it's a luxury spa package. Come to Google, we've got massage rooms! Join Spotify, we've got unlimited vacation! Work at Airbnb, our office looks like a boutique hotel! I've helped build these environments, crafted these employee value propositions, and watched as bright-eyed graduates fought for the chance to join companies based on travel, perks and benefits. According to a Glassdoor multi-country survey, 77 per cent of adults – across the US, UK, France and Germany – would consider a company's culture before applying to a job, and a significant majority view culture and company mission as more important than compensation.[22] This might explain why tech companies spend more on office perks than the GDP of Tuvalu. In 2019, Google alone spent more than $10 billion on perks[23] and facilities[24] – that's enough to run the entire Pacific island nation for 19 years.

In the experiential economy, work is supposed to feel special, exclusive, like you've somehow gamed the system by getting paid to work in what amounts to an adult playground. The 2021 LinkedIn 'Global Talent Trends' survey found that for job seekers worldwide, the top three priorities when choosing a new role were good life–work balance, followed by compensation and benefits, and then colleagues and culture.[25] They're buying into what organizational psychologist Adam Grant calls 'optimal distinctiveness' – workplaces that make them feel special and part of something exciting.[26] The theory, originally proposed by Marilynn Brewer, describes the tension between wanting to fit in (belonging) and wanting to stand out (uniqueness). Adam Grant uses it in *Give and Take* to talk about environments – teams, organizations, communities – that satisfy both needs.[27]

Examples abound: Google's famous campus, Hubspot's unlimited vacation policy, Salesforce's wellness rooms. These aren't just perks – they're part of a carefully designed process to make work feel less like work and more like a carefully crafted experience.

In what might be the most honest description of work I've ever experienced, during my research one tech worker, who elected to remain anonymous for this quote, said to me that their 'big-tech' motto was, 'get paid, have fun, go home', and that 'work feels more like a passport for other things, a means to a very fun end.' When I asked about their connection to purpose, they shared a story of a colleague who, as a first-generation immigrant, had shared their disillusionment with the purpose of their work in their role, but how important it was to their family that they made a better life for themselves. This doesn't mean that either of these individuals don't work incredibly hard, in fact the opposite seemed to be true when interviewed, but what is interesting is that the primary driver was so distinctly devoid of connection with the company purpose, mission or values, and so largely connected with its standing in the experiential economy.

This conversation crystallized something I'd been struggling to articulate about the experience economy: it's building, adding on top of, rather than distinct from the service economy in the world of work. The same fundamental value proposition exists – 'work here and we will pay you well' – but now it comes layered with experiential elements: 'and you'll have a fantastic time doing it'. This doesn't just mean ping-pong tables, cold brew on tap and 'unlimited' vacation policies, though, as it relates to Wrzesniewski's framework, there is a significant chance these experiences are also related to those who view work as a 'career'. Many of the experiential elements I've described in this section aren't necessarily about individual transformation or a sense of personal purpose; they're about making the transaction of trading time for money more pleasant, or setting towards a compelling career path, which within itself has a sense of meaning that can be deeply valuable.

One thing I've been consistently surprised with within my research is the subtle implication that if you prefer (or you find yourself in a workplace operating primarily within) the service or experiential economy, that there is something to be ashamed about, that you are missing a 'higher calling' of work and purpose. It is my strong belief that this is deeply false. There's nothing inherently wrong with any of these approaches, and there is no virtue in seeing your work as a job rather than a calling, or preferring travel opportunities over having a higher impact within your nine-to-five. In fact, there's something refreshingly honest about it. Many of the tech workers I interviewed spoke about how liberating it felt to stop pretending their job building productivity software was 'changing the world' and instead embrace it for what it was: interesting work that paid well, offered them career progression, and came with nice perks. We aren't saving humanity by making lives easier for those who use our API integrations, or cloud management, or data abstraction layer. We are, however, having a nice time, enjoying our work, and seeing the quality of our lives improve in conjunction: a win–win.

What's missing, still, from this equation is any real elevation into the world of genuine purpose, transformation and vocation. The experience economy makes work more enjoyable, but it doesn't necessarily (and I think this could be argued) make it more *meaningful*. The free lunches and meditation rooms might make Monday mornings a lot more palatable, but they don't answer the deeper questions about purpose and impact that many workers still grapple with. It's the difference between making work pleasant, enjoyable, and making it purposeful – a distinction that becomes particularly stark when times get tough and the perks start to disappear, as they did in 2020. Folks within the experiential economy are, generally, looking for a career that gives them some kind of meaning, although it may not be a transformational calling. Everyone I spoke to is on some kind of journey as individuals or within their community where work is able to contribute to that sense of fulfilment. This means that work may be something that offers them opportunities to travel, time to spend with their children, or a chance to work with best-in-class professionals; their work itself is not necessarily changing them by design of the company, but it remains the place they find the kindling or space to reach another purpose all of their own. This may look like those in the service economy who seek purpose from work as a *means to an end*: a way to feed their children, study or enjoy hobbies. In the experiential economy it may look like a tech worker who enjoys the opportunities for free, unstructured learning and development, and career progression through their work at a cloud-SaaS company. In neither of those examples is the relationship between purpose and work so close that the work *itself* is the transformation, but they offer the same opportunities for fulfilment and an enriching life.

The transformation economy

Picture working at Patagonia the day founder Yvon Chouinard announced he was giving away his $3 billion company to fight climate change, declaring, 'Earth is now our only shareholder'.[28] Not selling it to the highest bidder, not taking it public, but structuring it so that after paying regular taxes, all additional profits would go directly to fighting climate change. This wasn't a marketing stunt or a clever PR move – it was perhaps one of the purest examples of what happens when an organization fully commits to transformation as its core purpose.

The transformation economy is where we find organizations that can legitimately position purpose at the core of their customer and employee value proposition (EVP) – not because their marketing team crafted a compelling mission statement, but because their entire business model is built around creating meaningful change. This transformation can manifest in two distinct ways: organizations whose work genuinely transforms the world around them, and those whose work fundamentally transforms the people who do it.

The first type includes climate tech startups measuring success in carbon reduction, UN agencies whose existence is predicated on systemic change, and mental health organizations where patient transformation is the product itself.

The second type encompasses roles where the work itself changes you as a person; think of work training programmes where students emerge as fundamentally different professionals, intensive artistic residencies, or leadership development roles where personal growth isn't just encouraged but is literally the job. These might include executive coaching firms, elite training academies or organizations built around mastery of complex crafts where the practitioner is transformed through the practice itself.

Both types can legitimately centre purpose in their EVP because transformation – whether external or personal – *is genuinely what they deliver, not just what they promise.*

Employees are significantly more engaged when their organization's mission aligns with meaningful social impact and involves co-creation with its workforce; Deloitte's 2023 'Global Human Capital Trends' report shows that organizations co-designing with employees are 1.8 times more likely to have a highly engaged workforce.[29] The mistake many companies make is trying to position themselves as transformation economy workplaces when they're really experience or service economy operations at their core. Amy Wrzesniewski has noted that meaning at work doesn't require a grand, world-changing mission; in fact, focusing solely on such lofty goals can overshadow the genuine meaning people often create in more ordinary roles through everyday actions and relationships.[30]

As mentioned, when thinking of the transformation economy, and which workplaces fit easily into this framework, I think of two distinct categories. The first includes climate tech start-ups that measure success in carbon reduction alongside revenue, UN agencies and international NGOs whose very existence is predicated on systemic change, and mental health organizations where patient transformation is the product, not just the outcome of their quarterly earnings reports. The second encompasses organizations where the work itself fundamentally transforms the worker: intensive apprenticeship programmes where craftspeople develop not just skills but entirely new ways of seeing their trade; management consulting firms where analysts are systematically rebuilt into strategic thinkers; or research laboratories where scientists don't just conduct experiments but are fundamentally shaped by the process of discovery itself.

What sets these organizations apart isn't just their mission statements – it's their measures of success, their corporate governance, and their ownership structures. A regular company might celebrate a good quarter with higher profits. A transformation economy organization celebrates because fewer people are hungry, more rainforest was preserved, more lives were changed, or because their people have achieved new levels of mastery and personal growth that wouldn't have been possible elsewhere. Whether the transformation is external (changing the world) or internal (changing the worker), the profit is necessary but perhaps secondary to the transformation they're trying to create together.

According to Deloitte's 2023 purpose-driven organization study, only about 15 per cent of workers actually operate in truly purpose-driven organizations.[31] The rest work for companies that might talk about purpose but haven't fundamentally oriented their business model around transformation, with 78 per cent wishing they did.[32] It's the difference between a company that puts solar panels on their roof and calls themselves sustainable, versus one that exists to make sustainable energy more accessible to families in low income neighbourhoods.

This distinction becomes crucial when we think about employee engagement and meaning. Working for a transformation economy organization doesn't just mean buying into a nice-sounding mission statement – it means your daily work is directly connected to creating meaningful change, either within the world or within yourself. As Emory Sullivan, co-founder of Genba AI (with Bruce Kaufman), told me, 'We wanted to make sure that our corporate culture was in line with the ethos of the broader mission as well.' Emory Sullivan is the founder of Genba AI, a technology company focused on bringing modern tools to underserved blue-collar workers in manufacturing. The name 'Genba' comes from Japanese and means 'where the work is done',[33] specifically referring to the person doing the work on the factory floor. Emory describes her customers as people who had been largely ignored by the tech industry despite being 'the salt of the earth' who 'make all the things that we enjoy.' Emory doesn't see her business as directly within the transformation economy of work, but she has been inspired to co-create experiences with her team that are inspired by businesses in this space.

But transformation economy organizations face their own unique challenges. When your mission is to change the world, or your primary EVP is to change people's lives, how do you balance urgency with sustainability? How do you choose which parts of the world to save first, lest you leave some folks behind or unserved? When your work is deeply meaningful towards folk's fulfilment, how do you prevent burnout in employees who are deeply emotionally invested in the outcomes? Resources are often scarcer, teams more likely to be overworked, and ethical dilemmas conflicting. These organizations must navigate the delicate balance between pursuing transformative impact and maintaining operational sustainability.

The scarcity of true transformation economy organizations might explain why so many companies try to dress up service or experience-based work in transformational language. It's tempting to claim you're changing the world, or developing your employees in a way which is genuinely transformational at its core, when you're really just making a profit more efficiently (and trying to do some good, or at least not so much bad, while doing it, of course). But as we'll explore in the next chapter, this misalignment between claimed purpose and actual business model can create more problems than it solves.

Why does it matter which economy you're in?

Imagine two people working as cleaners in the same hospital. When asked about their work, the first says 'I clean floors.' The second says 'I help keep patients healthy.' Same role, same tasks, but profoundly different relationships with their work. This isn't just about positive thinking or reframing – it's about how individuals naturally construct meaning in their work, regardless of their position in the economic hierarchy.

This observation comes from Amy Wrzesniewski's research, which fundamentally changed how we think about the relationship between jobs and meaning. Her work revealed that the capacity for meaningful work isn't determined by whether you're a CEO or a custodian, whether you work in a purpose-driven nonprofit or a profit-focused corporation. Instead, it's shaped by how individuals personally connect with and make sense of their work. In other words, it is dependent on your 'ideal customer profile' and your ability to message to them (if you thought I was tired of talking about employees as customers after *Built for People*, you thought wrong).

Understanding which economy your organization operates in matters because it helps set realistic expectations about how meaning and purpose can authentically manifest in different work contexts, and for different types of people you may employ or wish to attract into your team. But as research would show, the story is far more complex than simply matching people to purpose-driven organizations…

Wrzesniewski's work sparked a whole field of research into how people find meaning through their work. Researchers like Justin Berg at Stanford expanded on her ideas by studying job crafting – how employees actively reshape their roles to align with their preferred orientation.[34] Research by

Blake E Ashforth and colleagues shows how workers in stigmatized occupations – such as those dealing with waste or pest control – are able to reframe their jobs by emphasizing societal purpose (e.g. helping families find pets, assisting individuals in financial difficulty), enabling them to experience their work as meaningful and identity-affirming.[35] These studies revealed something profound: the transformation economy wasn't just happening to work; it was happening *through* work. Companies like Google and Facebook didn't invent the idea of work as transformation when they 'started with why' – they just productized an existing human need to seek meaning through their labour. But in doing so, they may have fundamentally misunderstood one of Wrzesniewski's core insights: that these orientations are personal, organic and somewhat resistant to corporate manufacturing.

Chris Abbass, CEO of Talentful who transitioned from aspiring musician to successful entrepreneur, puts it bluntly: 'I think that's why a lot of companies have gotten it wrong. They think you should do what you're passionate about. I think that's total trash. I actually think you *decide* what you can be passionate about.'

So why does it matter which economy your organization operates in? Because when we understand the true economic context of our work, we can stop forcing false narratives and start building authentic relationships with our jobs. An organization which primarily operates within the service economy pretending to be transformational isn't just inauthentic – it's actively harmful, creating a disconnect and dissonance between expectation and reality that breeds cynicism and disengagement.

The parallel between purpose-driven organizations and the transformation economy is striking and inspiring from my point of view. Just as consumers increasingly seek transformative experiences over mere transactions, I watched colleagues longing for roles that would transform them, not just employ them, while others seek out deeper meaning *away* from their laptops, but through the resources or experiences their work gives them, and find purpose in their hobbies, families or creative pursuits.

I've seen it myself, in the last few years organizations claiming transformational opportunities at work; changing the world, learning and growth opportunities beyond the standard nine-to-five. Yet, somewhere between the promises of transformation and the reality of corporate life, disillusionment crept in. The same companies selling transformation to their candidates were often delivering transactional experiences to their employees. We witnessed 'purpose-driven' tech giants lay off thousands via email, 'mission-focused' start-ups burn out their most dedicated believers, and 'values-led' organizations reveal that quarterly targets trumped transformation every time. The pandemic had already cracked the veneer of corporate purpose, but 2023's tech industry upheaval shattered it completely. We discovered that many of these supposed vehicles for personal metamorphosis were actually just very well-branded coaches on the same old economic highway. The gap between Wrzesniewski's 'calling' and the reality of corporate 'purpose' grew into a chasm, leaving many of us wondering if we'd been sold a transformational experience but delivered a commodity job with better marketing.

As HR professionals, we find ourselves in an interesting position: we're product managers for the work experience. Just as a product manager wouldn't market a basic utility app as a life-changing platform, we need to be honest about the product we're building and selling. The goal isn't to make every workplace transformational to all of our employees – it's to create authentic alignment between what we promise and what we deliver to the customers of our workplace experience, at least if we are to have happier customers.

Dollar Tree doesn't try to be Patagonia, and McDonald's doesn't pretend to be a Michelin-starred restaurant. Yet both are highly successful because they understand their product and their market. And, in fact, Joe Pine may argue that both Patagonia *and* McDonalds are capable of experiential value, but it is about seeking the value in a way that is appropriate to our consumer, to our product's reality.[36] In HR, we need to bring this same clear-eyed approach to how we position our employee value proposition. A service economy organization might focus on competitive compensation, professional development, and work-life boundaries, and invest what would be spent on perks on better performance incentives and compensation for their team. An experience economy company might invest in distinctive culture and innovative ways of working. And yes, transformation economy organizations can lean fully into purpose and meaning – but only if that's genuinely what they're selling.

Purpose isn't a one-size-fits-all solution to employee engagement; it's one tool in a sophisticated toolkit. Sometimes the most purposeful thing we can do is stop trying to manufacture and stoke depth of meaning where it doesn't naturally exist. Instead, we might focus on creating fair, well-designed work experiences that allow people to find or develop their own sense of purpose, whether that's through the experiences provided within work itself or through what the work enables in their lives (resources, time, benefits).

This requires a more nuanced approach to talent attraction and engagement. Rather than trying to convince everyone that our organization is changing the world or changing them through the work itself, we might ask:

- What are we genuinely offering to them?
- What job do they want their job to do for them?
- Who is that most likely to resonate with (consider Wrzesniewski's framework of job, career, or calling)?
- How can we be transparent about both the opportunities and limitations of what we're building?

The answers to these questions will vary dramatically based on which economy we're operating in – and that's exactly as it should be.

Which economy do you exist within?

The distinction between these three economies might seem clear in theory, but in practice, organizations often send mixed signals (or may, in the case of some direct-to-consumer start-ups where there is a back office and logistics team, be selling two different experiences or 'work products'). A tech company might claim to be transforming the world while measuring success purely through transaction metrics. A traditional bank might invest in experiential perks without fundamentally changing its service-economy DNA. Even Patagonia, a poster child for the external view of the transformation economy, still needs to operate as a functional business and, apparently, wants all in the team to return to office, which has surprised quite a few remote-work fanatics in my network.[37]

So how do you cut through the corporate messaging to understand which economy your workplace truly operates in? It's not always as simple as reading the mission statement or tallying up the office perks. Instead, we need to look at specific indicators that reveal how an organization actually creates value, engages with employees, and measures success. Here's a practical framework for understanding where your organization sits on this spectrum...

Economic Spectrum Assessment

This assessment helps you determine whether your organization primarily operates in the service, experience or transformation economy. Remember, most organizations have elements of all three but usually demonstrate a dominant mode. Answer each section honestly, focusing on actual behaviours and outcomes rather than aspirational statements.

First, we will explore the way in which your company creates or thinks about value, then we will explore its messaging (specifically for recruiting and employment), and finally we will look at behaviours of your employees.

PART 1: VALUE CREATION

Rate each statement from 0–2 (0 = Rarely/Never, 1 = Sometimes, 2 = Frequently/Always), then count where you have the most points and then write down the points scored within each category to understand how strongly you present within it.

Service Economy Indicators   In my company...

1. Success is almost exclusively measured through operational metrics (efficiency, output, revenue) _____
2. Customer relationships are primarily transactional _____
3. Core value proposition centres on reliability and consistency _____
4. Processes are standardized and repeatable _____
5. Employee retention is primarily driven by competitive compensation and benefits _____

Total Points: _____

Experience Economy Indicators   In my company...

1. We invest heavily in how things feel to work here _____
2. Professional development budgets prioritize experiential learning over traditional training _____
3. Perks and facilities are considered a key part of compensation _____
4. Culture is actively engineered and marketed _____
5. Employee experience 'moments' are deliberately designed _____

Total Points: _____

Transformation Economy Indicators   In my company...

1. Impact is measured as well as more traditional metrics _____
2. Our core value proposition focuses on creating positive change in the world or the work being vocational to our employee base_____

3 Our business model aligns with these transformational goals _____
4 We would sacrifice profit for impact (on the world, our team, or our art) _____
5 Success, for us, can be measured in lives/systems changed _____

Total Points: _____

PART 2: LANGUAGE ANALYSIS

Review your organization's internal and external communications (primarily looking at all-company emails, career pages, and significant communications to your team or followers on LinkedIn) from the past three months and count instances of each type of language (or similar). You can consider weighting recent communications more heavily (last month = 3x, last 3 months = 1x). Again, count up the category with the most points and award 15 points for winning economic type.

Service Economy Language

1 Competitive compensation
2 Career progression
3 Core benefits: retirement man, paid time off
4 Flexible or additional opportunities for hours/reward
5 Job security
6 Total frequency: _____

Experience Economy Language

1 Unique culture
2 Perks/benefits
3 Career opportunities
4 Dynamic environment
5 Innovative workplace
6 Total frequency: _____

Transformation Economy Language

1 Changing the world
2 Making impact
3 Transforming lives

Mission/purpose

1. Fellowships, vocation, calling
2. Total frequency: _____
3. Primary Language used: _____

PART 3: BEHAVIOURAL INDICATORS

Answer these scenarios (these are mostly based on your imagination or projections, rather than lead by data), and award yourself five points for each question to the category that is most true for your business. Feel free to ask your colleagues the same questions below to see if their point of view differs.

The Monday Morning Test 'When people arrive on Monday morning, what do you imagine they are most likely to be thinking about from the three points below?'

1. Service: Getting through their tasks efficiently
2. Experience: What interesting challenges, conversations or problems await
3. Transformation: The impact of their work on their lives, their expertise, their vocation, or the world

The Departure Story Test 'When people leave here happy, what do they say about their time here?'

1. Service: 'It was a good job with benefits and opportunities to live a good life'
2. Experience: 'It was an amazing ride, met incredible people, I had some really interesting experiences'
3. Transformation: 'My time there really made a difference (to me, to the world)'

The Trade-off Test 'When forced to choose, what does your organization prioritize?'

1. Service: Efficiency over Experiences
2. Experience: Innovation over Consistency
3. Transformation: Impact and Purpose over Profits

The Crisis Test 'During difficult periods, what does your organization protect first?'

1 Service: Operations and customer commitments
2 Experience: Team culture and employee experience
3 Transformation: Mission and impact work

CALCULATE YOUR SCORE

Add up points from each section and convert to percentages for each economy type against a total possible score of 30. Your dominant economy is the one with the highest percentage. *Consider having others in your team complete it too, so you can compare perspectives and spot patterns.*

Remember, the goal also isn't to achieve the 'best', or what you perceive to be the most virtuous (there is no such thing!) economy type, but to operate authentically within your actual realities while being honest about what you do, can and cannot consistently offer employees (in fact, this framework is designed as morally neutral, there is no virtue or lack thereof in landing in any of these areas; the world needs all kinds of businesses to operate and serve the many different types of consumers of work that exist). Many organizations operate across multiple economies, but usually have a dominant mode, and you may find you have a reason to bridge, split, or feel like you have reasons to sit 'in between'. That's fine, this framework is designed to give these ideas a shared language so that you can build an authentic strategy, not to strap you into a box from which you cannot escape or innovate your own approach authentically.

A misalignment, for example, would be claiming to be in the transformation economy ('We're changing the world!') while operating consistently in the service economy by measuring performance *purely* on efficiency metrics, and making no managerial efforts to measure or assess the impact you are having on your company purpose. The most successful organizations are those that honestly understand which economy they primarily operate in (even if they do not use this language) and align their employee value proposition, and work experiences accordingly in order to share an authentic experience with their team, but also to design a meaningfully impactful strategy around motivating their team.

So finally, let's have a reality check. After scoring, ask these final questions:

THE AUTHENTICITY CHECK

1. Does this assessment match your gut feeling?
2. Does your organization's external messaging and claims match its day-to-day operational decisions?
3. Are your reward systems, promotion criteria, bonus structures and resource allocation aligned with your stated economy type?
4. Can this positioning survive hard times?
5. Could you defend these results with specific examples?
6. If your colleagues completed this assessment about your organization, do you think they would reach the same (or similar) conclusions?
7. If someone else in your team who read this book so far asked you where you sat, do you think they may agree or challenge you?

For us, this is urgent

There's a certain irony in the fact that while HR teams were crafting elaborate purpose statements and designing 'meaningful' workplace experiences, one of the fastest-growing online communities was /r/antiwork. The subreddit, which grew from 180,000 members in January 2020 to approximately 1.6 million in just a few months, became a digital town square for sharing stories about workplace disillusionment.[38] What's particularly fascinating is how many of the posts directly mock the very initiatives HR teams spent years developing – the 'pizza party' rewards, the 'we're a family' rhetoric, the carefully worded purpose statements. Screenshots of corporate communications about 'bringing your whole self to work' sit alongside bitter commentaries about lay-offs and exploitation.

The relationship between HR and /r/antiwork is like a funhouse mirror reflection – every well-intentioned initiative we created to make work more meaningful appears distorted and darkly comical in their feed. While we in HR were reading Gallup reports about employee engagement, workers were building their own narrative about work, one that saw our purpose initiatives not as solutions but as symptoms of a deeper problem. Perhaps most tellingly, the subreddit's description begins with 'A subreddit for those who want to end work' – a direct challenge to HR's fundamental project of making work better. It's a reminder that while we were trying to transform work from the inside, a significant portion of the workforce was questioning whether it needed to exist in its current form at all.

No matter where you work, there are likely folks in your team who feel this way, so understanding this perspective is crucial to doing your job well (presuming you don't feel this way yourself). The challenge for HR and People teams isn't to convince these employees that they're wrong – that's precisely the kind of corporate evangelism they're rejecting. Instead, we need to recognize that the growing anti-work sentiment isn't just cynicism or laziness; it's a rational response to decades of broken promises about what work would provide. When an employee rolls their eyes at your latest purpose initiative or quietly opts out of the company book club, they're not failing to engage, they're engaging differently, and perhaps more honestly, with what work means to them.

They're telling us what they want to buy may not be what we're selling. Work is a product that we are building, and our employees are consumers. Just as the best product teams obsess over user feedback and adapt their offerings accordingly, we need to listen when our employees are effectively leaving one-star reviews. The antiwork movement isn't a bug in our system, it's user feedback at scale. When millions of workers join online communities dedicated to rejecting our carefully crafted workplace experiences, they're not just venting; they're participating in one of the largest customer feedback sessions in HR history. And like any good product team faced with negative user feedback, we have two choices: we can either dismiss our users as 'not getting it,' or we can fundamentally rethink what we're building and why.

This is where we in HR need to make a fundamental shift in our approach. Instead of trying to convert everyone to a purpose-driven relationship with work, we need to create systems that accommodate multiple relationships with work, as well as those that are developed from a place of authenticity and alignment. Some of your employees might genuinely find deep meaning in their work: fantastic! Others might see their work as simply a means to fund their outside passions: also fantastic! The real failure of HR hasn't been in trying to make work better; it's been in prescribing a one-size-fits-all approach to what 'better' means.

The irony is that by acknowledging and accepting these different relationships with work, we might actually create more engaging workplaces than we ever did with our forced fun and mandatory meaning-making. After all, what's more respectful of human dignity: pretending everyone should find their life's purpose in their job, or creating space for people to define their own relationship with work?

Notes and further reading

1. Chaplin, C (1936) *Modern Times*, United Artists, US
2. Wilder, B (1960) *The Apartment*, United Artists, US
3. Judge, M (1999) *Office Space*, Twentieth Century Fox, US
4. Gervais, R and Merchant, S (2001–2003) *The Office*. BBC, UK. Daniels, G (2005–2013) *The Office*, NBC, US
5. Corporate Bro (n.d.) *Corporate Bro*. www.instagram.com/corporate.bro (archived at https://perma.cc/JX93-4KCY)
6. Reddit (n.d.) */r/antiwork*. www.reddit.com/r/antiwork/ (archived at https://perma.cc/AV2Z-ETLT)
7. Zitron, E (n.d.) *Ed Zitron*. https://twitter.com/edzitron (archived at https://perma.cc/TWD4-TCN9)
8. Zitron, E (2023) The anti-workforce, *Where's Your Ed At*, 4 December. www.wheresyoured.at/the-anti-workforce/ (archived at https://perma.cc/AH4B-E47Q)
9. Zitron, E (2023) The Layoff Speech Generator, *Where's Your Ed At*, 23 January. www.wheresyoured.at/the-layoff-speech-generator/ (archived at https://perma.cc/7VSG-JT92)
10. Pine, B J and Gilmore, J H (1998) Welcome to the experience economy, *Harvard Business Review*, 76(4), 97–105
11. Lindsley, D (2023) Built for People: Using product management principles to design work people love | Jessica Zwaan, Revisited. *Work For Humans*, 7 November. pod.link/series/work-for-humans (archived at https://perma.cc/7PGM-6D7S)
12. Lindsley, D (2024) The Progression of Value: How to deliver custom work experiences at scale | Joe Pine. *Work For Humans*, 9 July. https://podcasts.apple.com/podcast/the-progression-of-value-how-to-deliver-custom/id1612743401?i=1000673439265 (archived at https://perma.cc/9TUP-6VXZ)
13. Index Mundi (2018) Coffee, Other Mild Arabicas Monthly Price (US $/kg). www.indexmundi.com/commodities/?commodity=other-mild-arabicas-coffee&months=120 (archived at https://perma.cc/AEN7-VEEW). Nguyen Coffee Supply (2024) Robusta coffee prices in Vietnam in 2018, Nguyen Coffee Supply [Blog]. https://nguyencoffeesupply.com/blogs/news/robusta-prices-reach-30-year-high-what-does-this-mean (archived at https://perma.cc/9WUY-VDW9)
14. Lindsley, D (2024) The Progression of Value: How to deliver custom work experiences at scale | Joe Pine. *Work For Humans*, 9 July. https://podcasts.apple.com/podcast/the-progression-of-value-how-to-deliver-custom/id1612743401?i=1000673439265 (archived at https://perma.cc/7WSX-7LM7)
15. Future Data Stats (2025) *Pilates Market Size and Industry Growth 2030*. www.futuredatastats.com/pilates-market (archived at https://perma.cc/TR5H-6ZDP)

16   Wikipedia (2025) Think different. Wikipedia. https://en.wikipedia.org/wiki/Think_different (archived at https://perma.cc/VC9J-8BCQ)
17   Wrzesniewski, A, McCauley, C, Rozin, P and Schwartz, B (1997) Jobs, careers, and callings: People's relations to their work, *Journal of Research in Personality*, 31(1), 21–33. doi:10.1006/jrpe.1997.2162 (archived at https://perma.cc/4RVC-CPXW)
18   Kotler, P and Keller, K L (2016) *Marketing Management*. 15th edn., pp. 324–26, Pearson Education, Harlow
19   Trading Economics (2025) United States – Employment in services (percentage of total employment). https://tradingeconomics.com/united-states/employment-in-services-percent-of-total-employment-wb-data.html (archived at https://perma.cc/4SG4-C3ZT)
20   Bureau of Labor Statistics (2024) Employment by major industry sector. www.bls.gov/emp/tables/employment-by-major-industry-sector.htm (archived at https://perma.cc/M7UD-DGPE)
21   Walmart (n.d.) Careers – Walmart raises pay for store managers. Walmart store managers are the best leaders in retail, and we're investing in them – simplifying their pay structure and redesigning their bonus program, giving them the opportunity to earn an annual bonus up to 200 per cent of their base salary. https://careers.walmart.com/ (archived at https://perma.cc/9TA9-SWAR)
22   Glassdoor (2019) Culture over cash? Glassdoor multi-country survey finds more than half of employees prioritize workplace culture over salary, *Glassdoor Blog*, 11 July. www.glassdoor.com/blog/mission-culture-survey/
23   Tremayne-Pengelly, A (2024) Sundar Pichai explains why Google keeps spending on lavish office perks, *The Observer*, 21 October. https://observer.com/2024/10/google-ceo-sundar-pichai-defend-office-perks/ (archived at https://perma.cc/D5T3-Y6WU)
24   TheStreet (2022) Why Is Google spending $9.5 billion on offices in the work…, *TheStreet*, 13 April. www.thestreet.com/investing/googles-return-to-office (archived at https://perma.cc/R2WJ-MY9U)
25   LinkedIn (2022) Global Talent Trends 2022: A reinvention of company culture. https://business.linkedin.com/content/dam/me/business/en-us/talent-solutions-lodestone/global-talent-trends-2022.pdf (archived at https://perma.cc/637N-9ZXF)
26   Grant, A M (2013) *Give and Take: Why helping others drives our success*. Viking, New York
27   Brewer, M B (1991) The social self: On being the same and different at the same time, *Personality and Social Psychology Bulletin*, 17(5), 475–82. doi:10.1177/0146167291175001 (archived at https://perma.cc/N4A3-87LB)
28   Kolakowski, M (2022) Patagonia founder donates company to fight climate change, Investopedia, 15 September. www.investopedia.com/patagonia-donated-climate-change-6666257 (archived at https://perma.cc/J5NR-ZDR4)

29 Deloitte (2023) 2023 Global Human Capital Trends: New fundamentals for a boundaryless world. Deloitte Insights. www.deloitte.com/us/en/insights/topics/talent/human-capital-trends/2023.html (archived at https://perma.cc/Z8MM-PAJN)

30 Wrzesniewski, A (2022) Crafting your job into a calling. Yale Talk: Conversations with Peter Salovey, 28 February. https://salovey.yale.edu/sites/default/files/yale_talk_episode_25_amy_wrzesniewski_transcript.pdf (archived at https://perma.cc/RT8F-W6M7)

31 Deloitte (n.d.) 2023 US Impact Report – Purpose. Deloitte, US. www2.deloitte.com/us/en/pages/about-deloitte/articles/us-impact-report-purpose.html (archived at https://perma.cc/AU7F-NXC8)

32 Deloitte (2023) Deloitte research study finds today's workers want to find 'purpose', Crain's Detroit Business, 29 May. www.crainsdetroit.com/sponsored-content/deloitte-research-study-finds-todays-workers-want-find-purpose

33 Imai, M (1986) *Kaizen: The key to Japan's competitive success*. McGraw-Hill, New York

34 Berg, J M, Wrzesniewski, A and Dutton, J E (2010) Perceiving and responding to challenges in job crafting at different ranks: When proactivity requires adaptivity, *Journal of Organizational Behavior*, 31(2–3), 158–186. doi:10.1002/job.645 (archived at https://perma.cc/M526-GSUE)

35 Ashforth, B E, Kreiner, G E and Clark, M A (2007) Normalizing dirty work: Managerial tactics for countering occupational taint, *Academy of Management Journal*, 50(1), 149–74. doi:10.2307/20159845 (archived at https://perma.cc/NFF7-8BAN)

36 Pine, B J and Gilmore, J H (2011) *The Experience Economy*. Updated edn. Harvard Business Review Press, Boston, MA

37 Webster, S (2024) Patagonia became famous for letting staff cut out early to chase waves – now it's asking dozens of employees to relocate or leave because it's 300 per cent overstaffed', Fortune, 28 June

38 Darian, Z (2022) Reddit 'antiwork' forum booms as millions of Americans quit..., *Financial Times*, 9 January. www.ft.com/content/1270ee18-3ee0-4939-98a8-c4f40940e644 (archived at https://perma.cc/GQ5Q-92XP)

3

Emptiness and achievement

It's 5.45 am, and I am waking up to ride my bike to law school in Bloomsbury, London. Something indescribable is internally driving me on these freezing mornings as I slog across the city. I am working and studying, with an endless list of case law looking forward to me this weekend. In my mid-twenties, I had an almost endless appetite for achievement, with a list of things I wanted to do by the time I was 30, which I kept on a Post-it note next to my computer. When I graduated, I experienced something close to what has been described as 'post wedding blues'. The realization that I had done something incredibly difficult, often sacrificing huge chunks of shared memories and time with loved ones, was wonderful, but I began to wonder what I was really chasing; and I was not alone in these questions cropping up at inflection points like this.

In 2019, Genevieve Nathwani sat on a London bus, wrestling with a feeling she couldn't quite name. On paper, everything was perfect. She had landed a role in a prestigious venture capital (VC) firm, carved out a rare path as a left-field candidate, and was doing work that supposedly mattered. 'I had a lot of people around me being like "you've designed your dream job for yourself, you were like a left-field candidate for a VC and somehow got in and now you're doing all this cool work – why would you give that up?"' she recalls. Yet something felt fundamentally wrong.

The relationship between career success and personal fulfilment has been extensively studied in organizational psychology and behavioural science. One of the most notable examples comes from Daniel Kahneman and Angus Deaton's 2010 study published in the Proceedings of the National Academy of Sciences. Their research found that while emotional wellbeing and life satisfaction increased with income up to about $75,000 annually, beyond that threshold, higher income was not associated with greater emotional wellbeing.[1]

This is Peggy Lee syndrome – named after the jazz singer's famous ballad where she contemplates life's supposedly peak moments and repeatedly asks, 'Is that all there is?'[2] It's the existential emptiness that follows achievement, the quiet disappointment when reaching a long-sought goal feels nothing like you imagined. For Genevieve, it manifested as a physical rebellion: 'I just knew it in my bones that it wasn't right,' she says. 'I had a series of jobs that were really intense that hadn't felt great... I'd got to the end of enough iterations to be like "okay, this is a pattern I need to think about this on a deeper level and have a break."'

What followed was what Genevieve calls 'a homecoming', though not one her younger self would have recognized. 'I went through the whole of university and my early 20s being like, okay, nice big house near a park in a cool bit of London, kids, work that makes enough money to make all that happen,' she reflects. 'And if I'm being honest, work that gives me status among the people that I'm around.' Instead, she found herself leaving London's tech scene for the Portuguese countryside, trading investor meetings for ceramics classes, discovering that fulfilment meant 'going from that to intentionally choosing to be slow, intentionally choosing to be okay with good enough and not mega ambitious for a few years.'

Her story cuts to the heart of our complicated relationship with purpose and work. 'I had this real kind of spiral of like "what am I doing in this world that is actually addressing some of this stuff?" What I was looking for was meaning, a contribution that I could be proud of, not just work that was a means to fairly superficial ends... more money, big house, status and self worth in a capitalist economy,' she says. It's a question that resonates across industries and generations, as we witness a growing recognition that the traditional markers of success – the promotions, the prestigious titles, the carefully curated LinkedIn updates – can leave us feeling more empty than fulfilled. Genevieve found that 'the sense of belonging that I had in that job in tech was quite shallow actually in terms of connection to people and ideas and work that I cared about.' What if, in our relentless pursuit of purpose through work, we've been looking in exactly the wrong place?

'Wherever you go, there you are'

This pattern repeats across industries and decades. In 2012, Greg Smith, a Goldman Sachs executive director, famously quit via a *New York Times* op-ed, describing how achieving his dream job left him feeling morally bankrupt. In the piece titled 'Why I am leaving Goldman Sachs', he criticized what he saw as a deterioration in Goldman Sachs's culture and values, describing how he felt the firm had shifted from serving clients' interests to maximizing profits at clients' expense.[3] Alexi Robichaux reached the executive level at SaaS company Evernote by age 25, only to find himself having panic attacks in his corner office. He later co-founded BetterUp, telling Worklife, 'I was pretty discombobulated through that experience. I wasn't taking great care of myself. I wasn't setting great boundaries. I wasn't taking care of my wellbeing. I wasn't getting enough sleep. I felt burnt out, and I just didn't know what I wanted to do.'[4]

What's fascinating to me isn't just that these high achievers feel unfulfilled, it's that their stories keep repeating, even as each new generation promises to 'do work differently'. Despite two decades of purpose-washing and meaning-making in corporate culture, we're still confusing career growth with personal fulfilment, mistaking the climbing of ladders for the finding of purpose. When researching this chapter, I spoke with many executives and leaders who expressed some version of the same surprise: that reaching the top regularly didn't feel like they thought it would.

The phenomenon of high achievers experiencing emptiness despite their success was notably documented in a landmark study by Manfred F R Kets de Vries. His research on 160 senior executives revealed that many experienced what he termed 'Faust Syndrome' – a state of melancholia, depression, and loss of meaning that follows the sense of everything being completed, despite reaching the pinnacle of their careers.[5]

One particularly illuminating real-world example comes from Greg McKeown, author of *Essentialism: The disciplined pursuit of less*. In his work, McKeown shares his experience consulting with Silicon Valley executives who had achieved extraordinary professional success but felt increasingly disconnected from what they valued most. As he writes, 'Success can become a catalyst for failure. It leads to what Jim Collins calls "the undisciplined pursuit of more".'[6]

> I first saw this phenomenon in working with executive teams in Silicon Valley. When they were focused on what was essential it led to success. But success comes with so many options and opportunities that it can undermine the very focus that led to success in the first place. So, exaggerating the point in order to make it clear, success can become a catalyst for failure. It leads to what Jim Collins called 'the undisciplined pursuit of more.'[7]

I've had this conversation more times than I can count. Behind closed doors, in coffee shops or during late-night Slack messages, successful executives confide the same story with different details. There's Liz, who climbed from junior developer to staff engineer, who started making TikTok content for electronic dance music. There's Genevieve, whose series of perfectly executed career moves landed her a coveted executive position at a VC, who now spends her weeks walking, doing pottery, and coaching. They've all followed the prescribed path to success – and found it leads somewhere unexpected.

What's fascinating isn't just that these high achievers feel unfulfilled – it's that they almost universally express surprise at their unfulfilment, as if they've been somehow cheated. 'I did everything right,' a VP of HR told me, requesting anonymity because even admitting these feelings felt like career kamikaze. 'I got the promotions, I hit the compensation targets, I became the youngest person to reach my level. So why does it feel like I'm just collecting badges most days?' It's a question that cuts to the heart of how we've confused career growth with personal fulfilment, mistaking the climbing of ladders for the finding of purpose.

'Why would you leave Google?' It's a question Howard Wu faced repeatedly when he departed what many considered the pinnacle of tech success. With its massage chairs, free gourmet food, and generous stock grants, Google represented the apex of Silicon Valley achievement. Yet Howard found himself struggling to articulate why he was walking away from what others saw as the ultimate dream job. 'The company was crushing it, it will keep crushing whether I'm there or not,' he reflects. 'I have no way of knowing whether it did anything because of me… some other anybody in this role probably would just do as well.'

This disconnect between external markers of success and internal fulfilment, cuts to the heart of how we've misunderstood purpose at work. The tech industry, in particular, has mastered what Howard calls the 'fluffy stuff' – grand mission statements about changing the world and transforming humanity. But as he discovered through years at various tech giants, these lofty proclamations often evaporate the moment times get tough. 'When times are good and resources [are] rich, sure, go do those things, no harm,' he explains. 'But the moment they have to make a hard prioritization…' The sentence doesn't need finishing. We've all seen what happens next.

His perspective was crystallized by a recruiting experience with a prominent fintech company. After multiple rounds of interviews, they made their final request: fly from Seattle to London on 24 December for a Christmas Day meeting. It was a test of dedication, but for Howard, it revealed something deeper about how companies view the relationship with their employees. 'You're testing me for the ultimate culture fit,' he realized. 'Then I don't pass. You should hire someone else.'

This clarity – about what matters and what doesn't – comes from what Howard describes as the liberating experience of failure. 'Getting laid off wasn't that bad, company failing wasn't that bad, going to a completely different career than the one I was good at is not that bad,' he says. Each setback built resilience and, paradoxically, freedom. It's a stark contrast to what he sees in many high achievers who've never experienced significant failure: 'Their entire identity is built around excellence and just crushing it always… I can never fail, therefore I can never course adjust. I just need to go from success to success to success to success, just crush it all the way to the grave.'

Now, when Howard meets someone new and they ask what he does, his answer has nothing to do with his role as a CEO. 'We're travelling and exploring the world with my family,' he says. It's a shift that reflects a deeper understanding of purpose – one that doesn't need to be fulfilled entirely through work. He uses the Japanese concept of ikigai to explain this to his children: 'If you can find one thing that fits all five [elements of purpose] fantastic, do that, but that is incredibly rare… so you don't need one thing to give you all five.' Instead of seeking the perfect job that fulfils every aspect of purpose, he suggests finding the three elements that matter most to you and accepting that the rest can come from other parts of life.

This more nuanced view of purpose might seem less inspiring than the tech industry's grandiose mission statements. But it's ultimately more sustainable and honest. As Howard notes, wryly referencing a friend's experience at a major coffee chain that prided itself on being a 'family': 'Be careful about saying 'we are family and the mission is more important than profit' because there will be a day where you have to choose what family you have to trim and profit is not there… you're gonna have to blow up your entire company culture to make adjustments.' Perhaps real purpose isn't found in never-ending success or world-changing missions, but in the wisdom to know what actually matters – and the courage to choose it, even when it means stepping off the path of constant achievement.

The high achievement paradox

The disconnection McKeown witnessed in his Silicon Valley consulting work when writing *Essentialism: The disciplined pursuit of less* represents more than isolated cases of executive burnout. It points to a fundamental flaw in how our culture conceptualizes the relationship between achievement and fulfilment.

'These individuals start out unhappy, but they say to themselves, "It's OK because when I make it, then I'll be happy,"' explains Dr Tal Ben-Shahar, the Harvard-trained positive psychology expert. 'But then they make it, and while they may feel briefly fulfilled, the feeling doesn't last. This time, they're unhappy, but more than that they're unhappy without hope – because before they lived under the illusion that once they make it, then I'll be happy.'[8]

This phenomenon, known as arrival fallacy, perfectly illustrates why so many companies' approaches to purpose and meaning at work is fundamentally flawed. They promise transformation and fulfilment through work alone, when research consistently shows that true happiness and purpose come from a much broader life context.

What if, instead of trying to be the primary source of purpose and meaning in employees' lives, companies right-sized their approach based on their fundamental economic reality and asked, '*What job(s) are our teams asking their job to do for them?*' Service, experiential, or transformational; once that balance is struck, and the Venn diagram crosses over, we may see a stronger alignment with fulfilment and the work we're doing in our teams day-to-day.

Research from the field of positive psychology, particularly the work of Martin Seligman, helps explain this phenomenon. Seligman's PERMA model (positive emotions, engagement, relationships, meaning and accomplishment) suggests that wellbeing requires more than just achievement – it needs a balance of multiple elements that career success alone cannot provide.[9] This is further supported by Amy Wrzesniewski's research at Yale School of Management on work orientation. Her studies show that people who view their work as a 'calling' rather than just a career or job report higher life satisfaction. However, this sense of calling isn't necessarily correlated with professional status or achievement.[10]

The Harvard Grant Study, one of the longest-running longitudinal studies of human development, provides perhaps the most compelling evidence that career success alone doesn't guarantee fulfilment. George Vaillant, who directed the study for several decades, concluded that the warmth of relationships throughout life had the greatest impact on life satisfaction – far more than career achievement or wealth.[11] The study found that 'people's level of satisfaction with their relationships at age 50 was a better predictor of physical health than their cholesterol levels were' and that relationships were 'better predictors of long and happy lives than social class, wealth, fame, IQ, or even genes'. Vaillant famously summarized this as 'the key to healthy ageing is relationships, relationships, relationships'.

So what does this mean for us in HR and leadership?

The research presents a compelling case for reconsidering how organizations approach employee fulfilment. When we examine Seligman's PERMA model alongside organizational realities, we can identify practical implications for HR and leadership practices.

The fundamental truth emerging from the research is that companies cannot (and really should not) attempt to be the sole source of meaning in employees' lives. This isn't a failure of ambition or imagination on the part of HR departments; it's a recognition of basic human psychology and the limitations of what any workplace can authentically deliver. When I reflect on my own career journey, I can see how seductive this promise became. The idea that I could find everything I needed within the four walls of an office felt efficient, tidy and wonderfully convenient. No need to cultivate friendships outside work when I had brilliant colleagues! No need to pursue hobbies when my job was intellectually stimulating! No need to volunteer in my community when my company had a robust corporate social responsibility programme! It was a neat package, until it wasn't…

PERMA and the limitations of work-based achievements

Research from Seligman demonstrates that accomplishment is just one of five key elements of wellbeing.[12] A mentor of mine (who has been interviewed for this book, and you will be meeting Huw Slater very soon in the chapters to come!) suggested I read Seligman's book *Flourish* for the research in this book, and within it I found the PERMA model of wellbeing, which can easily explain why achievement alone isn't sufficient for complete wellbeing.

Seligman's research shows that true wellbeing consists of five essential elements of positive emotions (P), engagement (E), relationships (R), meaning (M), and achievement (A).[13]

POSITIVE EMOTIONS (P)
Think of positive emotions as the warmth and light in our daily lives – those genuine moments of joy, the feeling of gratitude when something goes well, or that quiet sense of contentment at the end of a good day. While career success can create moments of happiness, it doesn't guarantee sustained positive emotions, and in fact, research shows that achievement-related happiness often fades quickly (known as 'hedonic adaptation').[14]

ENGAGEMENT (E)

Engagement is being fully absorbed in meaningful activities (often called 'flow' states). While work can provide engagement, it needs to match our skills and interests. Pure achievement pursuit can actually reduce engagement if it focuses on outcomes rather than process.

RELATIONSHIPS (R)

The Harvard Grant Study found that relationship quality was the strongest predictor of life satisfaction, far outweighing career success. It comes as no surprise then that a crucial element of wellbeing is having strong, supportive connections with others.

Olivia Johnson, a Director of People Operations at a tech startup, captures this beautifully when she describes her motivation: 'I think for me, it's really relationally based… so much of my job is figuring out how can we make people's work-life experience better, so I'm very aware of it. We all spend a lot of time at work and so anything we can do to make it less stressful or more enjoyable is worth considering.'

MEANING (M)

The whole fabric of this book; feeling connected to something larger than yourself. While work can provide meaning, it's just one potential source, and research shows that people need multiple sources of meaning for robust wellbeing.

ACHIEVEMENT (A)

While important, achievement alone doesn't fulfil our other fundamental needs. Studies show that once basic financial needs are met, additional achievement-based rewards (like higher salary) have diminishing returns on happiness.[15]

The key limitation of work-based achievement is that it typically only strongly addresses one or two of these elements (achievement and sometimes engagement), while potentially undermining others. For example:

- Long hours pursuing achievement might reduce time for relationships
- Focus on external metrics might decrease internal sense of meaning and corrupt motivation
- Competitive environments might reduce positive emotions
- Pressure to perform might decrease natural engagement

This helps explain why highly successful people can still feel unfulfilled; they've optimized for achievement while potentially neglecting other crucial elements of wellbeing. The research suggests that sustainable wellbeing requires attention to all five elements, not just achievement.

Companies excel at providing opportunities for achievement but may struggle to authentically deliver on other elements like relationships or meaning in the same way that non-work contexts can.

For HR leaders and practitioners, the PERMA framework offers us a fresh lens to reimagine how we support employees at work. We've spent years – decades! – laser-focused on helping people find meaning in their work and celebrating achievement above all else. While this element is important, we've often overlooked the other vital ingredients that make up a truly fulfilling work-life. By expanding our focus to include positive emotions, engagement and relationships alongside meaning and achievement, we can create more balanced and effective approaches to workplace wellbeing. This shift isn't just about making people happier, it's about recognizing that when we nurture all five elements of wellbeing, we create an environment where both people and organizations can thrive. The challenge now is to move beyond our traditional achievement-centric mindset and build programmes and cultures that support the full spectrum of human flourishing at work.

Now that you have identified which employment type you align with (service, experiential, or transformation economy), applying the PERMA framework to your work in your People and Culture team gives you a new way to address the full spectrum of employee wellbeing.

Service economy focus

In service-oriented workplaces where the primary product is service delivery, PERMA elements can be explored through:

- **Positive emotions**
    - Team appreciation of service or delivery excellence
    - Financial or reward and recognition programmes
    - Daily team check-ins focused on positive service experiences (such as using Seligman's 'What Went Well' framework)
    - Positive psychology training for managers
- **Engagement**
    - Cross-training opportunities

- o Customer journey mapping involvement
- o Service innovation workshops
- **Relationships**
  - o Social events
  - o Flexible and family-friendly working (to allow for your team to have more time with their relationships outside of work)
  - o Community service initiatives
- **Meaning**
  - o Customer impact stories being shared in a simple manner
  - o Clear and specific service value articulation
  - o Avoiding superfluous messaging about purpose which isn't reflective of reality
  - o Community change programmes, and opportunities for corporate social responsibility
- **Achievement**
  - o Service quality metrics publicly shared
  - o Regular pay changes
  - o Personal development and on-job training

Experience economy focus

In experience-focused workplaces where creating experiences is key to your employee alignment and product:

- **Positive emotions**
  - o Perks and benefits
  - o Off-sites and travel experiences
  - o Creative expression opportunities
- **Engagement**
  - o Immersive learning programmes
  - o Design thinking sessions
  - o High-quality laptops and tooling for engaged working
- **Relationships**
  - o Gratitude Fridays and other 'kudos' initiatives

- o Collaborative design and cross-functional work
- o Social committees and workplace advocacy groups
- o Community experiences
- o Flexible working and family-friendly policies
- **Meaning**
  - o Sharing customer stories
  - o Aligning your purpose with the reality of your company's ethics
- **Achievement**
  - o Regular promotion cycles
  - o Personal growth outside of work, supporting MBAs and higher experiential programmes
  - o Mentorship programmes

Transformation economy focus

In transformation-oriented workplaces focusing on creating lasting change in the world:

- **Positive emotions**
  - o Donations to charitable causes
  - o Positive change storytelling
  - o Mentorship recognition programmes
- **Engagement**
  - o Change management involvement
  - o Innovation labs participation and 'think tanks' for future programmes
  - o Future-state design work
  - o Personal development challenges and skill-building programmes
  - o Cross-functional projects that stretch individual capabilities
  - o Leadership development opportunities for all levels
- **Relationships**
  - o Connecting with the community
  - o Job exchange programmes and charitable community programmes
  - o Peer learning circles and professional development groups
  - o Alumni networks for continued growth beyond the company

- **Meaning**
  - High levels of communication around purpose alignment
  - Change impact measurement
  - Inviting speakers from those impacted by the work of your company
  - Personal purpose alignment sessions and individual development planning
  - Storytelling about employee transformation journeys
  - Clear pathways showing how work contributes to personal mastery and growth
- **Achievement**
  - Impact milestone celebrations
  - Celebrating achievement as a team
  - Offering sabbaticals for significant achievements to extend further into purpose work
  - Nominating teams for awards, conferences and events to share their impact
  - Personal mastery certifications and skill advancement recognition
  - Individual transformation milestone celebrations (e.g. completing leadership programmes, mastering new competencies)
  - Creating opportunities for employees to teach and share their growth with others

As you can see, purpose and fulfilment don't need to be forced or inauthentically manufactured against your company's genuine alignments; it can emerge naturally when we create the right conditions for it to flourish. By understanding your organization's economic foundation, whether service-based, experience-focused or transformation-driven, you can thoughtfully apply the PERMA framework in ways that authentically align with your workplace culture. While staying true to your dominant economy, you can selectively borrow one to two elements from other frameworks if they genuinely fit your culture. The key is authenticity over comprehensiveness. Think of it like tending a garden: you work with the soil you have, choosing plants that will thrive in those specific conditions, rather than trying to grow tropical flowers in a desert.

The beauty of this approach is that it allows HR initiatives to flow naturally from your organization's core identity. Rather than implementing one-size-fits-all programmes, you can craft experiences that resonate with your unique workplace environment. It's about starting small and growing sustainably. Pick one element of PERMA that feels most relevant to your organization each quarter, create focused pilot programmes, gather real feedback from your people, and build thoughtfully on what works. Better yet, in your planning session, ask your team the question of whether your next initiative is benefiting the PERMA of your employees. Using a measured product-management approach, which I detailed in *Built for People*, helps ensure that your efforts to enhance workplace fulfilment take root and flourish over time.[16]

The work orientation framework

Another framework to think about achievement and the archetypes that may impact how achievement and disillusionment presents itself has already been explored in this book. Wrzesniewski's research into work orientation identifies three distinct ways people view their work.

Job (focus on financial rewards)

Like within the service economy, when someone views their work primarily as a 'job,' they approach it pragmatically as an economic transaction – trading their time and effort for financial compensation. These individuals often have rich, fulfilling lives, but they may find their primary source of meaning and satisfaction outside of work. For example, they might be deeply invested in their family life, passionate about hobbies, involved in community service or pursuing personal interests. This doesn't mean they perform poorly at work; almost everyone I've ever worked with has the desire to be proud of their work, and most people are excellent colleagues with professionalism and reliability. However, folks in this zone are likely to maintain clear boundaries between work and personal life, and they don't derive their core identity from their occupation. A person with this orientation might be a skilled accountant who does quality work during office hours but finds their true joy in coaching their child's soccer team on weekends. They might be perfectly content staying in the same role for years if it provides the stability and resources that they need to support what they consider most important in their lives. This orientation isn't inherently better or worse than viewing work as a career or calling – it's simply a different way of relating to work that can be equally valid, productive and healthy.

Career (focus on advancement)

Those who view their work as a 'career' are deeply invested in their professional advancement and find satisfaction in work experiences as much as climbing the organizational ladder. These individuals are often driven by measurable markers of success – each promotion, salary increase, or expansion of responsibility serves as validation of their progress and competence. They tend to think more strategically about their professional development, actively seeking opportunities to enhance their skills, expand their network, and increase their influence within their organization or industry. While they may enjoy their day-to-day work, their primary satisfaction comes from the trajectory of their career path rather than the specific tasks they perform. For instance, a sales manager with this orientation might be less focused on the immediate satisfaction of closing deals and more interested in developing leadership skills that will prepare them for a director role. They often invest significant time in professional development, industry networking and carefully planning their next career moves. Competition energizes them, and they frequently measure their success against their peers or industry benchmarks. This isn't merely about financial rewards, it's about the personal satisfaction of achievement and recognition, though they typically view monetary compensation as a tangible measure of their professional worth and progress.

Calling (focus on fulfilment and contribution)

For these individuals, their work isn't just what they do, it's an integral part of who they are. They find inherent meaning and satisfaction in the work itself, often describing it as what they were 'meant to do'. This orientation is characterized by a strong sense of purpose where the lines between work and personal fulfilment become blurred, not because they're workaholics, but because they see their work as an expression of their authentic selves. For example, a teacher with this orientation doesn't just educate students because it's their job; they see themselves as playing a vital role in shaping future generations and would likely be drawn to teaching-related activities even outside their formal role. Their satisfaction comes primarily from the impact they have on others and their contribution to a larger purpose, rather than from external rewards or career advancement. While they might appreciate good pay and recognition, these aren't their primary motivators – they often report that they would continue their work even if they had enough money to retire. This deep alignment between personal values and professional activity often leads to high levels of resilience in facing workplace challenges, as difficulties are viewed as part of a meaningful journey rather than just obstacles to overcome.

Importantly, Wrzesniewski's research shows that these orientations are fairly evenly distributed across occupations, suggesting that meaning comes from how people view their work rather than the specific role or status level. This pattern holds true even in prestigious professions; some doctors see medicine purely as a high-paying job, others focus on career advancement in medical leadership, while some view it as their life's calling. The implications of this on HR and leadership are compelling. This challenges some common assumptions that:

- Higher-status jobs automatically provide more meaning
- Certain professions are inherently more fulfilling than others
- You need to achieve more in your career to find more meaningful work

This may feel like it somewhat puts a spanner in the works of our purpose economy model introduced in Chapter 2, which is aligned to the type of workplace you are building, but doesn't easily allow for the fact that not *all* of your customers may be subscribing to the same work orientation, as in Wrzesniewski's research. While an organization might position itself within the transformation economy – focused on creating lasting change and development, transforming your employee 'consumers' – not all employees will approach their work with the same orientation or desired outcomes. For this reason, I want to explore how the work orientation model can deeply impact and change the way we think about workplace coaching and L&D, and how we can build workplaces which may be more aligned to one space in the purpose economy model, but which have varied 'customer types'.

You may have a business in which you have clearly identified your position within the experiential economy, but you want to understand your current 'customer base' using the workplace orientation model. This activity is designed to help individuals reflect on their work orientation in a non-judgemental way. It's important to emphasize that no orientation is better than others, they're simply different ways of relating to work. One challenge of this kind of exploration is a fundamental challenge in HR: employees often feel they need to give the 'right' answer rather than the honest one, especially when talking to HR or their managers. As Olivia Johnson candidly observes: 'Obviously, they're not going to outright say [I'm here for] a pay cheque. It might be the subtext, though... because there can be an element of the company wanting people who are 110 per cent in it, and not just here for the pay cheque. There's an expectation to believe in the company's mission, whether explicitly or implicitly stated.'

This expectation creates what Olivia describes as a scenario where 'there's a right answer to that question, and it's not "I'm here for a pay cheque."' The challenge is creating space for honest reflection without the performance pressure that typically accompanies these conversations.

'I don't think companies are transparent about the fact that we're okay with this not being your passion,' Melanie Naranjo, Chief People Officer at Ethena, told me. When candidates feel pressured to manufacture enthusiasm for company missions, 'everybody sort of says it with a wink, wink and a nod,' she explains. This disconnect, she argues, undermines trust before employment even begins.

In short, your team might feel pressure to present themselves as having a 'calling' orientation since it could seem more admirable or committed. For this reason, I encourage you to be open about using external facilitators, anonymous data-sources and sharing broader explorations of these ideas.

Provide participants with three sets of statements. Randomly sort the below questions and ask your team to stack rank them based on how much they resonate:

- **Set A (Job-oriented indicators)**
  - I primarily work to support my lifestyle
  - The best part of my work is the stability it provides
  - I most look forward to time off and the opportunities flexible work allows me to spend on my outside passions
  - My main focus is maintaining a good work-life balance
- **Set B (Career-oriented indicators)**
  - I'm excited about advancing to higher levels
  - I often think about my next career move
  - Professional development is very important to me
  - I enjoy competing for advancement opportunities
- **Set C (Calling-oriented indicators)**
  - My work feels like an important part of who I am

- I would recommend my type of work to others who are looking to improve something about themselves
- I find my work inherently rewarding within the day-to-day
- I feel my work contributes to something larger than myself

The card stacking method offers several psychological advantages over traditional survey approaches when exploring work orientation. By asking people to rank statements rather than simply agree or disagree with them, we create a more nuanced and honest assessment process.

When employees see statements mixed together randomly, they can't immediately identify which orientation each statement represents. This prevents them from gravitating towards what they perceive as the 'acceptable' response. As Olivia noted, there's often an implicit expectation that employees should be passionate about their company's mission. Card stacking removes this bias by obscuring the underlying framework until after people have made their choices.

The goal of understanding work orientations isn't to categorize or label people, but rather to gain deeper insights that support genuine development and engagement, as well as individual's alignments with purpose in reality and, crucially, not just how we'd like to see it. This understanding can transform how we approach coaching and L&D strategies, creating environments where all work orientations can thrive.

Consider how different support structures might resonate across orientations. For those with a job orientation, the focus should be on creating an environment that more directly respects the whole person's relationship with work as a means to an end. This means establishing clear boundaries around work hours without the subtle penalties that often come with strict adherence to work-life balance. It means developing transparent compensation structures that recognize both tenure and performance and implementing flexible work arrangements that acknowledge life beyond the office walls.

Career-oriented employees thrive in environments rich with opportunities. Leaders should construct clear developmental pathways supported by detailed competency frameworks. Regular career conversations – distinct from performance reviews and assessments! – provide space for aspiration and planning. Formal mentorship programmes, coupled with stretch assignments and cross-functional projects, offer practical growth experiences. Professional development and experiential support, whether through travel stipends or job-adjacent-education programmes, while teetering on the transformational, demonstrates organizational investment in their advancement and experiences which are an outcome of their role, but necessarily inherent within the work.

For those who view their work as a 'calling', a key is connection to purpose. While not every organization may have an obvious social or personal transformation impact, leaders can help these employees find meaningful ways to shape their roles around purpose. This might manifest through mentoring opportunities, where they can share their passion and expertise with others or through thoughtful role crafting that aligns their work with their sense of purpose within their work.

The successful implementation of these frameworks requires intentional effort from People teams. Performance evaluation systems need careful design to recognize and value contributions across all orientations, and include job orientation within the frameworks you are building. This means moving beyond the common bias that often elevates calling-oriented behaviours or career ambition as somehow more valuable to the organization, or else we risk our teams becoming disillusioned with their place within the team.

Not all organizations will seek out the 'ideal customer' of a specific job orientation, and many may choose to embrace this diversity of orientations. If that sounds like you, you might consider flexible benefit packages that allow employees to align their rewards with their values – whether that's higher compensation, additional vacation time, or robust professional development budgets. This approach recognizes that what motivates one employee might hold little appeal for another, and that's not just acceptable – it's valuable for creating a rich, diverse workplace culture.

Beyond achievement: Aligning work orientation with wellbeing

The goal isn't to abandon ambition, but to pursue it in a way that aligns with our authentic orientation and supports our overall success at work as individuals and as teams.

Understanding our work orientation, whether job, career or calling, can provide crucial insights into why we might experience achievement burnout differently. When we align our expectations with our true orientation, rather than what we think we 'should' want, we're better positioned to build sustainable success.

The PERMA model offers a complementary framework for maintaining balance. For instance, a career-oriented individual might need to consciously cultivate relationships and positive emotions to offset their intense focus on accomplishment, while someone with a calling orientation might need to set boundaries to prevent their sense of meaning from overwhelming other aspects of wellbeing.

My own journey from those pre-dawn bicycle rides to law school, like Genevieve's realization on that London bus, illustrates how achievement alone – even in pursuit of our supposed dreams – isn't enough. What matters is understanding our personal relationship with work and success, then deliberately crafting a life that honours all dimensions of wellbeing, not just purpose and ambition, but of course… that's not the only thing that can go wrong when we are myopic in our view.

Notes and further reading

1 Kahneman, D and Deaton, A (2010) High income improves evaluation of life but not emotional well-being, Proceedings of the National Academy of Sciences, 107(38), 16489–93. doi: 10.1073/pnas.1011492107 (archived at https://perma.cc/DH57-GETD)

2 Lee, P (1969) Is That All There Is?, *Is That All There Is?* [Album], Capitol Records

3 Smith, G (2012) Why I am leaving Goldman Sachs, *The New York Times*, 14 March. www.nytimes.com/2012/03/14/opinion/why-i-am-leaving-goldman-sachs.html (archived at https://perma.cc/529Q-XE83)

4 Worklife VC (n.d.) BetterUp CEO Alexi Robichaux felt like an imposter in Silicon Valley. Then he found himself, *Worklife Blog*. www.worklife.vc/blog/alexi-robichaux-betterup-ceo (archived at https://perma.cc/2N43-4GA3)

5 Kets de Vries, M F R (2009) The many colors of success: What do executives want out of life?, INSEAD Working Paper No. 2009/19/EFE/IGLC. https://ssrn.com/abstract=1389515 (archived at https://perma.cc/4FJK-4R5P)

6 McKeown, G (2014) *Essentialism: The disciplined pursuit of less*, Crown Business, New York

7 McKeown, G (2014) *Essentialism: The disciplined pursuit of less*, Crown Business, New York

8 Shilton, A C (2019) You accomplished something great. So now what?, *New York Times*, 28 May. www.nytimes.com/2019/05/28/smarter-living/you-accomplished-something-great-so-now-what.html (archived at https://perma.cc/4BZK-MGXQ)

9 Seligman, M E P (2011) *Flourish: A visionary new understanding of happiness and well-being*, Free Press, New York

10 Wrzesniewski, A, McCauley, C, Rozin, P and Schwartz, B (1997) Jobs, careers, and callings: People's relations to their work, *Journal of Research in Personality*, 31(1), 21–33
11 Vaillant, G E (2012) *Triumphs of Experience: The men of the Harvard Grant Study*, Belknap Press, Cambridge, MA
12 Seligman, M E P (2011) *Flourish: A visionary new understanding of happiness and well-being*, Free Press, New York
13 Seligman, M E P (2011) *Flourish: A visionary new understanding of happiness and well-being*, Free Press, New York, pp. 16–25
14 Diener, E, Lucas, R E and Scollon, C N (2006) Beyond the hedonic treadmill: Revising the adaptation theory of well-being, *American Psychologist*, 61(4), 305–314
15 Killingsworth, M A, Kahneman, D and Mellers, B A (2023) Income and emotional well-being: A conflict resolved, Proceedings of the National Academy of Sciences, 120(10), e2208661120
16 Zwaan, J (2023) *Built for People: How to create a product-led people experience*, Kogan Page, London

PART TWO

Career crossroads

4

Allowing for the contemplation of change

A few years ago I found myself, armed with a calculator and a masochistic urge to torture myself with financial what-ifs, totalling up a decade's worth of dubious life choices. I spent an hour or so on a Sunday night calculating how much money I would have if I had invested all the bar and taxi money I've spent between my first year of university and my 30th birthday. Every tequila shot, every 3 am taxi ride, every 'just one more drink' that turned into a sunrise-breakfast at a greasy spoon in East London – all converted into (near sadistic) compound interest calculations. The final figure stared back at me from my spreadsheet like a disapproving financial adviser: enough money for a house deposit, give or take a few karaoke nights.

For a moment, I wallowed in that special kind of self-flagellation reserved for thirty-somethings confronting their questionable decisions. But then I thought about what that alternate, financially responsible version of me would look like. Sure, she'd have a healthy savings account, but would she have crowd-surfed at Groezrock Festival in Belgium? Would she know the fastest way to get to know your funniest neighbours is the local Wednesday pub quiz? Would she have that story about accidentally missing a flight in Japan that still makes new friends audibly snort with laughter? Would she be able to list the best places to order a Guinness in the five boroughs? (Dead Rabbit in Fi-Di in case you're curious.)

This fiscally prudent doppelgänger might own property, but she'd never have learnt that the best conversations happen in the beer garden of the Shacklewell Arms, or that some friendships are forged only in the crucible of shared bad decisions and morning-after Gregg's runs.

My maths was probably pretty OK, but the logic was all wrong. You can't calculate the compound interest on experience and joy. There's no spreadsheet column for the value of knowing exactly which song will get your friend group on the dance floor, no amortization schedule for memories that make you laugh even 10 years later.

Besides, who wants to be the person whose epitaph reads 'Made sensible career decisions'?! Give me the one that says 'Knew all the words to Dolly Parton's *Baby I'm Burnin*'' any day.

Throughout the research for this book, I came across a similar kind of algebraic regret being performed by people looking back on their careers. They'd calculate the promotions not taken to stay close to family, the safer job chosen over the risky start-up, the steady pay cheque preferred over the creative pursuit. Their mental spreadsheets of regret were meticulous: if I had taken that job in San Francisco… if I had joined that start-up before its IPO… if I had worked harder in my twenties…

One senior software engineer I interviewed explained how he could have been a millionaire if he'd joined a successful Neo-Bank in 2014, instead of staying at his comfortable job. He'd clearly run these numbers many times before, a self-inflicted financial post-mortem that had become a personal mythology. But when I asked him what he'd been doing instead during those years, his face softened. *Travelling, learning piano, meeting people he'd otherwise never have met in his life.*

I wanted to show him my bar tab spreadsheet.

The truth is, we're terrible accountants when it comes to measuring the value of our choices. We track the losses with ruthless precision while treating the gains as rounding errors. That promotion you didn't take to stay near your ageing parents? Try calculating the compound interest on having one more year of Sunday dinners together. That 'safe' job you chose over the start-up lottery ticket? Maybe it gave you the stability to pursue your passion for photography on weekends, or the mental space to be actually present in your relationships instead of constantly checking Crunchbase.

This isn't an argument for never taking risks, nor is it one for choosing comfort over ambition. It's about recognizing that our lives aren't balance sheets where every decision can be neatly categorized as profit or loss. Some of the best returns on investment come in currencies that no spreadsheet can track; interesting problems, quiet moments, relationships that deepen over time, the luxury of being there when it matters.

I've started to think we need a new kind of accounting. One that measures wealth in stories you can tell over dinner, in friendships that have weathered decades, in the number of times you've laughed until you cried. One that values presence over potential profits, and connection over compound interest.

Bronnie Ware's 2011 book *The Top Five Regrets of the Dying* became an international phenomenon, with one of its lessons being that people on their deathbeds commonly regret working too much and not spending enough time with family.[1] The book's viral success spawned countless articles, social media posts, and workplace discussions, many echoing similar sentiments: people don't die wishing they'd spent more time at the office. It's the kind of wisdom that spreads like wildfire because it feels profound – a glimpse of clarity from life's final moments, telling us what truly matters.

Living in the present tense of purpose

When we talk about finding purpose through work, we often treat it as a static quest, as if the relationship between purpose and career should remain constant throughout our lives. And when building teams, we frequently make the same mistake, expecting people's motivations and aspirations to stay relatively fixed. But as Ben Gallacher, founder and CEO of the learning platform inrehearsal (a name that in and of itself expresses the beauty of a life incomplete and ever evolving), explained during his journey from actor to entrepreneur, purpose isn't a destination but a constantly evolving relationship. 'If you've got something that is firing you and that fire is never extinguished, you're very fortunate,' he reflects. 'But if you've got an absence of fire or something that's kind of motivating you to do that, it's hard to know where to deploy your time.'

This evolution of purpose isn't just natural – it's essential. Ben describes how his own source of motivation transformed from the pure creative joy of rehearsal and experimentation while deep in a career in acting, to something entirely different when founding his company. What is called the 'arrival fallacy' – the gap between what we expect to feel when achieving a goal and what we actually feel – plays a crucial role here. 'I was doing an audition... and what dawned on me was, imagine if you get this job. I was like, I don't want to get it. I don't even want to do it. And it was that stark moment of going, I'm competing against other people for something *I don't even want to do*.'

The challenge for organizations, then, isn't to try to prevent this evolution of purpose, but to create environments that accommodate and even celebrate it. As Ben notes about his own company's approach: 'I think leaning into an acceptance that everyone is on a journey to a destination that they haven't articulated or don't know where they're going.' This might mean accepting that someone who's been a stellar employee for years might wake up one day and decide to become a pilot – and that's not a failure of retention, but a success of personal growth. The goal isn't to chain people to their current path but to create spaces where they can honestly explore where their evolving sense of purpose might lead them, whether that's within the organization or beyond it.

The 'deathbed perspective' has become a sort of secular gospel in discussions about purpose and work. We believe that in this final vantage point, hopefully peacefully and surrounded by our loved ones, we will reflect on our lives as a whole – a transcendent perspective that offers some privileged insight into what really matters.

On 31 December 2024, when I was standing at the brink of a New Year, champagne in hand, I found myself wondering (hoping!) I was making decisions that my 80-year-old self will approve of.

Over the course of my research, however, I'm coming to see that we may be fundamentally misunderstanding what these end-of-life perspectives tell us. When we orient our entire working lives around avoiding the regrets of our dying selves, we risk missing something crucial: the validity of our present experiences, ambitions, and sense of purpose. Your 28-year-old self's drive to build something meaningful through your work isn't less valid than your imagined 80-year-old self's wish for more beach vacations. The excitement you feel tackling a challenging project at 35 isn't somehow less 'true' than your hypothetical deathbed desire for more family time.

This insight struck me during a conversation with Sophie Johnson, Managing Director at inrehearsal, the learning and development company founded in London by Ben who we met earlier in this chapter. Sophie had navigated multiple career transitions in her search for fulfilment within her career. 'I chose those jobs because of a fear,' she reflected. When asked to elaborate, she described a period where she kept making decisions based on external pressures and expectations rather than what felt meaningful in the present. She moved from role to role, each time telling herself she needed something specific – to learn about sales, to get mentorship from older colleagues – but never feeling fulfilled because she wasn't trusting her present experience.

'I looked around the room, and I was like, everyone's lovely but I'm still feeling like I don't think I'm going to get answers here,' she shared about one of her roles. 'I realized the answers weren't going to come from these older people I'm working with necessarily.' Her story illustrates how the pressure to make the 'right' career choices for our future selves can actually disconnect us from finding meaning in the present moment.

The real challenge for organizations isn't to minimize work's importance in their employees' lives – it's to create environments where people can find genuine engagement and purpose in their work while having the freedom to evolve, explore and balance their lives as their priorities shift. Some of the most innovative companies are already reimagining how to do this. They're moving beyond the false dichotomy of 'work less, live more' to ask more interesting questions: How can we make work itself more alive? How can we create space for people to change and grow without having to leave? How can we honour both the ambition of youth and the wisdom of experience?

Consider Shopify's Chaos Monkey initiative, designed to disrupt ingrained work habits by cancelling recurring meetings, limiting large group calls, and encouraging teams to re-evaluate how they collaborate – freeing up time for focused, high-value work,[2] or Patagonia's policy that supports employees taking two-month breaks to pursue environmental causes.[3] These aren't just perks – they're acknowledgments that a meaningful relationship with work (in either an experiential economy or transformation economy, both presenting themselves very differently programmatically) requires the freedom to change, explore, and occasionally step away.

In this chapter, we'll explore how organizations can create environments that validate both present engagement and future flexibility. We'll look at companies that have found innovative ways to support employees in finding purpose now while maintaining the freedom to evolve. Most importantly, we'll examine how rejecting the deathbed fallacy in favour of 'present purpose' can create more authentic, sustainable ways of working.

The goal isn't to ignore the wisdom of end-of-life or hypothetical perspectives, but to stop treating them as the only valid vantage point from which to judge our choices. After all, we don't live our lives in retrospect. We live them in the present, making decisions based on who we are now while trying to be thoughtful about who we might become. Perhaps it's time for organizations to do the same – to create cultures that honour both the present and the future, the ambitious and the balanced, the drive to achieve and the need to explore.

In the sections that follow, we'll examine practical strategies for:

- Building career development programmes that encourage exploration and evolution
- Designing work environments that validate multiple relationships with purpose

- Helping employees navigate career transitions without shame or judgement
- Balancing organizational needs with individual growth

The companies that get this right won't just avoid future regrets – they'll create environments where people can fully engage with their work today while maintaining the freedom to grow and change tomorrow.

Viewing purpose from the present tense

But what if, like Bill Perkins' approach to wealth in his book *Die With Zero: Getting all you can from your money and your life*, we thought about purpose as a resource to be allocated across different life stages?[4] Consider Abbie Pugh, a former consultant with experience in scale-ups and venture capital in the United Kingdom, I interviewed who spoke about her career in a way I'm going to refer to as 'purpose buckets':

'In my 20s, I optimized for learning and earning. I worked brutal hours, but I was building skills and enjoying the work. In my 30s, I shifted to a role that let me travel and experience the world while working remotely and starting my family. Now, I'm more focused on impact – ideally working with environmentally focused companies because I want to see my involvement in a better future,' said Abbie.

This 'purpose bucketing' approach challenges traditional career narratives in several crucial ways.

The false urgency of early purpose

There's a peculiar pressure that emerges in our early 20s, sometimes as a relentless push to discover our 'life's purpose' as quickly as possible. Career counsellors, LinkedIn influencers, and well-meaning mentors all seem to echo the same message: find your calling now, before it's too late. I myself felt it, at age 17, when I was trying to decide (unfathomable now) what I wanted to do for what I perceived as 'the rest of my life'. I choose journalism and communication, a body of study that, if I am honest, has been largely abandoned and forgotten (I say this while writing my second book, so perhaps not as much as I think). This cultural expectation creates an artificial sense of urgency around purpose, as if we're all racing against some invisible clock to unlock the secret of what we're 'meant' to do with our lives.

Ben Gallacher recounts his journey from actor to entrepreneur, which illustrates the flaw in this thinking. After graduating from drama school at 21, he spent seven years pursuing what he thought was his calling: a career in professional acting. 'You come from quite, you know, you come from a working-class background,' he reflects. 'There aren't very many people where I grew up who pursued an artistic career. So you are carrying around a little bit of judgement… the self-prescribed pressure that you're putting on yourself is that, well, I really want to do well because I've taken a chance, I've done something a bit different.'

This pressure to succeed at our chosen path can actually blind us to important signals about whether that path still serves us. Ben describes how shame about potentially 'giving up' kept him in acting longer than he might have otherwise stayed: 'I think shame is the one that it took me longer to stop the thing that was making me unhappy because of the shame that I felt about going, I'm giving up. I don't want to do it anymore.'

What's particularly interesting about Ben's story is how his relationship with purpose evolved. In his early 20s, purpose was deeply connected to artistic expression and the craft of acting. But as he moved through his career, his source of meaning shifted. 'If you think about acting, that sort of fire, or the north star that I had, was the pursuit of using the sort of skills and experience of going to drama school and using that to try and forge a career in the art… experimentation, rehearsing, becoming established as an artist.'

Yet when he later founded his company, InRehearsal, his sense of purpose transformed into something different: 'When I started InRehearsal the thing that really propelled me again was this sort of chip on my shoulder… I want to make this work because I've made this commitment to do this thing.' This evolution suggests that our relationship with purpose isn't static – it grows and changes as we do.

This natural evolution of purpose is actually healthy and normal. Just as our relationships, interests and values mature as we age, so too does our sense of what gives our work meaning. In our 20s, we might be driven by mastery of a craft or the excitement of proving ourselves. In our 30s, purpose might shift towards impact and influence. By our 40s and 50s, many find purpose in mentoring others or creating lasting institutional change. We might do it all exactly backwards to those examples, the point being that these journeys we are on as individuals are shaped by our experiences, the patterns we see in the world, and our surroundings.

Yet our cultural narrative around purpose remains stubbornly focused on that initial discovery – as if finding our purpose is a one-time event rather than an ongoing journey. This creates unnecessary anxiety for young professionals who feel they must have it all figured out immediately, while simultaneously making it harder for mid-career professionals to acknowledge when their source of purpose has shifted, and so too may their path in their careers.

Ben's observation about his current approach to running his company reveals how this understanding of evolving purpose can influence leadership: 'I think leaning into an acceptance that everyone is on a journey to a destination that they haven't articulated or don't know where they're going.' This perspective allows for a more nuanced and realistic approach to career development – one that acknowledges that what motivates us at 25 might be very different from what motivates us at 35 or 45.

The key isn't to find our perfect purpose as early as possible, but rather to remain open to how our relationship with purpose evolves over time. This might mean being willing to make dramatic changes, like Ben's shift from acting to entrepreneurship, or it might mean finding new sources of meaning within our existing career paths. What matters is recognizing that purpose isn't a destination we arrive at once and for all, but rather a journey that continues to unfold throughout our working lives.

Purpose as a lifetime portfolio

When we release ourselves from the pressure of finding a single 'perfect' career that fulfils all our purpose needs, we can begin to see how different types of purpose naturally align with different life stages. Rather than forcing our entire sense of meaning into our job role, we can recognize how our relationship with purpose naturally evolves over time. This comes with understanding the demographics of our teams, and adapting our messaging to suit those 'customer profiles' within our employee base.

Ben Gallacher's journey illustrates this evolution perfectly. 'What drew me towards performance and acting is rehearsal,' he explains, describing his early-career motivation. 'The concept of being able to rehearse and iterate, try new things, experiment.' Yet as he moved through different life stages, his source of purpose shifted dramatically. What began as a pure creative drive transformed into something else entirely when he founded his company – a desire to prove success on his own terms, deliberately rejecting the '5 am culture of entrepreneurship.'

This evolution extends to how we should think about building teams. As Ben notes, 'There's serendipity in employment, there's serendipity in leadership and management.' His company deliberately avoids 'defining people's motivations in a really rigid way because it is going to be really, really changeable and it's going to be based on so many other factors and influences over their life.' This approach acknowledges that some employees might crave constant change and challenge, while others find purpose in stability and mastery. 'There are some people who actually like "I really have this like incredibly rich beautiful family life that I have, I actually like that my job is very stable".'

The key for organizations is to create environments that can accommodate this spectrum of purpose-seeking. Ben's company demonstrates this through their approach to hiring, looking not for specific skills but for 'behaviours and qualities of people.' They seek what he calls that *je ne sais quoi* – the intangible qualities that suggest someone will bring unique value, regardless of how their strengths and motivations might evolve over time. This means moving beyond traditional career ladders and rigid progression paths to create what might be better described as career ecosystems: spaces where people can explore, evolve, and find different types of meaning at different stages of their journey.

This ecosystem approach to purpose requires a fundamental shift in how we think about retention and success in our teams. Success might mean supporting an employee's decision to become a pilot, as happened in Ben's company. 'We're not going to create, like, an internal pilot training programme,' he notes, but they can celebrate and support that evolution until the time comes for the person to take their next steps. It means recognizing that a 'successful' career path might look more like a meandering river than a straight line, with different tributaries of purpose feeding into the main flow at different times.

In practical terms, this means creating organizational structures and cultures that support multiple definitions of growth and success. It means offering opportunities for both stability and change, for both deep specialization and broad exploration. Most importantly, it means acknowledging that an employee's source of purpose today might be very different from their source of purpose five years from now – and that's not just okay, it's natural and healthy.

The challenge with building truly purpose-flexible organizations is that business needs often remain stubbornly concrete. While we might philosophically embrace the idea that people's sources of purpose evolve over time, quarterly targets don't pause for personal reinvention. As Ben notes from his experience leading a growing company, there's a delicate balance between supporting individual growth and maintaining operational stability: 'The biggest opportunity to get people motivated is to give them the tools, the time and the permission to do the things that they enjoy… but we are a small team, so everyone has to get on with what they're doing.'

This tension becomes particularly acute when we consider the real costs of supporting purpose evolution. When an employee decides to become a pilot, as happened in Ben's company, the celebration of their personal growth doesn't change the fact that their role still needs to be filled. The business impact is the same whether someone leaves to follow their dreams or leaves for a competitor. Companies face a practical paradox: they need to be simultaneously stable enough to deliver consistent results and flexible enough to accommodate changing individual desires.

The traditional corporate solution has been to create structured career paths – predictable progressions that attempt to align individual growth with business needs. But as Ben points out, this approach can be fundamentally limiting: 'I think the idea that there would be some sort of dedicated role that I would only ever do is suffocating, is stifling, it's unimaginable.' Yet the alternative – creating completely flexible roles that adapt to each person's evolving sense of purpose – risks organizational chaos. How do you plan resources when everyone might be on a different purpose journey?

Perhaps the answer lies in Ben's approach to hiring, where he looks not for specific skills but for 'behaviours and qualities of people,' seeking those who can bring unique value regardless of how their role might evolve. This suggests a middle path: building organizations that have clear business needs but flexible ways of meeting them. The goal isn't to create roles that can accommodate any possible purpose, but to build teams diverse enough in their motivations and skills that individual evolution becomes a source of organizational resilience rather than disruption. As Ben reflects on his own company's growth: 'You have to kind of find space and time to allow people to express their freedom, solve their own problems, to seek out solutions to things under their own remit and with their own autonomy.'

For this reason, I encourage you to approach this problem, as much as possible, through understanding your employees in cohorts of purpose-seeking. Who is seeking a place of learning and skill development, who is exploring and learning themselves, who may be seeking impact and leadership, and where in your team is there a desire for mentorship and reflection. Each of these stages correspond somewhat with age and experience, but don't let that blind you.

Rather than making assumptions based on age or experience level, try this simple but revealing exercise with your team. The goal isn't to put people in boxes, but to understand where they currently find their strongest sense of purpose and how that might be evolving.

- **Step 1: Individual reflection. Ask each team member to reflect on these questions:**
    - What energizes you most in your current work?
    - What were your proudest moments from the last 12 months?
    - What kind of activities (in and out of work) make you lose track of time?
    - If you had complete freedom, what would you spend more time doing?
    - What aspects of work feel most meaningful to you right now?
- **Step 2: Map responses to purpose patterns**
  Now, look for patterns that align with these four purpose-seeking modes:
    - *Learning and skill building*
        - Excitement about mastering new skills
        - Pride in technical accomplishments
        - Desire for feedback and improvement
        - Focus on personal growth
    - *Exploration and self-discovery*
        - Interest in trying different roles
        - Enthusiasm for diverse projects
        - Questioning current path
        - Seeking new challenges
    - *Impact and leadership*
        - Motivation to influence outcomes
        - Desire to shape strategy
        - Interest in mentoring others
        - Focus on organizational impact
    - *Legacy and mentorship*
        - Satisfaction in others' growth
        - Interest in system-building

- Desire to share knowledge
- Focus on long-term impact

As Ben observes, 'The biggest opportunity to get people motivated is to give them the tools, the time and the permission to do the things that they enjoy doing.' This exercise helps identify what those things might be for each person, while acknowledging that, as he put it, 'Everyone is on a journey to a destination that they haven't articulated or don't know where they're going.'

The key is to approach this not as a one-time categorization but as an ongoing conversation. Ben's experience shows how purpose can shift dramatically – from the creative drive of acting to the entrepreneurial motivation of building something larger than himself. Regular check-ins about where people find their sense of purpose allow you to spot these evolutions before they become crisis points or departure decisions.

Remember, as Ben notes about his own company's approach, the goal isn't to rigidly define people's motivations but to understand them well enough to create the conditions where different types of purpose-seeking can thrive.

This mapping exercise serves not as a final categorization but as a starting point for deeper conversations about how to align individual purpose with organizational needs. It helps leaders understand where their team members currently find meaning, while remaining open to how that might evolve over time.

Now that you understand more about where your team sits in terms of their associations with purpose, it's time to start building experiences that fit those needs, but doing it in a way that is scalable for your business, and encourages more effective work, deeper connection, and a sense of fulfilment.

Learning and skill-building years

In his 20s, Ben Gallacher immersed himself in the craft of acting, spending years at drama school and working in theatre doing what he loved: experimenting, rehearsing, playing, *learning*! This period of intense skill acquisition and mastery is characteristic of our early-career years, where the purpose often lies in the pure joy of learning and development (L&D) expertise. The focus isn't necessarily on the end goal, but on the process of growth itself.

For employees in their learning and skill-building years, purpose often comes from mastery and visible progress. As Ben's experience shows, it's not just about learning itself, but about having the space to 'rehearse, iterate, try new things, experiment.' Here are specific ways organizations can facilitate this:

- **Create deliberate practice opportunities**
  - Establish 'rehearsal spaces' where people can experiment safely without fear of failure
  - Build in time for structured experimentation and learning from mistakes
  - Create opportunities to test new skills in low-stakes environments before applying them to critical projects
  - Set up simulation exercises that allow for rapid iteration and feedback
- **Enable learning through observation**
  - Shadow programmes that allow people to observe more experienced colleagues
  - Regular demonstrations of expert-level work
  - Cross-functional project opportunities to see how different parts of the business operate
  - Access to senior meetings as observers to understand high-level decision-making
- **Build feedback loops**
  - Regular skill assessments that track progress over time
  - Clear competency frameworks that show the path to mastery
  - Frequent opportunities to demonstrate new skills and get feedback
  - Peer review sessions that encourage collaborative learning
- **Provide growth infrastructure**
  - Learning budgets that people can direct towards their interests
  - Protected time for skill development (like Google's famous 20 per cent time)[5]
  - Internal workshops led by experienced team members
  - Access to external training and certification programmes

The key, as Ben's journey suggests, is to understand that this stage isn't just about acquiring skills – it's about discovering what truly engages you through the process of mastery. As he found in his acting career, sometimes what you think will fulfil you turns out not to be what you expected. The goal is to create an environment where this discovery process is not just allowed but actively supported.

This approach needs to be balanced with business needs, of course. As Ben noted about his current team, 'everyone has to get on with what they're doing.' The art is in creating learning opportunities that align with actual business objectives – turning real work into learning experiences rather than treating learning as something separate from 'real' work.

Experience and exploration years

Ben's 30s brought a significant pivot, as he moved from acting into learning and development, and eventually entrepreneurship. This period was marked by what he calls 'the doldrums' – five years working at Central School of Speech and Drama (enjoying his work, and doing good work – I know, I was a very happy customer!) that he needed 'just floating around in the middle of the Atlantic not going anywhere to think about well I don't know... how do I get out of this.' This phase often involves testing different paths and finding unexpected connections between our accumulated skills and new opportunities. The purpose here comes from exploration and discovery rather than linear progression.

CREATE SPACE FOR EXPERIMENTATION

During this phase, people often need room to test different directions without fully committing to them. As Ben's story shows, sometimes what looks like 'doldrums' is actually crucial processing time. Organizations can support this by:

- Offering rotation programmes between departments
- Creating hybrid roles that span multiple functions
- Allowing people to take on side projects in different areas
- Supporting secondments to other teams or departments

ENABLE NETWORK BUILDING

Ben's transition from acting to L&D came through an unexpected opportunity at the Royal Academy of Speech and Drama, where he was able to step into a role where he was close to his acting expertise, but delivering training on public speaking and confidence at the institution. Companies can facilitate similar serendipitous connections by:

- Creating cross-functional project teams
- Encouraging mentorship relationships across departments
- Supporting attendance at industry events and conferences
- Building internal networks through social and professional events

SUPPORT REFLECTION AND DISCOVERY

As Ben notes, his time at Central wasn't directionless – it was necessary 'to think about, well, I don't know… how do I get out of this.' Organizations can support this reflection through:

- Regular career development conversations that go beyond immediate role progression
- Professional coaching or mentoring programmes
- Sabbatical policies that allow for deeper exploration
- Protected time for personal projects or learning

VALUE DIVERSE EXPERIENCE

Ben's journey from actor to entrepreneur shows how seemingly unrelated experiences can create unexpected value. Companies can embrace this by:

- Recognizing transferable skills from different domains
- Creating roles that combine different disciplines
- Valuing non-traditional career paths in hiring and promotion
- Encouraging people to bring their outside interests and experiences into their work

The key insight from Ben's experience is that this exploration phase isn't about aimless wandering – it's about finding unexpected connections and possibilities. As he puts it, discussing his company's current approach: 'What we were really attracted to were the kind of behaviours and qualities of people… So our recruitment was just based on, is this person going to bring something unique, different that we don't currently have.'

This period might look unproductive on a traditional career trajectory, but it's often where the most valuable insights and innovations emerge. Organizations that can create space for this kind of exploration while still maintaining business performance will often find themselves with more engaged, creative and capable employees in the long run.

Impact and leadership years

Now running InRehearsal, Ben's focus has shifted to creating systems and environments that enable others to thrive. His purpose has evolved from personal achievement to organizational impact: 'The biggest opportunity to get people motivated is to give them the tools, the time and the permission to do the things that they enjoy doing.' This stage often brings a natural transition from individual contribution to enabling and amplifying the success of others.

Drawing from Ben's evolution into leadership, here's how organizations can support employees in their impact and leadership years:

CREATE SYSTEMS FOR IMPACT SCALING

Ben's focus shifted from personal achievement to creating environments where others could succeed. Organizations can facilitate this transition by:

- Giving leaders autonomy to reshape team structures and processes
- Supporting the development of new systems and frameworks
- Providing resources for team development initiatives
- Encouraging innovation in management approaches

This is reflected in Ben's unconventional approach to work culture: 'I want everyone who works with me to only give 100 per cent (rather than 110 per cent) because I think there are more things important in life than virtue signalling and pretending that entrepreneurship is a reserve only for people that are prepared to work a lot, lot harder than everyone else.'

ENABLE TRUE LEADERSHIP DEVELOPMENT

Rather than just managing, Ben focuses on creating conditions for others to thrive. Companies can support this by:

- Allowing leaders to experiment with different management styles
- Providing coaching on how to develop and empower teams
- Creating opportunities for leaders to shape company culture
- Supporting initiatives that prioritize team wellbeing and growth

It's about leaning into an acceptance that requires a different kind of leadership than traditional command-and-control approaches. It's accepting that your team is happiest when able to find their own path in their career, be driven by their own motivations and genuinely uncover what feels true to them.

SUPPORT VALUE-ALIGNED LEADERSHIP

Ben's leadership style emerged from his own journey and values. Organizations can encourage authentic leadership by:

- Allowing leaders to define success in their own terms
- Supporting different approaches to team management
- Encouraging leaders to bring their full selves to work
- Valuing diverse leadership styles and approaches

This is exemplified in how Ben approaches team building, describing a time where 'we had an incredibly zero job role in mind… What we were really attracted to were the kind of behaviour and qualities of people and that was the thing.' What he was looking for in people was something close to an internal drive that he believed he could collaborate with and find unique and unexpected benefits, rather than seek out cookie cutters of what had worked before.

FOSTER COLLABORATIVE GROWTH

Ben's approach to leadership involves sharing in the company's success. Organizations can support this through:

- Creating shared ownership structures
- Developing clear profit-sharing mechanisms
- Building transparent growth targets and milestones
- Involving teams in strategic decision-making

As Ben describes his approach with his team: 'We want you to have skin in the game, we want you to be part of this growth… we've now got a destination we're trying to get to like evaluation of the company or kind of recurring revenue target that we all share.'

The key insight from Ben's experience is that the impact and leadership years aren't about exercising power or control – they're about creating environments where others can find their own path to success. This requires organizations to trust their leaders to experiment with new approaches and to measure success not just in traditional metrics but in the growth and development of their teams.

Legacy and mentorship years

While Ben hasn't reached this stage yet, his current thinking about leadership already shows signs of this longer-term perspective. He talks about 'leaning into an acceptance that everyone is on a journey to a destination that they haven't articulated or don't know where they're going.' This stage often involves passing on wisdom, building sustainable systems, and helping others navigate their own purpose journeys.

CREATE SUSTAINABLE KNOWLEDGE TRANSFER SYSTEMS

While Ben hasn't reached this stage, his current approach to leadership hints at how valuable institutional knowledge can be shared effectively:

- Developing formal mentorship programmes that connect experienced staff with newer team members
- Creating opportunities to document and share career journey stories
- Building systems to capture and preserve organizational wisdom
- Supporting the creation of playbooks and frameworks that outlive any individual's tenure

ENABLE MULTI-GENERATIONAL IMPACT

Ben's philosophy about accepting everyone's individual journey suggests a framework for longer-term impact:

- Supporting long-term projects that extend beyond immediate business needs
- Creating advisory roles that allow experienced staff to influence without direct management
- Developing 'elder statesperson' positions that focus on strategic guidance
- Building programmes that connect company veterans with early-career employees

FOSTER CULTURAL STEWARDSHIP

As Ben demonstrates in his current role, there's value in creating space for people to shape organizational culture: 'I'm very dismissive of that sort of

5 am culture of entrepreneurship... I want to be the antithesis of people who give 110 per cent.' Organizations can support this kind of cultural influence by:

- Creating forums for sharing workplace philosophy and values
- Supporting initiatives that challenge traditional workplace norms
- Enabling experienced staff to shape company policies and practices
- Encouraging the development of alternative working models

BUILD LEGACY PROJECTS

Drawing from Ben's focus on creating sustainable systems, organizations can support legacy building through:

- Long-term initiatives that focus on organizational transformation
- Programmes that develop future leaders
- Projects that codify and transmit company values
- Opportunities to shape the direction of the industry or profession

The key insight here is that legacy isn't just about looking back – it's about creating sustainable systems for the future. As Ben notes about his own company's approach: 'I think rewarding and recognizing people's value is really important, but I do think leaning into an acceptance that everyone is on a journey to a destination that they haven't articulated or don't know where they're going.' This suggests that true legacy work isn't about prescribing paths for others, but about creating environments where they can discover their own ways forward.

This stage requires organizations to think beyond traditional retirement transitions and instead consider how they can harness the wisdom and perspective of their most experienced people in ways that benefit both the individuals and the organization. It's about creating structures that allow people to gradually shift their focus from doing to guiding, from building to teaching, from achieving to enabling.

Let me help craft a polished ending that ties these themes together.

Allowing for new relationships with purpose frees us all

What's crucial to understand is that these stages aren't rigid boxes we need to fit ourselves into, but rather natural evolutions in how we relate to purpose and meaning in our work. Ben's journey from actor to entrepreneur to leader didn't follow a predetermined path – it evolved organically as his relationship with purpose shifted. As Ben explained it to me, some people are incredibly fortunate to find something that ignites them completely, a passion that burns steadily throughout their career without ever dimming. But for those who find themselves in seasons without that fire, the challenge becomes far more complex. When you lack that clear sense of direction or motivation, every decision about where to invest your time and energy feels fraught with uncertainty.

The real power in understanding these stages comes not from trying to force ourselves to align with them, but from recognizing that our sense of purpose naturally evolves as we move through our careers. This perspective frees us from the pressure of finding one perfect, purpose-aligned job that will satisfy us forever. Instead, we can focus on ensuring our current role aligns with our current relationship with purpose, while remaining open to how that relationship might change in the future.

This framework helps explain why so many of our interviewees found traditional purpose narratives lacking. They were being sold a one-size-fits-all approach to purpose when what they needed was a lifetime portfolio approach.

The implications for organizations are significant. Instead of trying to provide complete purpose fulfilment for all employees at all times, companies need to create environments that accommodate different purpose stages and support transitions between them. This might mean:

- Supporting employees in different purpose stages differently, recognizing that what motivates someone in their learning years might be very different from what drives them in their impact years
- Creating more flexible career paths that acknowledge purpose evolution, allowing for both vertical and horizontal movement
- Helping employees plan for purpose transitions, providing resources and support for career exploration
- Building alumni networks that support purpose shifts over time, maintaining connections with former employees who might return with new perspectives and purposes

This portfolio approach to purpose doesn't diminish the importance of meaningful work. Rather, it suggests that purpose might be better optimized when thoughtfully allocated across our lifetimes rather than frantically pursued at every moment. As Ben's experience shows, sometimes what looks like 'the doldrums' – those periods of floating and questioning – are actually crucial moments of purpose evolution.

The key is creating organizational cultures that can embrace this complexity. As Ben demonstrates in his approach to running InRehearsal, this means leaning into an acceptance that everyone is on a journey to a destination they haven't yet articulated or don't know they're heading towards. It means recognizing that someone deciding to become a pilot isn't a failure of retention but a success of personal growth. Most importantly, it means understanding that our relationship with purpose, like any meaningful relationship, will change and evolve over time – and that's not just okay, it's exactly as it should be.

Notes and further reading

1 Ware, B (2011) *The Top Five Regrets of the Dying: A life transformed by the dearly departing*, Hay House, Carlsbad, CA
2 Chan, J (2023) Shopify's 'Chaos Monkey' is coming for your meetings, *Business Insider*, 4 January.
3 Deloitte (2023) Sparking the sustainability cultural shift at every level: Patagonia Case Study, World Economic Forum Industry-Net-Zero Accelerator. https://initiatives.weforum.org/industry-net-zero-accelerator/case-study-details/patagonia---sparking-the-sustainability-cultural-shift-at-every-level (archived at https://perma.cc/73J9-UET3)
4 Perkins, B (2020) *Die With Zero: Getting all you can from your money and your life*, Houghton Mifflin Harcourt, Boston, MA
5 Mediratta, B (2007) The Google way: Give engineers time, *New York Times*, 16 October. www.nytimes.com/2007/10/16/jobs/16google.html (archived at https://perma.cc/U6YW-D8CQ)

5

The risks of leaping

I don't know if the internet has ever been a particularly quiet force (trite sayings like the 'quiet corners of the internet' have always bothered me), but it has absolutely been a *revealing* one.

On forums like Reddit, professionals share vulnerabilities about career paths they rarely voice in workplace settings. One architect lay bare their disillusionment: 'Extremely rigorous schooling, cut-throat internships, seven licensing exams that are four hours long, endless lay-offs, all for an average £70,000 in super HCOL (high cost of living) areas… that feeling of wasting decades. It can eat you up inside.' Without the protective masks we wear at work, these digital confessionals expose the raw emotions underlying career transitions – regret, uncertainty and the persistent search for meaning.[1]

This online candour reveals inner dialogues that shape workplace decisions and disengagement. Another professional on the Reddit thread admits: 'Over the past five years I've started to imagine how life would be if I was in other people's shoes. Like if I go to visit the dentist, I'll think to myself how a day in the life of a dentist or receptionist is.'[2] Even after one successful career change, they wonder if they're 'still not fulfilled', questioning whether 'the grass was greener on the other side'. These conversations expose not just career disappointments but deeper questions about identity, purpose, and the causes of professional restlessness that employees rarely discuss with their managers or company leaders.

It is almost certain that within your own organization (or even team) you have colleagues who are also struggling with these same questions of career and fulfilment. The difference is that these thoughts often remain unspoken in professional settings, hidden behind the polite facade of engagement or the subtle signs of quiet quitting.

As mentioned in Chapter 4, braiding the common threads of fulfilment and purpose is not as simple as upping and leaving the corporate world. The challenge extends beyond individual career choices to how organizations respond to these natural evolutions in professional identity. This chapter explores how companies can build environments that are dynamic and allow for change when someone has realized their role or career may not be for them: cultures that embrace rather than resist the career crossroads many employees inevitably face.

The decision to change careers carries inherent risks – financial uncertainty, identity disruption, and the very real possibility that the new path won't deliver the anticipated fulfilment. Yet organizations that acknowledge this reality and actively work to make current roles more meaningful often discover a powerful paradox: by creating environments where employees can honestly explore their evolving interests and what brings them fulfilment, companies actually reduce unnecessary turnover while facilitating more intentional transitions when appropriate. This approach transforms the traditional binary of 'stay or leave' into a more nuanced conversation about growth and alignment. When managers engage authentically with employees standing at career crossroads, they open possibilities for role redesign, internal transfers, or even supported external transitions that preserve relationships and institutional knowledge. The result is a workplace culture where risk becomes a shared consideration rather than a solitary burden, where purpose is regularly recalibrated rather than desperately sought elsewhere (after all, in times of silent crisis, it is easy to seek what may seem to be greener pastures), and where both individuals and organizations benefit from treating career evolution as an expected dimension of professional life rather than a failure of engagement.

The business impact of unaddressed career questioning can be astronomical. According to Gallup's 2017 'State of the American Workplace' report, replacing an employee typically costs between one-half to two times their annual salary when accounting for recruitment, onboarding and productivity losses.[3] More specifically, Josh Bersin's 2020 article 'The definitive guide to internal mobility' shows companies that excel at internal mobility retain employees nearly twice as long as those that don't, with average tenure increasing from 5.4 to 9.8 years.[4] Beyond simple retention metrics, as Harvard Business School Professor Boris Groysberg demonstrates in *Chasing Stars*, organizations that build strong systems to support employees through career transitions are far more likely to retain high performers and help them succeed in new roles, capturing value that might otherwise be lost to competitors.[5] The ROI becomes particularly compelling in light of LinkedIn's '2023 Workplace Learning Report', which reveals that employees who feel their company provides growth opportunities are 3.5 times more likely to be engaged than those who don't, regardless of whether they change roles internally or stay in their current position.[6]

Leaders often miss the subtle signals that employees are questioning their professional paths until exit interviews reveal what was happening beneath the surface. By then, it's too late. Understanding the behavioural indicators of career questioning can transform these moments from unexpected departures into opportunities for meaningful support and intervention. Think of it as preventive medicine rather than emergency treatment. Just as doctors look for early warning signs of health issues during routine check-ups, effective leaders develop regular practices that naturally surface information about their team's changing relationship with work. The goal isn't to catch people planning their inevitable escape, but to create an environment where you can recognize natural career evolution and respond proactively before it becomes a crisis.

The prevalence of these reflections points to a critical opportunity for organizations. While previous chapters explored how companies can identify and support purpose pathways, this persistent questioning suggests that responsibility doesn't rest solely on management's shoulders. Companies and employees that recognize these crossroads moments – and the complex feelings they generate – gain significant advantages in talent development, creating environments where purpose becomes an ongoing conversation rather than a private struggle.

Recognizing the signs of career crossroads

I once had a CEO tell me with absolute certainty that his head of product was 'more engaged than ever' just two weeks before they handed in their resignation. The executive team was blindsided, but the signs had been there for months – the gradually shortened time horizons in planning, sudden interest in marketing projects, the way they'd stopped challenging decisions which would have previously been fought tooth and nail over.

READING THE TEA LEAVES

Spotting career crossroads isn't about installing surveillance cameras in the break room or monitoring Slack discussions like we're all checked into Watergate Hotel. It's about developing the organizational equivalent of peripheral vision; the ability to identify subtle shifts in behaviour and engagement before they become obvious problems for all parties involved, not just for the company. The goal isn't to sneak up and catch people planning their inevitable escape, but to create an environment where you can recognize a natural career evolution when it's beginning to surface and respond proactively and supportively to find a solution which may be a more reciprocal solution. The ideal situation is that you are, as a leader within your organization, able to address places where a purpose gap may be addressable in your business operations and save any unnecessary attrition.

> The goal isn't surveillance or extracting loyalty pledges, but designing workflows that naturally illuminate when someone's professional compass starts pointing in a new direction that you can prepare for, or travel forwards together.

Some signs I've seen in interviews and throughout my career have been:

The incredible shrinking time horizon. Watch when someone who used to champion three-year strategies suddenly shows interest only in quarterly deliverables. This narrowing of focus often reflects uncertainty about their future with you. When they stop buying into the long-term plan, it may be because they're unsure how they should be seeing themselves in it.

The selective check-out. Notice the previously all-in team member who's now mysteriously unavailable for certain meetings but hyper-engaged in others. They're not being flaky; they may be experimenting with letting go of parts of their identity that no longer fit while doubling down on elements they might carry forward.

> The above example makes me think about Genevieve, who we met in Chapter 3 as she moved from VC to her new life in Portugal, when she spoke about, 'nurturing aspects of myself, my interests, and my personality that had been dormant for a long time.' This kind of thinking can look like someone reconnecting with a part of them which has previously felt 'cut off', and it can be sudden, but it can also be more gradual or exploratory, such as in the case of someone looking broader than their role and into new career interests within their current team.

- **Newly developed interests.** Take note when your marketing director suddenly volunteers for a data analytics project or your engineer starts hanging around sales calls. These may not just be random curiosities; they could present test flights into alternative futures. It's worth noting that I think these are also likely to be highly positive signs, and ones that should be a great opportunity to double down on understanding the driving factors. Seeing someone take on a new interest in design when they've been working as an engineer, or finance as they've been working in business operations, can be an opportunity for a more 'T-shaped' skill set that can be highly beneficial today while work is going through such a rapid development in the face of technological advancement.

- **The purpose interrogation.** Pay attention when an employee begins openly questioning the fundamental premises of the organization's mission. This goes beyond typical workplace critique – it's a more fundamental challenge where they start dissecting the company's stated purpose, challenging presentations about organizational impact, or raising pointed questions during meetings that reveal a deeper scepticism about the work's meaning. When someone moves from being a participant to becoming a persistent interrogator of the organization's core narrative, it can signal that they're no longer aligned with the underlying purpose and are actively seeking to understand – or expose – potential misalignments between the company's stated mission and its actual practice.

The key insight here isn't just recognizing these signals, but understanding that they represent valuable opportunities for investigation and potential mutual intervention. Each behaviour is a potential conversation starter that could transform a potential departure into a meaningful realignment to benefit you, your colleague and your team at large.

Creating systems to spot career crossroads signals

Identifying career questioning shouldn't rely on managerial mind-reading or invasive monitoring. Instead, organizations can establish thoughtful mechanisms that naturally surface these signals while respecting employee autonomy:

- **Structured check-in frameworks.** Replace vague 'how's it going?' conversations with structured career check-ins that normalize discussions about evolving professional identities. Questions like 'Which aspects of your work energize you most right now?' and 'What skills are you eager to develop that you aren't using regularly?' can reveal shifting interests without triggering defensive responses.

Project post-mortems with a twist. Expand project reviews beyond 'What went well/what didn't' to include reflections on personal engagement: 'Which parts of this work did you find most meaningful?' and 'If you could redesign your role in the next project, what would you change?' These discussions create natural openings for employees to express evolving preferences without feeling they're initiating a difficult conversation.

Team temperature maps. Have department leaders discuss which strategic initiatives generate authentic enthusiasm from team members versus what may feel more like compliance-level engagement. Tracking these patterns over time can reveal when previously enthusiastic champions begin shifting their energy elsewhere – often a precursor to deeper questioning.

Learning allocation trackers. Make a system which gives oversight to where employees choose to invest their developmental time and energy: the projects they volunteer for, the skills they develop independently, the feedback they request. These self-directed investments often reveal emerging interests that might signal new directions. A great way to do this systemically can be through your learning management system (LMS). Leveraging modern systems like Sana to gain deep insights into employees' self-directed learning trajectories can be very revealing for predictors of behaviour. These platforms provide granular analytics that go beyond simple course completion rates, revealing the nuanced learning patterns that signal emerging interests and potential career shifts. Track metrics like time spent in specific learning modules, voluntary skill acquisition across different domains, and the progression of learning paths that deviate from standard role-based training. When an engineer begins consuming marketing strategy courses, or a sales representative dives deep into data analysis modules, these are not just casual explorations but potential indicators of broader career questioning and evolving professional identities.

> 'Unlike scheduled learning sessions where engagement can be performative, learning in the flow of work reveals genuine curiosity and emerging passions. Traditional LMS systems tell you who completed what course, but they miss the most revealing data: spontaneous questions, topics explored during downtime, moments when people choose to dig deeper.

'We've found that the richest learning insights come from capturing these authentic moments in the flow of work – when someone's struggling with a concept outside their expertise, or during a coffee break when they want to understand something a colleague mentioned. This is why we developed an AI tutor that's available in these real moments of need, creating a detailed map of genuine interests and emerging competencies through voluntary interactions.

'When you can see where people choose to spend their learning energy – not where they're required to – you get a much clearer picture of where their careers might go.'

Rita Azevedo, Senior Engagement Manager, Sana

Cross-functional exposure initiatives. Create structured opportunities for employees to experience different functions through rotation programmes, shadowing opportunities or cross-functional projects. These experiences not only provide development opportunities but also surface valuable data about where employees' interests naturally gravitate. They can also be fantastic ways to get proactive cross-functional contributions into certain projects, pieces of work or places where diverse perspectives will benefit the overall delivery.

The strength of these approaches lies in their integration into normal business operations rather than appearing as special 'retention initiatives'. They create natural opportunities for career questioning to surface within the context of everyday work, allowing leaders to respond to emerging signals before they become resignation letters.

Most importantly, these systems work best when they're genuinely bidirectional – not just tools for managers to extract information, but frameworks that help employees articulate and explore their evolving relationship with work in a supported environment. The goal is creating conditions where both the organization and individual benefit from increased transparency around career evolution.

Creating a culture of career transparency

The modern workplace hosts a curious paradox: we've developed sophisticated frameworks for professional development, yet many employees still feel compelled to hide their deepest questions about purpose and meaning. Organizational psychologist Adam Grant has critiqued how modern career architectures – despite their sophistication – can feel restrictive, turning what should be journeys of growth into rigid trajectories that diminish personal fulfilment. In multiple episodes of *WorkLife with Adam Grant*, Grant has explored how organizational systems can inadvertently box people in. For instance, in 'The Problem with all-stars' and 'A world without bosses', he talks about how formal career ladders and rigid structures can limit creativity and fulfilment.[7]

The consequence is predictable: employees develop a kind of workplace code-switching, presenting professionally acceptable versions of their career interests while keeping their deeper questions private. This disconnect between sophisticated systems and authentic employee needs isn't just about career structure – it extends to how we approach engagement itself. Burnout researcher Christina Maslach, who has spent decades studying workplace engagement, has shown that organizations often focus on surface-level engagement initiatives while neglecting deeper drivers of meaning and purpose at work.[8] This gap runs deeper than job satisfaction and speaks to our fundamental need to connect our work to our sense of identity.

The irony is palpable. Companies tout mission statements, invest in elaborate performance management systems, and create intricate career development programmes, all while maintaining an unspoken culture that discourages employees from honestly exploring their professional aspirations. As one senior HR leader confided during my research, 'We talk endlessly about career paths, but rarely about the underlying human questions of purpose and fulfilment.'

This reluctance to engage in genuine dialogue about career purpose isn't just a communication problem, it's a fundamental misalignment between organizational structures and human needs. Employees are left to navigate their professional uncertainties in silence, treating career questioning as a form of disloyalty rather than a natural part of professional growth.

The quest for purpose at work is not a one-size-fits-all journey. Just as businesses can move into different economic stages as we've discussed – between goods, to services, to experiences and to transformations – so, too, can employees' relationships with their professional lives between job, career and calling. Creating a culture of career transparency means recognizing that purpose manifests differently for each individual, whether they're seeking a straightforward job, an enriching career experience, or a transformative professional path.

Beyond the one-dimensional career narrative

Traditional workplace cultures have treated careers like fixed railroad tracks – linear, predetermined, with little room for deviation. This approach fundamentally misunderstands how modern professionals view work. As Amy Wrzesniewski's research reveals, people relate to work through three distinct orientations: a job (service), a career (experience), or a calling (transformation).[9] Consider the bank teller who views work as a reliable means to support their family, the tech designer who sees their role as an exciting journey of creativity, and the artist driven by the mission of connection and self-discovery through their work. Each finds meaning differently, yet traditional organizational structures often fail to accommodate these diverse perspectives.

THE SPECTRUM OF PROFESSIONAL PURPOSE

Creating a culture of career transparency requires acknowledging this spectrum of purpose introduced in Chapter 2:

1 **Service economy professionals**: These individuals seek clear expectations, fair compensation, and work-life boundaries. Transparency for them means honest, straightforward conversations about roles, compensation and advancement.

2 **Experience economy professionals**: These employees want more than just a pay cheque, they're seeking workplace experiences that feel special, distinctive… Transparency here means creating environments that support professional exploration, skill development, and personal growth. For these professionals, career transparency means: clear visibility into potential growth trajectories that go beyond linear promotions; regular, structured dialogues about how their current role can evolve to match their emerging professional interests; and insight into how their current work connects to broader organizational opportunities.

3 **Transformation economy professionals**: These are the purpose-driven individuals who see work as a vehicle for meaningful change for themselves and, perhaps, for the world. They're not just looking for a job or an experience, but an opportunity to develop themselves through their work; a true calling. For transformation economy professionals, transparency means radical authenticity.

MECHANICS OF TRANSPARENT CAREER DIALOGUES

Transparent career conversations go beyond traditional performance reviews. They're collaborative explorations of an employee's evolving professional identity. Instead of asking, 'Are you planning to stay?', leaders might ask:

- What aspect of your work feels most meaningful to you right now?
- How does your current role align with your broader professional aspirations?
- What transformations are you seeking in your professional journey?
- And – perhaps difficult to ask – Do you feel your role helps you achieve whatever purpose looks like in your life; how can we help you feel like the work you're doing gives you fulfilment, whatever that is for you?

> Note: Remember that for some this may be supporting their family, but for others it may be saving the Great Barrier Reef; not all answers will be the same or directly related to your company's mission and that is okay!

THE ROI OF AUTHENTICITY

Helen Tupper and Sarah Ellis, authors of the bestselling *The Squiggly Career*, argue that 'the career ladder is dead.[10] We're now in an era of career rock climbing – where movement isn't just vertical, but can be lateral, diagonal, and sometimes even requires letting go to find a better grip.' Their research shows that organizations embracing 'career lattices' (multi-directional career frameworks) see significant benefits.[11]

Organizations that create space for honest career discussions often experience lower turnover. Research from *MIT Sloan Management Review* shows that while most employees desire career advancement, many lack access to transparent development paths; this disconnect contributes to dissatisfaction and turnover.[12] As Gallup notes, 'Employees who have regular, meaningful conversations about their goals and successes are significantly more likely to be engaged – and engaged employees are much less likely to leave' (Gallup, 2023).[13] When employees feel their professional evolution is genuinely supported – if that evolution might eventually lead them elsewhere – they remain more engaged and productive while they are in your team.

The infrastructure underpinning most organizational career discussions remains stubbornly antiquated. As Alison Lands, Head of Strategy at talent technology company Skyhive, observes: 'In the past, we've operated largely off of jobs and occupation-based paradigm where we're using job titles, job descriptions, occupational categories, infrastructure that was largely created at the turn of the 20th century, it was part of the industrialization of our economy. And those practices have largely been in place, and we continue to operate them. The challenge is that we've had several economic evolutions in the intervening century that have dramatically changed how we work.'[14]

Organizations serious about supporting genuine career transparency must move beyond annual performance reviews and vague 'development discussions' towards practices that reflect how people actually grow and evolve professionally.

PRACTICAL IMPLEMENTATION STRATEGIES

Creating this culture requires:

- Regular, structured career exploration discussions
- Internal talent marketplaces that make lateral moves visible
- Leadership training emphasizing coaching over controlling
- Compensation systems that reward T-shaped growth, not just hierarchical advancement

At its core, career transparency is about recognizing a fundamental truth: careers are complex, multidirectional explorations. Some seek a simple relationship with their work to focus elsewhere on their fulfilment, others seek experiences, and some seek transformation. The most progressive companies understand that an employee's potential growth might occasionally mean growing beyond current organizational boundaries, and that's not a failure, but an opportunity for mutual evolution.

INTERNAL PATHWAYS FOR PURPOSE EXPLORATION

'Find your passion and stick to it' may be the most dangerous career advice of our generation. With AI reshaping entire industries and the future of work constantly shifting, adaptability matters more than unwavering commitment to a single path.

Professional restlessness isn't a problem to solve, it's the new reality to embrace. The most progressive companies are creating deliberate mechanisms for employees to explore, experiment and evolve within their walls rather than watching them leave to do it elsewhere. The companies doing this aren't just being nice, they're being strategic. In a world of constant change, organizations need employees who can pivot, adapt, and grow in multiple directions.

The most effective rotation programmes go beyond simple exposure, and are designed more as systematic experiments in professional strengths. Unlike traditional job shadowing or temporary assignments, these programmes create genuine learning laboratories where participants can test hypotheses about their interests while contributing real value to the organization.

ROTATION PROGRAMMES: THE CAREER EXPLORATION SANDBOX

Rotation programmes can serve as powerful 'discovery engines' for personal and professional development – providing structured, low-risk environments where employees gain meaningful exposure to different functions. At Spotify, for example, the Finance Analyst Rotation (FAR) programme gives early-career analysts a holistic, meaningful two-year experience across Spotify's finance organization. Similarly, the Rotational Product Management (RPM) programme immerses participants in different roles, helping them explore and grow in the product space before settling into a long-term track.[15] In 2018, I worked with my team at McCann Worldgroup to build CANVAS, a new kind of rotation programme, which went on to win Gold at the Inhouse Recruitment Awards in the UK. This programme was designed around the premise that junior talent often joins agencies with little understanding of what they actually want to do – and that's perfectly fine. Rather than forcing early-career professionals into rigid specialization tracks, CANVAS gave participants 15 months to explore different disciplines within the agency ecosystem.[16]

The programme structure was deliberately flexible: participants spent time across account management, strategy, creative, production and business development, with each rotation lasting three to four months. What made CANVAS different was its emphasis on genuine integration rather than observation. Participants weren't just shadowing – they were contributing to real client work, attending pitch meetings, and taking ownership of specific deliverables.

The results exceeded our expectations. Not only did we see significantly higher retention rates among CANVAS graduates, but many discovered passions in areas they'd never considered. Perhaps most importantly, the programme created a cohort of professionals who understood the business holistically, making them invaluable as they progressed in their careers.[17]

Key design principles for rotation programmes:

1. **Clear learning objectives for each rotation:** Define specific skills, knowledge, or insights participants should gain from each placement. These should align with both individual development goals and organizational needs.
2. **Structured mentorship and reflection processes:** Assign mentors in each rotation who can provide context, guidance and honest feedback. Build in regular reflection sessions to help participants process their experiences and identify patterns in their interests and strengths.
3. **Tangible project outcomes that add value to the organization:** Ensure rotations involve meaningful work, not make-work. Participants should leave behind completed projects or improvements that demonstrate their contribution and give them concrete achievements to reference.
4. **Transparent pathways for pursuing discovered interests:** Create clear mechanisms for participants to transition into roles or departments that sparked their interest. This might include priority consideration for openings, structured transition periods, or exploratory role creation.
5. **Cross-functional skill mapping:** Track how skills and knowledge transfer between rotations, helping participants and the organization understand how diverse experiences create unique value propositions.
6. **Outcome tracking and programme evolution:** Monitor where participants land post-rotation, their satisfaction levels, and long-term retention. Use this data to continuously refine programme design and demonstrate ROI to leadership.

Implementation considerations:

- **Duration and pacing:** Most successful programmes run 6–24 months total, with 2–6 month rotations allowing enough time for meaningful contribution without losing momentum
- **Selection criteria:** Balance high-potential employees with those showing career uncertainty or restlessness, both groups benefit significantly
- **Manager buy-in:** Invest heavily in training receiving managers to maximize the learning experience and minimize disruption
- **Budget for transition costs:** Account for the productivity dip during role changes and the mentoring time required

SABBATICAL AND EDUCATION POLICIES: BEYOND TRADITIONAL LEARNING

What is one of the most radical things you can do as an employer? Tell someone fantastic to stop working for *you… temporarily.*

Modern sabbatical and education policies are ditching the old 'send them on a compliance course' mentality for something far more interesting: giving people permission to pursue what genuinely excites them. Smart organizations have realized that an engineer who spends six weeks building wells in rural communities, or learning oil painting in Italy often returns with more valuable insights about creativity and problem-solving than any corporate training could provide.

Patagonia exemplifies this approach by actively encouraging employees to take time for environmental activism.[18] They've discovered that passion exploration isn't a distraction from work: it's fuel for their transformational strategy. When someone returns from defending old-growth forests, they don't just bring back environmental knowledge; they bring renewed energy, fresh perspectives, and often unexpected connections between their cause and their day job.

Consider the experiential-aligned company that funds a product manager's month-long immersion in design-thinking workshops in Copenhagen, or the marketing team that sponsors an employee's documentary filmmaking course. These aren't feel-good perks – they're strategic investments in human potential that traditional L&D budgets could never match.

The companies brave enough to bet on their people's curiosity consistently find that what looks like time away from work becomes the foundation for their most innovative thinking when employees return.

Essential elements for building a sabbatical programme:

- **Set clear eligibility criteria:** Define minimum tenure requirements (typically three to five years), performance standards, and application processes. Consider offering different sabbatical lengths based on seniority or service years.

- **Establish funding frameworks:** Decide what you'll cover (salary percentage, specific costs, or stipends), set annual budgets, and create approval processes. Some companies offer 50–100 per cent salary for shorter sabbaticals or partial funding for longer ones.

- **Create structured application and planning processes:** Require detailed proposals outlining objectives, timelines and expected outcomes. Build in manager approval workflows and ensure adequate coverage planning for the employee's absence.

- **Design re-entry and knowledge-sharing mechanisms:** Plan structured debriefs, presentation opportunities, or internal blog posts where returning employees can share insights. This maximizes organizational learning and helps justify the investment.
- **Start small and measure impact:** Launch with a pilot group, track metrics like retention, engagement and innovation outcomes. Use early results to refine the programme and build a business case for iterations.

> Tip: Make sabbaticals a competitive advantage by promoting them during recruitment – top talent increasingly values these opportunities as much as traditional benefits.

Designing roles with purpose variability

The most radical approach to purpose exploration is redesigning roles themselves to be inherently flexible. It's something I seem to never stop talking about (apologies in advance if you've listened to my podcasts before, just know that it's important!). In the rapidly evolving landscape of AI and technological disruption, the concept of T-shaped roles has become increasingly critical for organizational adaptability and innovation. T-shaped professionals are characterized by deep expertise in one specific area (the vertical bar of the T) combined with broad knowledge across multiple disciplines (the horizontal bar), making them uniquely valuable in complex, interdisciplinary environments.[19]

T-shaped professionals represent a new paradigm of workforce development; individuals who combine deep expertise in a specific domain with a broad understanding of interconnected fields. This approach goes beyond traditional skill silos, creating professionals who can navigate complex, multidisciplinary challenges with nuance and creativity.[20]

The design of these roles requires a fundamental rethinking of how organizations approach talent development. It's no longer sufficient to hire for a narrow set of technical skills or expect employees to remain static in their capabilities. Instead, companies must create environments that actively encourage exploration, cross-pollination of ideas, and continuous expansion of a role scope.

As technological disruption and sustainability challenges grow increasingly complex, the ability to move fluidly across disciplines has become a

FIGURE 5.1 T-shaped people and roles

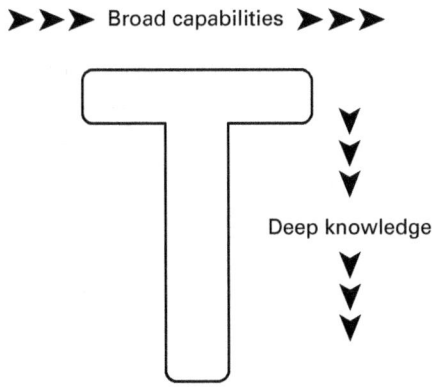

Can apply their more fluid skills across various situations, while maintaining functional knowledge on specific problems when needed

critical organizational capability. It's forcing us to fundamentally reimagine how teams form, how knowledge flows, and how breakthrough innovation emerges at the intersection of different domains.

When T-shaped professionals collaborate, their deep expertise anchors the work while their broad knowledge creates unexpected connections. The result isn't just additive, it's multiplicative.[21] Cross-pollinated teams of T-shaped individuals consistently outperform traditional siloed structures because they can see problems from multiple angles simultaneously, identify solutions that single-discipline teams miss, and execute with a sophistication that comes from truly understanding the broader ecosystem they're operating within.

In a world where the most pressing challenges exist at the intersection of technology, human behaviour, and systems thinking, T-shaped collaboration isn't a nice-to-have, it's the competitive advantage that separates thriving organizations from those struggling to keep pace.

The economic implications are profound. Organizations that can create more flexible, adaptable workforce structures will have a significant competitive advantage. This means designing roles that are not constrained by traditional job descriptions, but instead are built around the ability to solve complex, evolving challenges.

REAL-WORLD EXAMPLE
Making T-shaped potential visible

Most organizations struggle with working out how to identify people who can grow beyond their current role. Traditional performance reviews tell you who's good at their job today, but they're often quite flawed at predicting who could adapt, learn and contribute across different areas tomorrow.

DealMaker, a fintech company that prides itself on making data-informed decisions, faced exactly this challenge. Their performance management focused on standard metrics that only look backwards: sales numbers, project delivery, technical competencies. But these measures only captured current performance, not future potential. When they needed people who could work across functions or take on broader responsibilities, leaders knew they weren't data-informed and felt more like they were guessing.

The company's approach was typical of many organizations: their efforts concentrated on quality of hire but had no reliable way to check for quality of employees. They relied on interview questions designed to surface tenacity and adaptability beyond their immediate function. Managers would ask what candidates what dissatisfied them (and they can't wait to fix) or which topics they chose to lead in peer discussions. But this only worked during hiring and they had no systematic way to identify these qualities in existing employees. The limitation became particularly evident during calibration meetings. Leaders would have ill-informed debates about who deserved promotions or stretch assignments, often defaulting to whoever was most vocal about their achievements or had the strongest advocate in the room. The process felt subjective and political.

The good news is there are new ways that are emerging with technology to give leaders more granular (technology enabled!) insights into these kinds of questions, which are almost impossible for a single human to ascertain a solid and repeatable answer to. When DealMaker adopted Incompass Labs – a 360-degree evaluation tool focused on organizational network analysis and incentive-compatible grading – they gained visibility into behaviours that signal adaptability and tenacity: pushing limits, finding a way, innovating and driving outcomes. The platform captured peer observations about traits like effectiveness outside of their function/team, tenacity and resilience, which are crucial for T-shaped individuals who are likely candidates to be successful at DealMaker.

The results surprised them. Some high performers on traditional metrics scored poorly on adaptability measures, while others who seemed average in their current roles showed deep network connections and strong potential for growth. The data revealed patterns that were gathered during interviews that standard employee reviews had missed entirely.

The change wasn't just about better data – it shifted how the organization made decisions. As their VP of People and Operations, Kara Wilson Oliver, explained: 'The power of this approach is that it extends decision-making into the hands of the broader organization. There is inherent wisdom in the crowd. Long gone are the days of myopic reviews where only the manager's opinions count, and we all sit around and pretend we can calibrate a bunch of sentiment data ourselves. Getting performance assessment right, including surfacing T-shaped employees, should be a key focus for all heads of People. In fact, I would contend it's the most important work we do.

But the tool also revealed hidden and uncomfortable truths, ones that enabled them to optimize their workforce. Some long-term employees who'd been passed over for development opportunities actually had strong T-shaped potential that had never been recognized. This forced DealMaker to reconsider how they'd been making promotion and development decisions.

The real test came when they had to choose people for a new cross-functional project. Instead of defaulting to obvious choices, they could identify employees who demonstrated the behavioural markers for success in ambiguous, collaborative environments. Six months later, several of these selections had exceeded expectations, validating the approach. The case highlights both the promise and complexity of measuring potential rather than just performance. While tools like this can surface hidden talent, they also expose how many organizations have been making talent decisions based on incomplete information.

Some practical steps on how to build a future that is more T-shaped:

1. Building 20 per cent time principles into job descriptions.
2. Creating role frameworks with explicit exploration components.
3. Developing compensation models that reward learning and exploration.
4. Implementing performance evaluations that prioritize growth over static performance.

The organizational mindset shift

Implementing these pathways, programmes and management methodologies requires more than new policies, it demands a pretty fundamental reimagining of how organizations view talent. Within that new exploration, the most progressive organizations I've worked with and spoken to have learnt a counter-intuitive truth: sometimes, the most valuable thing you can do for an employee is to help them leave. This isn't an admission of failure, but a sophisticated understanding of talent, purpose and organizational evolution.

Melanie Naranjo, Chief People Officer at Ethena, shared her perspective with me over an interview (and several unrecorded conversations thereafter). In her view, work is not a lifelong commitment, but a series of experiences that help individuals achieve their personal goals. 'I hope that I was happy and that I enjoyed the short time that I had while I was here,' she shared, capturing a nuanced approach to professional journeys that goes beyond traditional notions of loyalty. This philosophy shapes how she thinks about careers. Work isn't a lifelong commitment, but a series of (often quite temporary) experiences that help people achieve their personal goals.

Modern workforce dynamics have rendered obsolete the old paradigm of treating departing employees as defectors. Instead, forward-thinking companies are recognizing that an employee's journey doesn't end when they walk out the door, it transforms. The relationship between an organization and its talent has become more fluid, more nuanced, and potentially more valuable in the long term.

Alumni networks have emerged as a strategic imperative, not a nostalgic afterthought. These are living ecosystems of professional relationships that extend far beyond traditional employment boundaries. A departing employee is no longer seen as a loss, but as a potential future collaborator, client, advocate, or boomerang hire.

Chris Abbass, Founder and CEO at Talentful, demonstrates this in practice. When economic realities forced difficult decisions during the 2023 downturn, his approach remained consistent: 'I think we genuinely care about people. There have to be decisions that don't suit everyone, but I think when we make decisions, we take people into consideration quite significantly.'

This philosophy paid dividends. Within twelve months of recovery, nearly 80 former employees returned to the company. Abbass reflects on why people chose to come back: 'Out of all the places that I could do this job, the place that I'm going to learn the most.' This approach transforms the traditional employer-employee relationship from a transactional exchange to a long-term professional partnership.

The mechanics of ethical off-boarding require a fundamental shift in organizational mindset. It's about creating structured, supportive processes that:

- Preserve professional dignity
- Maintain appropriate transparency
- Facilitate knowledge transfer
- Maintain meaningful connections
- Recognize the individual's contribution beyond their current role

Organizations that approach external transitions with this kind of approach signal something truly compelling to their entire workforce: we value your professional journey, even when that journey takes you beyond our immediate boundaries. This approach changes the traditional employer-employee relationship from a transactional exchange to a more respectful professional partnership.

Ethical off-boarding is not a cost centre or a compliance exercise, it's a strategic investment in organizational adaptability, reputation and future talent acquisition. In an era of unprecedented professional mobility, how an organization says goodbye may be just as important as how it says hello.

Measuring success beyond retention

The pursuit of dynamic career pathways sends most traditional organizations into full panic mode. I've sat in countless boardrooms watching executives clutch their pearls at the mere suggestion of these programmes. The pursuit of progress inevitably challenges traditional organizational thinking! I've been on the side of the desk arguing for these kinds of programmes unsuccessfully before, including in established businesses where workforce development is viewed through a lens of stability and specialization, fearing that transparency and flexibility might undermine the very foundations of organizational effectiveness.

The objections come thick and fast, delivered across a colourful spectrum of professional panic: 'Systematic exploration of workplace fulfilment threatens institutional knowledge!' they cry. 'It reduces deep expertise! Creates unpredictable team dynamics!' The traditional wisdom brigade insists that mastery requires laser focus and robotic consistency. Career paths, they declare with the confidence of people who haven't changed jobs in decades, need predictability for both individual and organizational planning.

Yet the most progressive organizations are reimagining these constraints. They understand that measuring success extends far beyond simple retention metrics. The true value lies in creating an ecosystem where professional growth becomes a strategic asset rather than being seen as an operational challenge.

For this reason, it's crucial that we are both diligent and critical in measuring the success of these programmes, because without justification and ongoing evidence of ROI, not only will credibility be erased, but it could further damage future programmes that seek to bring our teams closer to a sense of purpose and fulfilment in and out of work.

As I wrote in *Built for People*, within a chapter that still gets most of the attention of all I've ever written, I said, 'In People Operations, as well as Product Management, what to measure, how to measure it, and how to know things are going wrong before they can no longer be arrested are both a science and an art. Even more operational than that, I am often met with pleading questions around which tools to use, and how to collect data on a "data budget (when you don't have elaborate software and dashboarding tools)".'

Developing meaningful metrics for success in this specific area requires a reimagining of how we view professional development's outcomes: success is no longer about keeping employees in fixed positions for as long as possible, but about creating environments that allow for continuous learning, cross-functional exploration, return on investment, and purposeful career evolution.

The most compelling organizations are those that can calculate the return on investment of transparent career practices not just in financial terms, but in organizational adaptability, innovation potential, and employee satisfaction. This means tracking metrics that capture skill diversity, knowledge transfer effectiveness, and the ability of teams to rapidly reconfigure in response to changing business needs.

Critically, this approach isn't universal. An accounting firm operating in a service economy may approach career development differently from a mission-driven non-profit in the transformation economy. The key is understanding your organization's fundamental economic position and designing career support strategies that align with your core operational model.

The most progressive people leaders I've had the pleasure of working with recognize that measuring success is not about counting bodies in seats, but about understanding the intricate ecosystem of talent development, the relationship with company success (and growth, profit, revenue and commercials!). This means developing metrics that reveal the qualitative and quantitative dimensions of professional purpose.

Recruitment and employer branding, too, become powerful tools in this new landscape. By showcasing genuine commitment to employee growth and professional exploration, organizations can differentiate themselves in competitive talent markets. The most attractive employers are those who see careers not as fixed trajectories, but as dynamic journeys of continuous learning and personal development.

The future of work as a purpose ecosystem

The journey from rigid career ladders to dynamic professional exploration represents more than a few hours in a workshop to spin up an organizational strategy. Leaders facing disconnected teams must recognize that purpose is not a one-size-fits-all concept, but a deeply personal, evolving experience that requires nuanced, empathetic support.

For HR professionals and organizational leaders, the path forward is clear: create environments of radical transparency, where career questioning is not just tolerated, but actively encouraged. This means developing systems that allow employees to explore, experiment, and evolve without fear of professional repercussion. The most progressive organizations will treat themselves not as fixed destinations, but as dynamic ecosystems that support individual growth, even when that growth might eventually lead an employee elsewhere. Practical action steps are deceptively simple yet profound:

- Create structured conversations about personal purpose
- Design roles with intentional flexibility
- Develop cross-functional exploration opportunities
- Measure success through learning and adaptability, not just retention
- Treat departures as potential future collaborations, not betrayals

The individual experience transforms dramatically under this approach. No longer constrained by linear expectations, professionals can view their careers as ongoing journeys of discovery. Work becomes a platform for personal growth, not a prison of predetermined paths. By acknowledging that purpose is fluid, contextual and deeply personal, organizations can create environments where employees feel genuinely seen, supported, and empowered to continuously reimagine their professional identities.

The future of work is not about holding onto talent, but about celebrating its natural evolution.

Notes and further reading

1. Reddit (n.d.) Do people constantly think about changing their careers?, r/careerchange. www.reddit.com/r/careerchange/comments/19aatxy/do_people_constantly_think_about_changing_their/ (archived at https://perma.cc/7FQZ-BZLY)
2. Reddit (n.d.) Do people constantly think about changing their careers?, r/careerchange. www.reddit.com/r/careerchange/comments/19aatxy/do_people_constantly_think_about_changing_their/ (archived at https://perma.cc/7FQZ-BZLY)
3. Gallup (2017) State of the American Workplace, Gallup, Washington, DC. www.gallup.com/workplace/238085/state-american-workplace-report-2017.aspx (archived at https://perma.cc/7F37-CNXZ)
4. Bersin, J (2020) The definitive guide to internal mobility, *Josh Bersin*, 27 January. https://joshbersin.com/2020/01/the-definitive-guide-to-internal-mobility/ (archived at https://perma.cc/Q73F-AB4G)
5. Groysberg, B (2010) *Chasing Stars: The myth of talent and the portability of performance*, Princeton University Press, Princeton, NJ
6. LinkedIn (2023) 2023 Workplace Learning Report. www.devlinpeck.com/content/employee-training-statistics (archived at https://perma.cc/7RD5-M7CB)
7. Grant, A (2022) *WorkLife with Adam Grant: The problem with all-stars*. TED Audio Collective, 15 February
8. Maslach, C and Leiter, M P (1997) *The Truth About Burnout: How organizations cause personal stress and what to do about it*, Jossey-Bass, San Francisco
9. Wrzesniewski, A, McCauley, C, Rozin, P and Schwartz, B (1997) Jobs, careers, and callings: People's relations to their work, *Journal of Research in Personality*, 31(1), 21–33. doi:10.1006/jrpe.1997.2162 (archived at https://perma.cc/7N97-XEAE)
10. Tupper, H and Ellis, S (2020) *The Squiggly Career*, Portfolio, London
11. Lattice (2024) What is a career lattice?, *Lattice Blog*, 10 June. https://lattice.com/articles/what-is-a-career-lattice (archived at https://perma.cc/9JMR-229Y)
12. Downs, M and Swisher, M (2023) Why companies should help every employee chart a career path, *MIT Sloan Management Review*, 65(1). https://sloanreview.mit.edu/article/why-companies-should-help-every-employee-chart-a-career-path/
13. Gallup (2023) State of the Global Workplace 2023 Report, Gallup, Washington, DC. www.gallup.com/workplace/349484/state-of-the-global-workplace.aspx (archived at https://perma.cc/P3JT-NLEF)
14. Lands, A (n.d.) Career lattice: How to shift from traditional career ladders, *AIHR Blog*. www.aihr.com/blog/career-lattice/ (archived at https://perma.cc/4T9M-K3WC)

15 Spotify (2023) Less is more (impactful) with tailored early career programs, *Spotify HR Blog*, 25 May. https://hrblog.spotify.com/2023/05/25/less-is-more-impactful-with-tailored-early-careers-programs (archived at https://perma.cc/GG9N-8SW2)
16 Marjoram, S (2021) McCann London's Sheryl Marjoram put focus on partnerships, Ad Age. https://adage.com/article/special-report-leading-women/mccann-londons-sheryl-marjoram-put-focus-partnerships/2343471/ (archived at https://perma.cc/NM3K-6WTJ)
17 Zwaan, J M (2018) On being BOLD. *Medium*. https://jessicamayzwaan.medium.com/on-being-bold-f7f551c63564 (archived at https://perma.cc/JE6E-ZCZH)
18 Patagonia (2025) Environmental internships. www.patagonia.com/environmental-internships/ (archived at https://perma.cc/Z9AW-PCPS)
19 Wikipedia (2025) T-shaped skills. https://en.wikipedia.org/wiki/T-shaped_skills (archived at https://perma.cc/23J2-96F4)
20 Hansen, M T (2001) Introducing T-shaped managers: Knowledge management's next generation', *Harvard Business Review*, March
21 Lighthouse Labs (2024) T-shaped team members: The key to versatile and effective teams, *Lighthouse Labs Blog*, 24 October. www.lighthouselabs.ca/en/blog/t-shaped-team-members (archived at https://perma.cc/2XKD-7EST)

PART THREE

Walking away

6

Identity and life outside work

For decades, companies have pushed a narrative that our jobs should be the primary source of meaning in our lives. We're told to *'find our calling'*, to seek roles where *'we feel we never work a day in our lives,'* to discover that mythical perfect position where work doesn't feel like work at all. So much so that when I ran a workshop on the topics in this book in May 2025, a member of the audience described their team's relationship with purpose as one of 'longing', a word that I was both surprised and melancholic to see come up on the workshop's screen. When we discussed this as a group later, I brought this word up in the conversation and the answers were interesting; the reflection was that many folks in their teams felt that they were seeking something they couldn't seem to find but felt 'others had', which was a sense of purpose within their organization's mission.

Here's the inconvenient truth: for most people, their deepest sense of purpose comes from somewhere else entirely than their company's purpose. For myself, my interests outside of work are varied, and broadly deeply creative. Music production, art, writing. I love my work, don't get me wrong. I'm lucky enough that I've found a way to truly express myself, my interests and things I'm learning, through my work. Doing this kind of work fills my cup, brings me community and challenges me in a way that I find incredibly fulfilling. That said, I've personally been fascinated by the journeys and challenges of people around me who have chosen to invest in creative work for their income. Part jealousy, part curiosity, part self-doubt. I have often wondered if I would be happier, more engaged, more fulfilled, if I had pursued music or theatre as I'd imagined I would as a child and young adult.

A part of the joy of writing a book like this is the ability to test and understand the truth behind these beliefs. Chris Abbass, CEO and Founder of Talentful, an embedded recruitment process outsourcing (RPO) serving the tech sector, offers another compelling perspective on the relationship between passion and profession. His journey began far from the recruitment world, with aspirations of becoming a professional musician. 'Everything I did was focused on being a musician,' Chris recalls, having moved to London specifically to study music, only to later realize that his musical ambitions weren't materializing as he'd hoped.

Faced with limited options, determined not to return to his hometown of Blackpool, and armed with an ambition to make something of himself, Chris found himself working at Waitrose while pursuing door-to-door sales for commission – hardly the creative fulfilment he had envisioned. The turning point came from a simple but profound realization about the nature of work and passion. 'I think that's why a lot of companies have gotten it wrong,' Chris reflects. 'They think you should do what you're passionate about. I think that's total trash. I actually think you *decide* what you can be passionate about.'

This insight guided Chris as he navigated from reluctant retail worker to successful entrepreneur. Unlike the common narrative that one should chase a pre-existing passion, Chris discovered that professional satisfaction could come from mastering whatever path he chose. 'I think mastery is the aim… being amazing at something and being able to do that every day and get better and better. That's ultimately what people want.'

His experience at Waitrose crystallized this perspective. Observing colleagues who had been there for decades, Chris remembers thinking, 'This cannot be it for me. This cannot be it. I could not be there in another year [from that point].' This desperation became the catalyst for seeking something with 'good upwards potential', rather than pursuing an inherent passion in music.

Today, as the leader of a multimillion-dollar company that has scaled across Europe and the US, Chris approaches workplace culture with refreshing pragmatism. Rather than selling grandiose visions of changing the world, he focuses on creating a company aligned with the experiential economy of work (my words not his), an environment where talented people can excel alongside other high performers. 'If you keep your bar really high, if you hire the best people, you can do the best work you possibly can [in that workplace]. That attracts people.'

It reminds me of Ben Gallacher, who we met in a previous chapter. Ben found himself confronting an uncomfortable truth: the very thing he'd trained for, the career he'd invested years in developing (acting), wasn't bringing him the fulfilment he'd imagined.

'What drew me towards performance and acting is rehearsal,' Ben explains. 'The concept of being able to rehearse and iterate, try new things, experiment.' But the reality of professional acting turned out to be quite different. 'The problem with, like, any kind of performance role is that the success is actually quite boring because then you have to do the same thing over and over and over again.'

Ben's journey from actor to entrepreneur wasn't driven by finding his 'true calling' or 'following his passion'. Instead, it was sparked by a clear-eyed recognition of what wasn't working, combined with a desire for autonomy and the freedom to evolve.

Today, as the founder of InRehearsal, Ben approaches leadership with this hard-won wisdom. Rather than pushing his team to find ultimate fulfilment in their roles, he embraces the reality that careers evolve and people change. 'I think there's serendipity in employment, there's serendipity in leadership and management,' he reflects. Many times in our conversation he's articulated his belief that everyone is on a journey to a destination that they haven't articulated, or which may surprise them.

This disconnect between societal messaging (you must do what you love in order to be fulfilled) and human reality (not all of us can be writers, actors, artists professionally) creates a peculiar pressure. We're made to feel somehow deficient if we don't find our ultimate fulfilment in quarterly objectives and team off-sites. It's as if having interests outside of work has become a guilty secret, something to hide rather than celebrate.

One of the attendees at my May workshop with TroopHR said that she has seen people feel 'shame' and 'guilt' at leaving roles because they were seeking more financial reward, rather than staying in their current role and buying further into the company's purpose and mission as their motivation. This social pressure only serves to make our team feel a greater sense of discontent and longing, isolated from the stark reality that, as Chris so eloquently said, 'I think people need to realize that for most of us your job is your job, and [one of] the primary functions of your job it is for professional satisfaction.'

So what if we've got it backwards? What if having a rich life outside of work actually makes us better at our jobs? What if the best thing companies could do for their employees' growth isn't another leadership training programme, but rather the space and encouragement to develop interests that have nothing to do with their job descriptions?

The high cost of work-as-identity

When our professional roles become the primary anchor of our identity, we create a precarious foundation for our sense of self. This phenomenon – what organizational psychologists refer to as 'work-identity fusion' or 'overidentification with work roles' – has accelerated dramatically in recent decades, particularly in knowledge work sectors.[1] As an example, Blake E Ashforth (Professor at Arizona State University's W P Carey School of Business) has conducted extensive research on organizational identity and identification processes.[2] His work provides valuable insights into how people incorporate work roles into their sense of self. Ashforth's research shows that while some identification with work roles is positive and motivating, excessive identification increases vulnerability to psychological distress. When work identity becomes too central, individuals experience greater psychological distress during organizational changes, job transitions or retirement. For example, his framework of 'role transitions' explores how individuals manage boundaries when moving between roles, highlighting identity disruption and emotional strain in the absence of supportive separation mechanisms.

The consequences extend far beyond mere job dissatisfaction, creating ripple effects that touch every aspect of our wellbeing and organizational health. The relationship between work-identity fusion and burnout is well-documented. When we tie our fundamental worth to our professional achievements, we transform ordinary workplace challenges into existential threats. A critical comment in a performance review isn't just feedback – it's a referendum on our value as a human being. A missed deadline isn't merely a scheduling issue – it's evidence of personal failure.

Christina Maslach, the psychologist who pioneered burnout research, identifies 'lack of control' and 'values conflict' as two of the six primary causes of burnout.[3] Both intensify when work becomes our identity. We feel we cannot step away (lack of control) because who would we be without our work? And when company decisions conflict with our personal values, the dissonance is more painful because it feels like a betrayal of self, not just a disagreement with an employer.

As one tech industry veteran told me, 'I spent over five years building products I genuinely believed were making the world better. When I finally admitted to myself that the company's priorities had shifted to shareholder value over anything else, I didn't just feel disappointed, I felt like a fraud. Like everything I'd told myself about who I was had been a lie.'

As I heard in the TroopHR workshop, there's a particular anxiety that haunts many professional spaces today: the fear of not being 'passionate enough' about one's job. This anxiety stems directly from the cultural mythology built over the last few decades that our work should be our calling. The pressure to demonstrate passion creates a peculiar form of emotional labour – what organizational psychologist Alicia Grandey calls 'surface acting' – where employees feel compelled to perform enthusiasm they may not genuinely feel.[4] This performance becomes exhausting over time, creating a secondary burden beyond the actual work itself.

Chris Abbass's perspective offers a refreshing counterpoint: 'I think mastery is the aim… being amazing at something and being able to do that every day and get better and better.' This focus on craft rather than emotional attachment creates a healthier relationship with work – one where improvement and skill development take precedence over the expectation of constant passion.

When work-as-identity becomes embedded in organizational culture, it creates several problematic dynamics:

- First, it enables exploitation. Employees who derive their primary sense of self from their professional role are more likely to accept unreasonable demands, unpaid overtime, and boundary violations. 'We're changing the world' becomes the justification for burnout-inducing expectations.
- Second, it hampers honest feedback and genuine collaboration. When criticism of one's work feels like criticism of one's identity, defensiveness naturally follows. Innovation suffers when teams cannot candidly evaluate ideas without triggering identity threats.
- Third, it creates unhealthy competition. When professional achievement becomes the measure of personal worth, colleagues transform into rivals in a zero-sum game of status and recognition. This undermines the cooperation essential for organizational success.

Perhaps the most devastating cost of work-as-identity becomes apparent when that professional role is suddenly disrupted or lost. The Covid-19 pandemic provided a mass-scale demonstration of this vulnerability.

When millions found themselves furloughed or unemployed, those who had most strongly fused their identities with their professions often experienced not just economic hardship but a profound identity crisis. Interestingly, research on leaders during the pandemic revealed both the risks and potential resilience strategies associated with work-identity fusion. A qualitative study published in *Frontiers in Psychology* examined how senior leaders navigated the Covid-19 disruptions and found that their 'leader role identity, as part of their work identity, was amplified by the pandemic.'[5] The leaders interviewed had to rapidly adopt new roles – strategist, technology expert, entrepreneur, coach, mentor and team member, simultaneously – to ensure organizational survival and employee wellbeing.

What's particularly revealing is that while these leaders experienced an intensification of their work identities, those who adapted most successfully did so by developing greater identity flexibility. One participant noted, 'My brain changes six or seven times a day, depending on what kind of call I have,' suggesting that spreading their identity across multiple professional roles actually created a form of resilience rather than vulnerability. Yet this same research highlighted the precarious nature of work-identity fusion: leaders reported having to manage not only their own changing roles but also the identity threats experienced by their team members who were 'dealing with loss of loved ones, general fear, and manual processes.'

The pandemic revealed a paradox to us: while strong work identity helped some leaders navigate crisis by providing motivation and direction, it simultaneously created psychological vulnerability for countless others whose professional identities were disrupted through job loss, furlough, or dramatic role changes. This suggests that the healthiest approach involves cultivating what organizational psychologists call 'identity diversification' – maintaining robust identities outside of work that can provide stability when professional roles inevitably shift or disappear.[6]

Even voluntary career transitions become unnecessarily traumatic when work has been our primary identity. As Ben Gallacher's story illustrates, leaving a career path – even one that isn't bringing fulfilment – can trigger a crisis when that path has been central to how we understand ourselves. 'And I come from quite, you know, from a working-class background. There aren't very many people where I grew up who pursued an artistic career. So you are carrying around a little bit of judgement. And most people do want you to do incredibly well. But there's certainly a tension between you're doing a traditional typical thing that everyone else is. So the self-prescribed pressure that you're putting on yourself is that, well, I really want to do well because I've taken a chance, I've done something a bit different.' Ben describes here the challenge of disturbing his professional path of pursuing acting due the judgement he felt for initially entering the field at all; in short, he felt a conflict about leaving a profession that initially brought him a sense of purpose, when that no longer was the case.

The economic turbulence of recent years has further exposed this vulnerability. Tech industry lay-offs, affecting even high-performing employees, have left many confronting versions of the same question: 'If I'm not a [job title] at [company], then who am I?'

Recovery from job loss takes significantly longer for those who lack robust identities outside of work. The folks who struggle most aren't necessarily those facing the greatest financial pressure. They're the ones who've invested so completely in their professional identity that they have no ready answer to the question of who they are without it.

This pattern creates a paradoxical reality: the very commitment and dedication that organizations claim to value makes their employees more vulnerable to devastating personal crises when organizational needs change. And in today's economy, those needs will inevitably change.

The healthiest approach – both for individual resilience and organizational adaptability – involves maintaining identity diversification: developing and valuing multiple facets of who we are beyond our professional roles. This doesn't mean caring less about our work; it means creating a more stable foundation for our sense of self by drawing meaning from various domains of life.

As Chris Abbass pragmatically put it: 'For most of us your job is your job.' This perspective isn't lowering the bar – it's setting a realistic one that protects both individual wellbeing and organizational health.

REAL-WORLD EXAMPLE
Talentful's boomerang effect

When the 2023 economic headwinds forced many tech companies into painful workforce reductions, Talentful wasn't immune. Like others in the industry, they faced the difficult reality of making lay-offs during a prolonged market downturn. Yet unlike most organizations that saw these departures as permanent, Talentful's approach during this crisis laid the groundwork for something extraordinary: within 12 months of recovery, nearly 80 former employees returned to the company – some for the second or even third time.

1. Clear, honest communication during exits

When economic realities forced workforce reductions, Talentful's leadership maintained the same transparency that characterized their daily operations. CEO Chris Abbass explained their position directly: 'I think we genuinely care about people. There have to be decisions that don't suit everyone, but I think when we make decisions, we take people into consideration quite significantly.'

Rather than sugar-coating the situation or creating elaborate narratives, the company communicated the economic realities plainly. There was no denying the economic realities of the market the business found itself in: Talentful leadership shared openly the work they were doing to rebuild its client base and remain the market leading tech-RPO. This honest communication during departures established trust that would prove crucial for future returns.

2. Reinforcing experiential economy values

Talentful had already embraced the experiential economy approach to work – focusing on what employees actually wanted rather than manufactured purpose to drive motivation. During the crisis, they reinforced this philosophy. 'Great people fundamentally want to work with great people,' Abbass explains. 'If you keep your bar really high, you do the best work you possibly can. That attracts people.' This meant, even during the most difficult period of the company's history, rather than lean in on purpose messaging, the team leaned in on developing their existing team, holding the bar high for their clients and maintaining strong relationships with high-quality work.

This wasn't about promising life-changing experiences or revolutionary missions. As Abbass puts it more directly: 'Most people are like, "Yeah, I know what I'm doing, I don't need any wool pulled over my eyes. I want to come in and do my job and have things be sensible and have a nice life outside of work, get paid fairly."' As soon as the market signals began to return, Talentful proactively raised compensation among their team who had remained within the business, and began a tireless 12-month campaign to regain trust and stability in their employment model.

3. Sustained investment in recovery and growth

While many companies went into survival mode, Talentful continued investing in their brand and market position. 'I think one of the big decisions that were made in 2023,' Abbass notes, 'was the fact that we continued our brand. And we really invested heavily in making sure that our name was still out there and we still demonstrated we were doing the most we could for our clients.'

Abass's perspective on downturns shaped this approach: 'You zoom out, the graphs are always like this. You look at the S&P, but if you zoom into a month out of that year, it dropped 20 per cent.' By maintaining a long-term view, Talentful positioned itself for recovery rather than retreat.

4. Learning from mistakes and transparent path forward

Perhaps, most importantly, Talentful acknowledged what hadn't worked before the downturn. 'We learned from the mistakes we made before the downturn in 2023,' Abbass explains, 'and we were committed to building a workplace that was sustainable, transparent and took care of our team long term.'

This wasn't just internal reflection, it was communicated openly to the team. As Abbass notes, 'I think we're a pretty consistent organization in our approach. People might not always agree with the approach, but I think that the logic behind how we make decisions is pretty consistent.'

5. Establishing career development over purpose theatre

While many companies position themselves as transformational experiences, Talentful took a different approach. Rather than claiming to 'change the world', they focused on being 'the absolute best' within their vertical of recruitment.

Abbass explains the reasoning: 'There's limitations to how impactful recruiting can be. But within that vertical, can we be the absolute best?' This honest positioning attracted people who wanted to excel professionally without being sold on grandiose missions.

The results: Trust through consistency

The effectiveness of this approach became clear during the recovery period. As departing employees watched Talentful navigate the crisis with as much dignity and transparency as possible, many chose to return once the market improved.

'Out of all the places that I could do this job,' Abbass reflects on the returners' perspective, 'the place that I'm going to learn the most, or get to do the most cool stuff is here.'

The validation wasn't just in the numbers (80 returning employees is impressive no matter how you think about it) but in what it represented: a workplace that had regained and earned genuine loyalty through professional respect rather than emotional manipulation.

The lesson: Sustainable retention through honest practice

Talentful's success offers a clear model for other organizations facing similar challenges:

- Communicate clearly during difficult times – Don't create false narratives, share realities
- Focus on professional satisfaction if you are in the experiential economy of work – Most people want good conditions, smart colleagues, and fair treatment
- Continue investing in genuine strengths – Don't retreat, position for recovery
- Be transparent about lessons learnt – Acknowledge and address past mistakes
- Build career opportunities, not cult-like purpose – People want to develop professionally, not surrender their identity

As Abbass concludes, 'By treating work as what it actually is – professional engagement between competent adults – we built an organization that people actually want to return to.'

In a tech environment often characterized by extremes of idealism and cynicism, Talentful demonstrated that the most powerful retention tool might be the simplest: honest professionalism combined with genuine care for people's growth and autonomy.

Building identity frameworks across work economies

The challenge of work-identity fusion isn't unique to any single type of workplace culture. Whether an organization operates in the service economy (where work is primarily transactional), the experiential economy (where work delivers professional satisfaction and growth), or the transformational economy (where work promises to change the world or its employees as 'consumers'), employees benefit from developing robust identities beyond their professional roles. The question then becomes: How can companies actively support this identity diversification, regardless of their economic approach?

Creating space for non-work development

Progressive companies are beginning to recognize that supporting employees' non-work identities isn't a drain on productivity – it's an investment in resilience and long-term performance. Some approaches include:

- **Learning stipends with no restrictions:** Rather than limiting professional development funds to work-related skills, some companies offer stipends that can be used for any learning pursuit – from pottery classes to language lessons to financial planning courses.
- **'Identity time' policies:** Beyond traditional PTO, some organizations offer specific time off for pursuing non-work projects, whether that's training for a marathon, volunteering, or writing a novel.
- **Showcase diversity of interests:** Creating forums where team members can share their non-work passions and projects, moving away from the mindset that personal interests should be hidden or apologized for.
- **Celebrating exits and transitions where appropriate:** Rather than treating departures as failures or betrayals, acknowledging them as natural parts

of career evolution, particularly if they are at a junction in someone's life where the transition is a positive one for their wellbeing and life experience, such (but not limited to!) as travelling, study, or family.

Modelling identity diversification at leadership levels

When leadership openly embraces and discusses their non-work identities, it creates permission for others to do the same:

- **Transparency about personal priorities:** Leaders sharing how they balance work with family, creative pursuits, or personal development builds a downward culture of permission that ripples through the entire organization. When a CEO mentions taking piano lessons during a town hall, or a department head openly discusses attending their child's soccer game during their lunch break, it fundamentally shifts what's acceptable and admired within the company culture.

- **Demonstration of boundary setting:** Showing that high performance is compatible with having rich identities outside work. Many organizations unwittingly promote a zero-sum mindset where time and energy spent on non-work identities are viewed as resources 'stolen' from professional excellence. Leaders who openly discuss how they structure their days to accommodate both professional excellence and personal pursuits provide practical blueprints for others.

- **Acknowledgement of life transitions:** Openly discussing how personal changes have influenced professional growth goes beyond mere mention of life events to create a culture where major life transitions are seen as catalysts for professional development rather than obstacles to be overcome, for example, sharing how learning patience and multi-tasking through raising children has fundamentally improved their approach to work, but also that challenges faced by balancing work and external responsibilities is something that is both acknowledged and appreciated by the business as a necessary part of a full and fulfilling life.

Designing work that accommodates diverse identities

Rather than expecting employees to conform to standardized professional personas, companies can create structures that allow for authentic expression:

- **Flexible schedule architecture:** Beyond remote work, building systems that accommodate different peak performance times and life circumstances includes asynchronous core hours, job sharing options, and compressed work weeks. These structures recognize that productivity doesn't always align with traditional schedules and that life circumstances like caregiving or health needs require workplace flexibility.

- **Multidimensional role definitions:** Allowing employees to shape roles that draw on their full range of interests and skills creates positions that evolve as individuals bring unexpected strengths to bear. This approach moves beyond rigid job descriptions and encourages your team to embrace how an accountant's theatre background might enhance client presentations or a developer's interests in art improves design thinking. For example, your team can publicly celebrate instances where non-traditional skill combinations create business value, reinforcing that diverse backgrounds enhance rather than distract from professional roles.

- **Rotation and experimentation opportunities:** Creating pathways for employees to explore different aspects of the business without career penalty includes sabbaticals in other departments, cross-functional innovation projects, and learning budgets for learning outside one's current role. These programmes satisfy human needs for growth while building organizational resilience through employees who understand multiple facets of the company.

Investment in community beyond work

Supporting employees' broader identities often means investing in their connections outside the workplace:

- **Community engagement programmes:** Rather than treating community involvement as a corporate branding exercise, truly supporting employees' community connections means providing resources for their existing volunteer commitments and neighbourhood projects. This could include offering flex time for coaching youth sports, providing stipends for materials for community garden projects, or allowing employees to use company resources for skill-sharing workshops they lead in their communities. The distinction here is following the employee's existing community interests rather than directing them towards company-selected charitable initiatives.

- **Location flexibility:** Prithwiraj Choudhury's book, *The World Is Your Office* talks deeply about the positive impacts of an organization's move beyond remote work policies to create true 'live anywhere' positions.[7] True location flexibility means allowing employees to make residential choices based on their broader life priorities – proximity to extended family, access to outdoor recreation, affordable housing, or community connections – rather than requiring them to live in specific career hubs. This goes beyond simple remote work to include supporting employees who choose to live in smaller towns for quality of life, near ageing parents for caregiving responsibilities, or in communities that align with their cultural or spiritual values. It might involve providing co-working space stipends, adjusting compensation for cost-of-living differences, or supporting alternative transportation arrangements for occasional in-person requirements.

- **Family and relationship support:** Professional performance often hinges on personal stability, particularly the strength of relationships at home and with extended family networks. Organizations can recognize this reality by providing resources for family therapy, relationship counselling, or eldercare support, understanding these as business investments rather than mere benefits. This might also include policies that respect family rituals like regular dinners together, school events, or caregiving responsibilities for ageing parents, acknowledging that these relationship maintenance activities directly impact workplace productivity.

Practical implementation across economies

These frameworks can be adapted to different work economy contexts. Service economy organizations might focus on creating clear boundaries between work and personal life, ensuring that transactional work doesn't consume identity. Experiential economy organizations (like Talentful in our real-world example above) can emphasize that professional excellence and personal fulfilment outside work are complementary, not competing forces. Transformational economy organizations face the biggest challenge, as their purpose-driven cultures often unconsciously encourage work-identity fusion. These companies might need to actively create counterbalances – explicitly validating that work transformation is one aspiration among many valid life goals, and that the work may never be fully complete, so we must allow our team the space for a life measured by wellbeing as well as professional fulfilment to the company's higher purpose.

The business case for identity diversification

Supporting diverse identities isn't just ethically sound – it's strategically smart. When organizations invest in their employees' full identities, rather than demanding professional tunnel vision, they discover something counter-intuitive: the benefits ripple through every aspect of business performance.

Consider resilience first. When the next organizational restructuring hits (and if the last few years have taught us leaders anything, it will) companies discover that employees with rich lives outside work navigate change with remarkable stability. A marketing director who is also a dedicated rock climber and volunteer literacy tutor may not suffer the same emotional challenges when their role shifts during a merger. They possess psychological anchors that help them weather professional uncertainty without losing their sense of self. These employees become the steady forces that help entire teams through turbulent transitions.

This resilience feeds directly into enhanced creativity. A software engineer who spends weekends restoring vintage motorcycles brings a maker's mindset to debugging. An accountant who volunteers at a local theatre company approaches financial storytelling with unexpected narrative flair. When people live fully beyond their job descriptions, they return to work carrying a portfolio of perspectives that enrich problem-solving. The most innovative solutions often emerge from the intersection of professional expertise and seemingly unrelated life experiences.

The retention story tells itself in exit interviews and return rates. People don't leave companies that genuinely support their entire lives – they leave, or feel disengaged, when work starts consuming their identity. Organizations that respect and encourage their employees' non-work passions create environments where 10-year tenures become common rather than exceptional. These employees weather career plateaus more gracefully because work isn't their only source of meaning. They stay through professional challenges because their companies have demonstrated commitment to their full selves, not just their output.

Burnout, a persistent plague of modern workplaces, finds its antidote in reduced professional stakes. When an employee's identity eggs sit in multiple baskets, work criticism loses its power to devastate. A poor quarterly performance review remains just that – a professional reflection, not an existential crisis. This psychological distance creates space for honest self-assessment and improvement rather than defensive reactivity. Teams function more effectively when individuals can accept feedback without protecting their core sense of worth.

Perhaps most surprisingly, succession planning flows more smoothly in organizations that normalize diverse identities. Employees who understand themselves as multifaceted beings handle career turmoil with greater ease. They can step into new roles without abandoning previous identities, and they can step away from roles when the time comes without losing their sense of purpose.

These benefits compound over time, creating organizational cultures where excellence and humanity reinforce rather than compete with each other. Companies that embrace identity diversification find themselves attracting the kind of resilient, creative, committed talent that sustains long-term success, precisely because they've stopped demanding that success require personal sacrifice.

Perhaps most fundamentally, companies need to expand their definition of professional development to include personal development. Rather than seeing these as separate or competing priorities, forward-thinking organizations recognize them as mutually reinforcing. Companies that support this journey – rather than trying to control or redirect it – create environments where people can do their best work while maintaining the flexibility to evolve as multifaceted individuals with a healthy relationship with purpose and work.

The most sustainable organizations may be those that master the paradox of being simultaneously professional and personal: places where excellent work happens alongside acknowledgement that excellent work is just one dimension of excellent lives.

Notes and further reading

1 Wikipedia (2025) Identity fusion. https://en.wikipedia.org/wiki/Identity_fusion (archived at https://perma.cc/MLK5-XCE2)
2 Ashforth, B E, Harrison, S H and Corley, K G (2008) Identification in organizations: An examination of four fundamental questions, *Journal of Management*, 34(3), 325–74
3 Maslach, C and Leiter, M P (1997) *The Truth About Burnout: How organizations cause personal stress and what to do about it*, Jossey-Bass, San Francisco
4 Grandey, A A (2003) When 'the show must go on': Surface acting and deep acting as determinants of emotional exhaustion and peer-rated service delivery, *Academy of Management Journal*, 46(1), 86–96
5 Meadows, S and De Braine, R (2022) The work identity of leaders in the midst of the Covid-19 pandemic, *Frontiers in Psychology*, 13:958679. www.frontiersin.org/journals/psychology/articles/10.3389/fpsyg.2022.958679/full (archived at https://perma.cc/9YKU-KJPM)

6 Unsworth, K L (2023) Managing multiple, geographically separated identities: Integration and separation strategies in work–life configurations. Unpublished manuscript
7 Choudhury, P (2025) The World Is Your Office: How work from anywhere boosts talent, productivity, and innovation. *Harvard Business Review Press*, Boston, MA. www.hbs.edu/faculty/Pages/item.aspx?num=66927 (archived at https://perma.cc/JUG4-RQX4)

7

Quiet quitting

In August 2022, a simple TikTok video sparked a workplace revolution. A video posted by Zaid Khan, a young engineer, is often credited with sparking the initial viral wave. 'I recently learned about this term called "quiet quitting",' explained user @zaidleppelin, 'where you're not outright quitting your job, but you're quitting the idea of going above and beyond.'[1] Within weeks, the hashtag had millions of views, thousands of response videos and spawned countless think pieces across mainstream media. One study I read in the research for this chapter begins, 'A Google search of "quiet quitting" yields over 350 million results, which is remarkable given that the term is only a few years old.'[2] What began as a social media trend quickly revealed itself as something far more significant: a mass reckoning with our relationship to work.

My own journey of working across industries, as well as across continents, has given me a somewhat unique (or, at least specific!) point of view on the cultural differences which shape our relationships with work. When I moved to London, I encountered a culture where working hours were worn as badges of honour, yet my British colleagues maintained a certain ironic distance from corporate devotion, openly preferring the pub to the office (and rightly so, frankly). The Netherlands introduced me to a refreshingly direct approach, colleagues who would glance at their watches at 5pm and announce without apology, '*Borreltijd!*' (wine, beers and snacks after work – truly a hidden element of Dutch culture that should be celebrated worldwide). Finally, now, in the US, I witnessed the complex relationship between the American dream's promise of meritocracy and the grinding reality of hustle culture. These experiences showed me how deeply language and cultural context shape our relationship with work – not just in how we perform our jobs, but in how we conceptualize the very role of work in our lives. What might be seen as admirable dedication in one culture registers as concerning workaholism in another; what's framed as healthy boundaries in the Netherlands might be interpreted as lack of commitment in the US. The contrasts made me realize that work isn't just what we do, it's a cultural construction shaped by shared stories, linguistic frames and collective expectations.

The German concept of *Feierabend* (translated into 'celebration evening') offers a fascinating counterpoint to our current fascination with quiet quitting. While both concepts deal with work-life boundaries, they emerge from radically different cultural perspectives. *Feierabend* isn't about resistance or resignation, it's a culturally endorsed ritual of transitioning from work to leisure, marked by the phrase '*Schönen Feierabend!*' (essentially, 'Have a nice evening off!').[3] It represents a collective understanding that work, while important, is just one part of a well-lived life.

Contrast this with quiet quitting, a term that emerged from Western corporate culture's tendency to frame any limitation on work as a form of rebellion. The very phrase suggests guilt. 'Quitting' implies abandonment of duty, while 'quiet' suggests shame, or perhaps more sinister, *secrecy*. Even as we advocate for boundaries, our language betrays our cultural assumption that work should be all-consuming, that doing only what we're paid for is somehow subversive.

The difference is potent. *Feierabend* is built into German workplace culture, where shops close reliably early, emails after hours are discouraged, and there's a different view on cultural kudos for being 'always on'. It's not just about leaving work; it's about actively celebrating the transition to personal time. Meanwhile, US and UK workers post TikToks about 'acting their wage', framing basic boundaries as acts of defiance, rather than an expected part of the workplace agreement.[4] Where *Feierabend* expresses 'This is how things are', quiet quitting says 'What I agreed to isn't enough'.

This linguistic framing reveals profound cultural differences in how we conceptualize the relationship between work and life. In many European countries, leaving work on time isn't seen as a lack of commitment, it's simply the natural order of things. The Polish *fajrant* and Czech *fajrumt*, both derived from the German concept, similarly celebrate rather than apologize for the end of the workday.[5,6] These cultures have institutionalized the belief that a good worker is also a well-rested one, that productivity comes not from endless hours but from sustainable engagement.

The irony of the quiet quitting phenomenon is that, despite the provocative name, most of its practitioners aren't disengaged saboteurs (it turns out, most people in the world are actually *not* performing mindlessly malicious acts). They're simply people recalibrating their relationship with work to something more sustainable; doing what they're paid to do competently, but refusing to sacrifice their health, relationships and personal interests on the altar of corporate expectations. Yet our cultural frame positions this basic boundary setting as a form of rebellion, casting reasonable limits as a failure of commitment.

This chapter explores this disconnect, why setting healthy boundaries at work has become framed as an act of resistance rather than a foundation for sustainability. We'll examine how different cultures approach work-life boundaries, what psychological forces drive both overwork and boundary setting, and how organizations might respond to quiet quitting in ways that address underlying needs rather than symptoms. We'll consider whether this trend represents not a problem to be solved, but a necessary correction to unsustainable work expectations, a cultural shift that might bring us closer to the celebration of *Feierabend* than the guilt of quitting. Most relevant to this book, I want to explore what this means for purpose and its relationship with work in today's working world.

The anatomy of quiet quitting

The quiet quitting phenomenon has generated endless hot takes, concerned LinkedIn posts, corporate think pieces and scathing op-eds. I find the whole conversation excruciating and tedious, frankly, but the exact parts of the discussion that frustrate me most are: obviously blatant anti-worker sentiment, an implied reliance on meritocratic workplaces and a damning lack of *specificity of the harm*. When quiet quitting was in the headlines at its peak, it was never quite clear to me what exactly these supposedly problematic employees were doing or *not* doing. It felt like pearl-clutching about a corporate rebellion with no discernible substance I could quite make out from the noise.

Ed Zitron, writing in his newsletter 'Where's Your Ed At', identified this glaring lack of specificity with characteristic precision: 'What's frustrating me is how many people are simply accepting this term on its merits without interrogating a single thing about the underlying concept, and it's because of one very simple problem: nobody seems to be asking bosses what they think workers are not doing. This simple little question is so important because not a single damn article on this subject seems to be concerned with the supposed damages of quiet quitting.'[7]

This absence of concrete examples reveals something about the entire debate which makes it feel a little more like a paper tiger than a genuine workplace crisis. When business commentators like Kevin O'Leary advise workers to avoid quiet quitting, they're remarkably vague about what harm this behaviour supposedly causes.[8] The criticism remains abstract because, as Zitron notes, there appears to be 'no enumeration of what exactly quiet quitting does, how it hurts companies, or how it hurts anyone.'

The specificity problem

When we drill down into what quiet quitting actually looks like in practice, we often find employees who are:

1 Arriving at work on time and leaving at the designated end time as per their contract of employment.
2 Completing their assigned tasks to the standard expected of them.
3 Participating in required meetings and discussions around their work.
4 Responding to emails during business hours (rather than evenings and weekends).
5 Declining optional social events or after-hours activities if they do not wish to attend or have other plans.
6 Focusing on their job description's expectations.

Put this way, quiet quitting starts to sound remarkably like doing your job. The behaviours being pathologized are precisely the ones that previous generations would have considered normal, healthy workplace expectations. In fact, many may have seen this as the kindling of high performance. So then the real question becomes: when did fulfilling your actual job requirements become *insufficient*? And what does that have to do with our relationship with *work and purpose*?

At the heart of the quiet quitting debate lies the concept of 'discretionary effort', the extra work that employees choose to do beyond their basic job requirements. Modern workplaces have become increasingly dependent on this voluntary contribution, often without acknowledging or compensating for it appropriately.[9] Quiet quitting is the withholding of discretionary effort, even when reasonable capacity exists.

The problem isn't that employees are unwilling to go above and beyond; it's that 'above and beyond' has become much closer to (if not *the*) baseline expectation, and that this expectation is often connected with a false belief that meritocracy genuinely exists within workplaces.[10] When discretionary effort becomes mandatory, it ceases to be discretionary. What we're witnessing isn't employee rebellion but a rational response to workplaces that have normalized exploitation while dressing it up as passion and purpose.

What makes this even more interesting, the study by Henry, Bolino, and Whitney shared how supervisors respond to quiet quitting, finding that perceptions of reduced discretionary effort often trigger a range of managerial reactions (from punitive measures to increased support) depending on the leader's underlying attributions about the employee's motives. Their work highlights that the supervisor's interpretation of the behaviour is as consequential as the behaviour itself.[11] What's worrying is that this means quiet quitting isn't judged by some objective standard… it's judged through the lens of a manager's personal biases.

Consider the software engineer who stays late to fix bugs that could wait until tomorrow, or the marketing coordinator who checks emails during weekend family time. What might once have been recognized as exceptional dedication has, over time, become an unspoken job requirement. Failing to meet these informal expectations can invite a wide and unpredictable range of managerial responses – shaped less by objective standards and more by individual bias.

Quiet quitting, then, in my opinion represents employees recalibrating these expectations back to sustainable levels, and aligning them with their own emergent need for individual purpose within and outside of their work. For a long time, companies and management have been able to live relatively lazily (sorry if this feels blunt, I myself have had to grapple with my own contributions to this dynamic!), by spouting purpose statements, claiming meritocratic opportunities for promotions and growth based on 'going above and beyond' but without additional incentives, genuinely calibrated compensation and reward frameworks, and a light or absent application of out-of-work support frameworks. Those days seemed to be changing, and it has (as most change does) scared those firmly benefiting from the status quo.

The language of rebellion

The term quiet quitting itself reveals dark patterns within our cultural assumptions about work. The word 'quitting' implies abandonment, failure, giving up. Yet the behaviours it describes are actually about staying: staying employed while maintaining boundaries, staying productive while preserving personal time, staying engaged while avoiding exploitation. Language matters, and alternative framings tell different stories; where we could have learned from the Germans, Polish and Czechs we learnt about earlier in this chapter, we didn't. Boundary setting. Work-life integration. Sustainable engagement. Acting your wage. Each phrase carries different implications about whether the behaviour is problematic or healthy. The choice to label these behaviours as 'quitting' rather than 'boundary setting' reveals whose perspective shapes the narrative.

In many ways, quiet quitting represents a logical endpoint of decades of workplace boundary erosion. As technology made us perpetually reachable, as economic pressures increased competition for jobs, as corporate culture increasingly demanded emotional investment alongside professional output, the distinction between work and life gradually dissolved. Quiet quitting can be understood as employees attempting to redraw those boundaries that were slowly erased without their explicit consent.

Beyond disengagement

Perhaps, most importantly, as I have been writing this book and exploring these concepts, I realize that what is most important is the work we must do to distinguish between quiet quitting, and genuine disengagement and resentment. How we identify the employee who does the minimum required work *while actively undermining* team goals or customer service represents a different phenomenon entirely from one who completes their responsibilities excellently but declines to work unpaid overtime. The former of these colleagues contributes to a working environment which negatively impacts the team, the clients, the work, where the latter deserves to manage their life's time (and find their purpose within their work and life) as they are. In short: true disengagement involves emotional withdrawal, reduced quality of work, and often passive-aggressive behaviours that genuinely harm organizational effectiveness. Quiet quitting, by contrast, typically maintains professional standards while simply not continuing to provide free labour. Understanding this distinction is crucial for organizational responses that address real issues rather than manufactured ones.

Another deeply uncomfortable aspect of the quiet quitting conversation is its focus on employee behaviour rather than workplace conditions. Rather than asking why talented people are choosing to limit their investment in work, the discourse centres on how to convince them to resume providing discretionary effort. This framing suggests that the problem lies with employee attitudes rather than organizational practices: a convenient narrative for leaders unwilling to examine whether their workplaces have become unsustainably demanding. When speaking to one of the senior technology leaders I spoke to for my research, I was hit by a quote, 'Because the mental health struggle is not worth it anymore. It's like, no, I did the rat race and the rats won.'

In the spirit of language mattering: How do we build workplaces where no one needs to see ourselves or our colleagues as rats in an analogy?

As we'll explore further, the quiet quitting phenomenon intersects directly with questions of purpose and meaning at work. When employees feel manipulated by artificial purpose narratives while being asked to provide ever-increasing effort for stagnant compensation, boundary setting becomes not just rational but necessary for psychological survival (and thriving!). The real question isn't how to eliminate quiet quitting, but how to build workplaces where such protective measures become unnecessary.

The purpose paradox

There's a cruel irony at the heart of the quiet quitting phenomenon: many of the employees setting firmer boundaries work for organizations that have spent years telling them their jobs should be their passion, their calling and one of their primary sources of meaning in life. The same companies that plaster mission statements about 'changing the world' on their walls are often the ones most confused when employees decline to work weekends for that world-changing mission.

This represents what I call the purpose paradox, the more aggressively organizations (and specifically service and experiential companies) push purpose as a motivational tool to extract more discretionary effort, the more likely they are to create the very disengagement they're trying to prevent. When purpose becomes a performance rather than a genuine shared commitment, based on genuine relationships with purpose in the workplace, employees develop sophisticated defences against manipulation, including the protective boundaries that get labelled as quiet quitting.

Consider the cognitive burden of being constantly asked to care deeply about *everything*. The morning all-hands meeting about 'our mission to revolutionize human productivity'. The afternoon workshop on 'living our values'. The evening team-building event designed to 'strengthen our shared purpose'. For many employees, this relentless emotional labour becomes exhausting, particularly when the actual work involves mundane tasks that bear little resemblance to the grandiose mission statements.

The same senior leader mentioning her exit from the rat race shared, 'Nine out of ten of my friends that are not in technology, they wouldn't even know what work they do [as it relates to their company purpose]' and, 'at the time [working in big tech] my purpose was to get my kids through college. So my transaction was my purpose, and I still feel like I sold a bit of my soul to do that.' This kind of exhaustion often manifests as what psychologists describe as emotional labour fatigue – a drain that arises from constantly performing emotions one does not genuinely feel.[12] The strain of emotional dissonance, particularly in roles that require surface acting (displaying emotions that don't reflect one's true feelings), can deplete emotional resources and lead to burnout. Studies have demonstrated that such emotional labour is strongly associated with emotional exhaustion, especially in professions that involve sustained interpersonal demands.[13] When organizations demand not just professional competence but emotional investment in corporate narratives that employees find hollow or exaggerated, the natural response is protective withdrawal. Quiet quitting becomes a way of preserving psychological energy for things that actually matter to employees themselves, their families, their communities, and their relationship with purpose and work.

The demand for authentic emotional investment in corporate purpose creates a particularly modern form of workplace stress. Previous generations of workers weren't expected to find their life's meaning in their employer's mission statement. They could take pride in doing good work without having to pretend that processing insurance claims or debugging software was their personal passion. Today's employees face the additional burden of performing enthusiasm for corporate purposes that may conflict with their personal values or simply feel artificially inflated.

Purpose-washing and its many discontents

Purpose-washing is the practice of creating elaborate mission statements and values frameworks without genuine commitment to living them. This practice, in my recent experience, has become so prevalent that employees have developed finely tuned detection systems for corporate authenticity. When companies talk about 'family culture' while conducting lay-offs via email, or promote 'work-life balance' while expecting constant availability, employees quickly learn to discount corporate messaging entirely, particularly that which connects to their already tenuous and often somewhat manufactured connection to the company purpose and mission.

This erosion of trust has profound implications for discretionary effort. Research shows that employees are willing to go above and beyond when they believe their extra effort serves something meaningful. But when purpose feels manufactured or manipulative, that same discretionary effort starts to feel like complicity in their own exploitation.[14]

The tech industry provides numerous examples of this dynamic. Employees join companies attracted by missions to 'democratize information' or 'connect the world', only to find themselves optimizing advertising algorithms or managing data collection practices that feel increasingly problematic. The disconnect between an organization's stated purpose and employees' daily reality can produce what psychologists call moral injury: the profound psychological harm that occurs when individuals are compelled to act against – or pretend to align with – work and purpose they no longer believe in.[15]

When purpose becomes a tool for extracting additional labour rather than a genuine expression of agreed motivation, employees may naturally develop resistance. Quiet quitting can be understood as a form of conscientious objection, not to work itself, but to the emotional manipulation that often accompanies modern workplace culture. It is a pattern which is entirely avoidable, but requires a delicate dismissal of leadership ego, to acknowledge that for most employees and teams (service and experiential primarily), that purpose and work's connection may be a means to an end, or a method of developing career and life experience, more than it is a deep and unquestioned commitment to a company's purpose.

There's growing evidence that organizations with a genuine connection between purpose and daily work experience less quiet quitting – not because employees sacrifice everything for the mission, but because authentic meaning reduces the need for protective boundaries. When purpose resonates with employees' real work-purpose orientation – whether transformational, experiential, or service-based – it triggers three positive effects:

1 **Intrinsic reward:** The work becomes rewarding in itself, reducing feelings that effort is being extracted from unaligned tasks.
2 **Sustainability of engagement:** Organizations with authentic purpose understand that burnout undermines impact, and thus structure work to preserve energy and engagement.

3 **Mutual trust:** Rather than mandating enthusiasm, these organizations model trust by allowing employees to manage their own engagement, because they believe in the work's inherent value.

> A 2021 Kumanu Harris poll found that employees are twice as likely to stay and four times more engaged at organizations that genuinely embody their stated purpose. This underscores how authentic purpose can drive loyalty and discretionary effort, rather than deepen cynicism.[16]

For the research of this book I met with Emory Sullivan, the founder of Genba AI, a technology company focused on bringing modern tools to underserved blue-collar workers in manufacturing. Emory describes her customers as people who had been largely ignored by the tech industry despite being 'the salt of the earth' who 'make all the things that we enjoy'. When I met with Emory to talk about building a workplace which was service in nature, but had a deep impact and opportunity for individual connection to the community, Emory talked to me about her low turnover, high team engagement, and how she created authentic alignment between company values and employee treatment. 'I made a great effort to bring the engineers and the team like on site to meet the people who were actually using the technology. And so I think having that loop closed, and having them meet the people and see their technology out in the wild is really impactful.'

When asked about compromising the mission for money, Emory said: 'I couldn't look at myself in the mirror if I were to… I really loved our customers, I knew them all by name, and I spent years, passionately thinking about how to solve this problem and make people's lives better, and I built a team around this idea of making these people's lives better… once you hire a team around that mission, there's an added pressure, in a way, to stay true to that.'

From my conversation with Emory, three themes emerged: authentic connection through direct customer engagement, sustaining mission-driven work without compromising values, and fostering trust through employee autonomy:

- Authentic connection reduces need for boundaries – Emory's team didn't need protection from manipulation because their relationship to the company's mission was genuine and evidenced through direct customer contact, regardless for where they were personally deriving their sense of purpose in their work

- Sustainable operation within the service economy – Genba AI empowered employees with flexibility and autonomy, showing they understood that sustainable engagement serves the mission better than extraction
- Trust-based engagement – Employees were 'fully empowered to make decisions on their own' rather than having enthusiasm mandated

Emory's approach explains a really crucial and somewhat surface-level insight as it relates to engagement and management: authentic purpose doesn't eliminate the need for boundaries; it creates cultures where healthy boundaries are seen as essential to mission success rather than obstacles to it. The organizations struggling most with quiet quitting are often those trying to use purpose as a substitute for fair compensation, reasonable workloads, and respectful management.

The relationship between meaning and discretionary effort is more complex than most corporate wisdom suggests. While meaningful work can indeed inspire additional discretionary effort, this inspiration cannot be mandated or manipulated. Think of a time where inspiration struck you in your work, where you felt genuinely 'in flow'... perhaps when solving a particularly challenging problem or creating something you were proud of. That state emerged naturally from the conditions: you likely had clarity about what you were doing, felt capable of the challenge, received immediate feedback on your progress, and importantly, weren't being coerced into caring.

Flow states require psychological safety and autonomy – they can't be manufactured through motivational slogans or guilt. According to self-determination theory, autonomy is essential for intrinsic motivation and flow.[17] Moreover, studies in workplace settings reveal that autonomy support enhances psychological safety, which in turn enables peak performance.[18] Flow itself depends on conditions like balanced challenge and skill... not on external pressure or moral obligation. When organizations try to manufacture meaning through corporate messaging while maintaining exploitative practices, they often achieve the opposite of their intended effect. Employees recognize the disconnect between the rhetoric of 'changing the world' and the reality of being asked to work unpaid overtime, and this contradiction breeds the very cynicism that purpose initiatives were meant to prevent.

Genuine discretionary effort stems from intrinsic motivation, which is deeply rooted in fulfilment derived from autonomy, mastery and purpose. When employees feel empowered by these drivers, their effort arises organically rather than being coerced or rewarded externally.[19] But when purpose becomes a management tool rather than an authentic shared commitment, it undermines the very autonomy that makes discretionary effort feel voluntary rather than coerced. Studies on corporate social responsibility programmes show us that employees are remarkably sophisticated at distinguishing between authentic purpose and corporate theatre.[20] Your team, just like you, can sense when mission statements were crafted by marketing teams rather than emerging from actual organizational values. They *will* notice when purpose gets invoked primarily during difficult conversations about compensation or workload. This sophistication explains why purpose-washing often backfires, creating cynicism rather than engagement.

Cultural recalibration or crisis?

The quiet quitting phenomenon suggests that many employees have reached a breaking point with inauthentic purpose narratives. Rather than continuing to perform enthusiasm for missions they don't believe in, they're choosing to focus their energy on doing good work within clear boundaries. This represents not a rejection of purpose itself, but a rejection of purpose-as-manipulation. It also represents a reason to change our approach, and why adjusting our purpose messaging to be more aligned with the purpose-economy spectrum may result in a higher level of both engagement and honesty within our teams. For the most positive results:

- **In service economy businesses,** leadership focuses on the team's and company's purpose as it relates to work to enable family time, hobbies, study, travel or relationships within the community. *How does our company meeting our purpose and mission help others achieve theirs outside of work?*
- **Whereas in the experiential economy** as long as the company purpose is not contributing harm to the world, most folks are connecting their sense of purpose at work to their career, growth, relationships and ways of working. Leadership would benefit from proudly sharing what kind of quality of life the company's success can offer them, be that development or perks, as well as sharing insights towards the company's positive impact.
- **Finally, in the transformation economy,** as long as the company purpose is clearly and honestly articulated, your team would expect an involvement and transparency in their relationship with purpose and the company mission and their own transformational work experiences. They are deeply motivated by this element of their work, and are looking for these connections to their own (or the world's transformation).

The challenge for organizations isn't to find better ways to convince employees to care about existing corporate missions, but to create conditions where authentic care and flow can emerge naturally. This requires moving beyond purpose as only a shallow motivational tool toward more output, and instead as a genuine expression of shared values and meaningful work. When that happens, the protective boundaries of quiet quitting may become less necessary because the work environment lacks these elements of dissonance or manipulative messaging, and more connected to the drivers behind the employee's lives and motivations.

> As we'll explore in the next three chapters, this shift requires organizations to examine their workplace cultures. This means that, even with reconsidering your company purpose and mission statements, and how you communicate them, you may need to recognize some of your cultural norms have become unsustainably demanding. There is a world where what they're calling quiet quitting actually represents a healthy correction towards more humane working conditions.

These dang lazy kids

All this talk of quiet quitting often comes with another, perhaps more subversive and consistent set of messaging: these dang lazy kids. The accusation that younger generations are uniquely lazy represents one of humanity's most enduring clichés, with a pedigree stretching back millennia. Socrates reputedly complained that young people in ancient Athens 'have bad manners, contempt for authority', and 'show disrespect for elders'.[21] A Sumerian tablet from 2800 BCE supposedly grumbled about 'degenerate' youth who will 'never amount to anything'.[22] Every generation seems convinced that the one following them represents civilization's inevitable decline, despite the inconvenient fact that society has generally progressed rather than collapsed.

The World War II generation called baby boomers spoilt and self-indulgent. Boomers denounced Gen X as slackers and cynics. Gen X dismissed millennials as entitled and narcissistic. Now millennials and Gen Z are supposedly work-shy and demanding, lacking the proper work ethic that previous generations supposedly possessed in abundance. This pattern reveals less about actual generational character than it does about human psychology's tendency to romanticize our own struggles while dismissing those of others, particularly those younger and with less experience than us *old folk*.

The older worker who remembers grinding through 60-hour weeks at their first job conveniently forgets that those same 60-hour weeks bought them a house, supported a family and led to a pension – luxuries largely unavailable to today's young workers despite similar efforts. What looks like laziness from one generation's perspective often represents rational adaptation to entirely different economic realities.

The economic context of 'disengagement'

I think if we had a moment to reflect with some intellectual honesty, we may see that much of the discussion around quiet quitting is in fact a reaction to various economic challenges that the current working population has endured. These are people who entered the workforce during the Great Recession, watched their older siblings struggle with student debt that previous generations never faced, and then lived through a pandemic where 'essential workers' were simultaneously called heroes and denied basic protections while executives worked safely from home. They've seen tech companies lay off thousands of employees via Zoom calls after record-breaking profit quarters, watched housing prices become completely detached from wages and witnessed the hollowing out of benefits that their grandparents took for granted.

And yet, somehow, when these workers decide that maybe working unpaid overtime for companies that view them as disposable isn't the path to prosperity, we get think-pieces about their character deficiencies rather than examinations of the economic conditions that shaped their entirely rational responses to an increasingly extractive employment landscape. The generational difference isn't that younger workers are lazier or more entitled, it's that they've had front-row seats to watch the complete breakdown of the social contract between employers and employees, and they're responding accordingly by refusing to participate in a system that demands everything while promising nothing.

If quiet quitting is real, and people are disengaged from their work and not going the extra mile, it's probably because they've lived through millions of lives taken by a pandemic, all while living in crushing fear that they themselves might die, while watching the majority of aid go to companies that then posted record profits, none of which seemed actually to trickle down to the majority of people. Workers have been told they're demanding for wanting to work from home, entitled for wanting better pay and seeking it out through other employment, and then lazy for feeling burnt out as every new day in the world produces some new macroeconomic or social nightmare.[23]

The productivity paradox

It's especially ironic that while workers are more productive than ever, they're also significantly more stressed and less satisfied. Data consistently shows that productivity gains have come at a steep emotional cost.[24] Technology that was supposed to liberate us has instead created an always-on culture where, as research suggests, having email on our phones and tablets has increased our working day by roughly 10 per cent on average, with 35 per cent of folks saying these tools *significantly* pushed up working hours.[25, 26] But rather than improving our productivity, it has created more stress, and stress leads to being less productive.[27]

Consider this: Charles Dickens wrote 15 books, 200 short stories and edited a weekly publication… and didn't work in the afternoons. Instead, he went for walks, often ten to twelve miles. 'Nowadays we'd put him on performance review, to get his hours up', as productivity expert Bruce Daisley notes. Above all, sitting at your desk rarely leads to creativity or innovation.[28]

What actually works

The solution isn't to berate workers for having boundaries, it's to create working conditions that make discretionary effort feel worthwhile rather than exploitative. The direct correlation between employee happiness and profitability is demonstrated time and time again across research. Harvard psychologist Daniel Goleman's book *Primal Leadership* cites research where, for every 2 per cent increase in employee happiness, revenue grew by 1 per cent.[29] Similarly, a three-year Willis Towers Watson study of 41 global companies found that operating margins improved nearly 4 per cent on average in organizations with high employee engagement levels and declined about 2 per cent in those with low engagement levels.[30]

Companies need to go above and beyond for their workers if they expect them to do so for the company. The solution is deceptively simple: pay people more, give them a career path, provide great working conditions, and align their sense of purpose and fulfilment at work with a genuine reality. Their work should be rewarding in the sense that they are *rewarded for doing the work well* in the forms of monetary compensation, career progression, opportunities for new experiences, or the work offering something genuinely transformative. It goes without saying, wherever possible, they should work less than the statutory maximum hours within a week if their work can be handled in that time, and if they work over that amount, you should be compensating them for doing so.

This means supporting union contracts, being generous with paid time off, aggressively policing toxic management, reducing micromanagement, being explicit with what's expected and rewarding those who exceed it monetarily and when things are tough, treating people better than usual. Why? Because doing these things shows workers that you're loyal and place their experience as a core part of the economic value of your business, which in turn means they'll be more likely and willing to go above and beyond for you when necessary.

Work as product, employee as customer

Perhaps, most importantly, employers need to recognize that as the 'supplier' of work experiences, they need to provide their employees (their customers) with something that is reliable, honest and valuable, without it necessarily having to change the world (not something people are frequently out to 'buy' from their job). This product-thinking approach requires honesty about what you're actually offering. If you're a service economy company, focus on competitive compensation, professional development, and work-life boundaries rather than manufacturing artificial meaning. If you're genuinely in the transformation economy; then yes, lean into that calling and purpose as a means of benefiting your team (but, seriously, *only* if that's authentically what you're selling).

The cure for quiet quitting isn't better motivational messaging or more pizza parties. It's treating work as what it actually is: a value exchange where both parties need to benefit and that benefit must be honest and fair. When that exchange feels fair, sustainable and honest, engagement follows naturally. When it doesn't, you get entirely rational boundary setting that gets unfairly labelled as laziness by people who fundamentally misunderstand both human motivation and basic economics.

A future filled with *Feierabend*!

The quiet quitting phenomenon reveals a fundamental truth about humans and modern work: employees aren't lazy or uncommitted. They're responding rationally to workplaces that have become unsustainably demanding while offering diminishing returns. What we're witnessing isn't a crisis of character but a necessary correction towards more humane working conditions and a more authentic connection with work and purpose.

The lesson embedded in this cultural shift is that sustainable engagement cannot be manufactured through motivational messaging or purpose-washing. It emerges when organizations create genuine value exchanges, where employees receive fair compensation, meaningful development opportunities, and respect for their boundaries in return for their contributions. This requires employers to abandon the fantasy that passionate speeches about 'changing the world' can substitute for competitive wages, reasonable workloads and trustworthy management.

Perhaps most importantly, the quiet quitting conversation forces us to confront an uncomfortable reality about how we've constructed modern work culture. As one research participant reflected, 'the one lesson I have learnt is that you must put more good into the world than it costs to sustain your life within it. If you are successful, you should not be spending your time stopping those who are not.'

The path forward isn't about eliminating quiet quitting. It's about creating workplaces where such protective measures become unnecessary. When leaders like Emory recognize that 'once you hire a team like around that mission, there's like an added pressure, in a way, to stay true to that mission,' they understand that authentic purpose creates accountability that works both ways. This means treating work as what it actually is: a product that must deliver authentic value to its primary customers, the employees. When organizations embrace this perspective, moving beyond extraction towards genuine exchange, they'll find that discretionary effort flows naturally from conditions of trust, fairness and mutual respect, rather than from guilt, manipulation, or manufactured purpose.

The alternative to this cultural recalibration isn't a return to some mythical golden age of unlimited employee dedication. It's an accelerating cycle of disengagement, cynicism and turnover that serves no one's interests. The choice, ultimately, is between sustainable engagement built on honest foundations or continued deterioration of the employment relationship disguised as motivational leadership.

Notes and further reading

1. Wolfe, J (2022) The year in quiet quitting, *The New Yorker*, 29 December. www.newyorker.com/culture/2022-in-review/the-year-in-quiet-quitting (archived at https://perma.cc/W7XD-HSKF)
2. Henry, S E, Bolino, M C, and Whitney, J M (2025) Keep up the good work… or else! Exploring supervisor responses to quiet quitting, *Human Resource Management*. https://doi.org/10.1002/hrm.22319 (archived at https://perma.cc/WFF3-CNWK)
3. The Expath Team (2025) What does the German word *Feierabend* mean? www.expath.de/what-does-the-german-word-feierabend-mean/ (archived at https://perma.cc/K6CH-4EYJ)
4. Wikipedia (2025) Work-to-rule. https://en.wikipedia.org/wiki/Work-to-rule (archived at https://perma.cc/B3JV-ZYTW)
5. Wiktionary (2025) *fajrant*. https://en.wiktionary.org/wiki/fajrant (archived at https://perma.cc/GGE6-Y3HD) (meaning: knock-off time, leisure, quitting time; borrowed from German *Feierabend*)
6. Reverso Context (2025) Translation of 'to *fajrant*'. https://context.reverso.net/translation/polish-english/to+fajrant (archived at https://perma.cc/JUD4-TWKQ) (Usage example: 'we are done for the day' – a colloquial nod to 'fajrant'.)
7. Zitron, E (2022) Quiet quitting and the death of office culture. *Where's Your Ed At*, 22 August. www.wheresyoured.at/quiet-quitting-and-the-death-of-office/ (archived at https://perma.cc/GZ7X-X7LM)
8. CNBC Make It (2022) Kevin O'Leary calls 'quiet quitting' a really bad idea, CNBC Make It. www.facebook.com/CNBCMakeIt/videos/quiet-quitting-describes-the-experience-of-doing-your-job-without-going-above-an/432362342243346/ (archived at https://perma.cc/V4RW-WX25)
9. Daniels, A C (n.d.) Discretionary effort is the level of effort people could give if they wanted to, but above and beyond the minimum required. www.aubreydaniels.com/discretionary-effort (archived at https://perma.cc/6G8K-JG6T)
10. Cooper, M (2015) The false promise of meritocracy, *The Atlantic*, December. www.theatlantic.com/business/archive/2015/12/meritocracy/418074/ (archived at https://perma.cc/5KYP-2BSA)
11. Henry, S E, Bolino, M C, and Whitney, J M (2025) Keep up the good work… or else! Exploring supervisor responses to quiet quitting, *Human Resource Management*. https://doi.org/10.1002/hrm.22319 (archived at https://perma.cc/E72G-5H6L)
12. Chen, C-C, Lin, Y-L, and Chang, S-L (2022) The effect of emotional labor and emotional exhaustion on the physical and mental health of health professionals, *International Journal of Environmental Research and Public Health*, 19(1). www.mdpi.com/2227-9032/11/1/104 (archived at https://perma.cc/9X84-XB3G)

13 Peng, P (2023) The hidden costs of emotional labor on withdrawal behavior, *BMC Psychology*, 11, Article 12392. https://bmcpsychology.biomedcentral.com/articles/10.1186/s40359-023-01392-z (archived at https://perma.cc/7UPY-DTJB)
14 Soren, A (2023) Meaningful work, well-being, and health: Enacting a… (open access article). https://pmc.ncbi.nlm.nih.gov/articles/PMC10454804/ (archived at https://perma.cc/7ZMV-DDMN)
15 *Psychology Today* (2022) How to identify and address moral injury at work. www.psychologytoday.com/us/blog/positively-different/202204/how-identify-and-address-moral-injury-work (archived at https://perma.cc/CN76-R79J)
16 Kumanu Harris (2021) Purpose-driven organizations: Engagement and retention insights. https://www.wtwco.com/en-us/insights/2022/10/quiet-quitting-the-real-story-dont-blame-gen-z (archived at https://perma.cc/YVH5-PGBL)
17 Deci, E L and Ryan, R M (2012) Motivation, personality, and development within embedded social contexts: An overview of self-determination theory, Ryan, R M (ed.) *The Oxford Handbook of Human Motivation*, Oxford University Press, Oxford
18 Buvik, M P and Tkalich, A (2021) Psychological safety in Agile software development teams: Work design antecedents and performance consequences. arXiv
19 Pink, D H (2009) *Drive: The surprising truth about what motivates us*. Riverhead Books, New York
20 Kim, H and Lee, M (2022) Employee perception of corporate social responsibility authenticity: A multilevel approach, *Frontiers in Psychology*, 13, Article 948363. https://doi.org/10.3389/fpsyg.2022.948363 (archived at https://perma.cc/PV5W-H58M)
21 Freeman, K J (1907) *Schools of Hellas: An essay on the practice and theory of ancient Greek education from 600 to 300 BC*. George Allen & Unwin, London. (Quoted paraphrase regarding youth behaviour in ancient Greece)
22 Quote Investigator (2012) Ancient tablet: The world is speedily coming to an end, *Quote Investigator*, 22 October. https://quoteinvestigator.com/2012/10/22/world-end/ (archived at https://perma.cc/SLP8-7PF7)
23 Fortune (2025) Gen Z whines about everyone else calling them lazy workers: 'People like to talk about us but not talk to us', Fortune Workplace Innovation Summit, 22 May. https://nypost.com/2025/05/22/lifestyle/gen-z-whines-about-lazy-worker-label-in-workplace-debate/ (archived at https://perma.cc/4JU4-BK2H)
24 Gallup (2023) Globally, employees are more engaged – and also stressed, Gallup Workplace Insights. www.gallup.com/workplace/506798/globally-employees-engaged-stressed.aspx (archived at https://perma.cc/2HVR-5KVM)

25 National Bureau of Economic Research (2020) You're right – you are working longer and attending more meetings. Working Knowledge, Harvard Business School. www.library.hbs.edu/working-knowledge/you-re-right-you-are-working-longer-and-attending-more-meetings (archived at https://perma.cc/G3T6-TKUF)

26 Pew Research Center (2014) Email and the internet are the dominant technological tools in American workplaces. www.pewresearch.org/internet/2014/12/30/email-and-the-internet-are-the-dominant-technological-tools-in-american-workplaces/ (archived at https://perma.cc/EK7E-X43D)

27 Insightful (2024) Stress in the workplace report 2024: The disengagement dilemma. www.insightful.io/reports/stress-at-work (archived at https://perma.cc/6EQZ-Y5XU)

28 Daisley, B (2019) Bruce Daisley on understanding workplace culture, Armadillo, 24 May. https://armadillocrm.com/bruce-daisley-on-understanding-workplace-culture/ (archived at https://perma.cc/3UM2-JYG8)

29 Happy.co.uk (2021) Happy workplaces are more successful. www.happy.co.uk/blogs/happy-workplaces-are-more-successful/ (archived at https://perma.cc/CH9Q-EBVW)

30 Willis Towers Watson (2012) Engagement at risk: Driving strong performance in a volatile global environment. www.wtwco.com/en-US/Insights/2012/07/2012-global-workforce-study (archived at https://perma.cc/2RLA-UFGF)

PART FOUR

Building with purpose

8

Transforming corporate cultures

Do you remember when finding out what it was like to work somewhere required knowing someone who knew someone? When the only way to get the inside scoop on a company's culture was through hushed conversations over coffee, or that friend-of-a-friend who'd 'heard things' about the management team? Those days feel positively quaint now, don't they?

Then Glassdoor arrived in 2008 and absolutely obliterated one of corporate culture's best-kept secrets: the gap between what companies claimed to be and what employees actually experienced. Suddenly, every passive-aggressive manager, every toxic team dynamic, every 'we're like a family' company that treated people like expendable relatives was capable of being aired out for the entire world's viewing pleasure. I remember the time pretty clearly, it felt like someone had installed a giant digital spyglass into workplaces across the globe.

I'll never forget the moment I discovered just how powerful this transparency could be. I was helping a friend to research a role at what seemed like a dream company on paper: great benefits, impressive client list, all the right buzzwords on their careers page. But something felt off during her interviews. The hiring manager kept emphasizing how 'resilient' and 'thick-skinned' she'd need to be. Amber flags were raised at half-mast. At this point in time, at least for me in the UK, Glassdoor was used but not at its peak. Once we reviewed the company's Glassdoor reviews, the picture became clearer. I don't recall the precise quotes but, 'management by intimidation' comes to mind. Review after review painted a common theme, a consistent picture began to form: a company that confused cruelty with high performance, where 'pushing people to their limits' was mistaken for leadership excellence.

Now, don't get me wrong, I'm not here to sing Glassdoor's praises. The platform itself is deeply flawed. Anonymous reviews can become weapons for disgruntled employees to target individual managers rather than systemic issues. There's no way to verify if that scathing review came from someone who was legitimately mistreated or someone who got fired for cause and wanted revenge. The rating system reduces complex cultural dynamics to star ratings, as if workplace experience could be Yelp-ified. Also, a crucial bias that is often ignored by those reading the profiles, in my experience, is that people are far more motivated to write reviews when they're angry than when they're content, creating an inherent negativity bias. Glassdoor was once a unique and newly developed peek behind the scenes, but what I see now is a system which is inherently flawed and deserves a significant overhaul. Either way, the truth remains: if the momentum of Glassdoor tells us anything, we need a way to understand when a company is delivering what they're selling.

Criticism aside, what fascinates me about this cultural transparency revolution, flawed execution and all, is that it hasn't just exposed the bad actors or corporate bullies. It also illuminated something that I think is quite fantastic, that the companies where folks were already getting it right, they were often doing it without even realizing how rare they may have been. While some organizations scrambled to manage their online reputation or game the system with planted positive reviews, others discovered they'd built something people actually wanted to talk about authentically. The culture whisper network didn't just change how we research potential employers, it fundamentally shifted the power dynamic between companies and talent, even if the execution was messy. Suddenly, authenticity wasn't just nice to have; it became table stakes. You couldn't hide behind corporate-speak and hope for the best, but you also couldn't control the narrative through perfectly curated review platforms. The emperor's new clothes had been revealed, and employees everywhere realized they had agency in ways previous generations could only dream of, even if that agency sometimes came with its own set of problems.

Which brings us to the central tension of modern workplace culture: in an age where every company claims to have an 'incredible culture', every job posting promises 'work-life balance', and every review site can be gamed, corrupted, or weaponized, how do you actually build something worth whispering *about*? More importantly, how do you create an environment so genuinely engaging that people don't just stay – they become advocates, not because you asked them to write positive reviews, but because they can't help themselves?

The answer, as I've discovered through conversations with leaders who've cracked this code, is probably what you're expecting to read at this point in the book (but perhaps not when you first cracked it open to page one!). It's not about ping-pong tables or unlimited paid time off (PTO) or purpose statements that sound like they were written by a motivational poster generator. It's about something far more fundamental, and far more challenging: the courage to acknowledge that work is just one vehicle in people's lives, not the destination itself.

Companies that cracked the code

In the heart of London's bustling tech scene, a quiet revolution is taking place. It's not about disrupting markets or chasing unicorn valuations, though success has certainly followed. Instead, this revolution centres on a more fundamental question: What if the true measure of a company's worth lay not in its profit margins, but in its capacity to nurture human flourishing? How can a company bring a sense of purpose that is genuine to their teams?

For Nick Taylor, CEO of Unmind, this question isn't theoretical. When he cofounded the workplace mental health platform in 2016, he wasn't just launching another digital health start-up. Drawing from his background as a clinical psychologist, Taylor envisioned a future where workplaces actively contributed to their employees' mental wellbeing – not as a peripheral benefit, but as a core purpose.[1]

In his podcast *Lead From Within* Nick spoke to Loren Schuster, Chief People Officer from the LEGO Group. Within the hour-long discussion, they discuss the impact of loneliness and community at work, the inspiration of children, and the power of purpose in your daily working lives. '*Sometimes the discussion gets overly anchored on [benefits] rather than what is far more fundamentally important: do I have the opportunity to operate in an environment, in a system that creates that sense of meaning and purpose... Do I belong?*'[2]

This reframing of corporate purpose isn't unique to Unmind or to LEGO. Across London's entrepreneurial landscape, a new generation of founders is emerging who share a common conviction: that authentic purpose and profitable enterprise aren't competing priorities, but complementary forces that amplify each other. From Oliva's similar mission of transforming workplace mental health support to Wonderbly's mission of inspiring creativity through personalized storytelling and books, business leaders are writing a new chapter in the story of business – one where purpose isn't just a statement on a wall, but the foundation upon which everything else is built.[3,4]

In this chapter, we'll meet some pioneers of this purpose-driven revolution. Through their stories, we'll explore how they've translated lofty ideals into tangible organizational practices, navigated the tensions between purpose and profit and built cultures that attract and retain not just the best talent, but the most aligned talent. Their experiences offer valuable lessons for any leader seeking to build an organization that serves both its balance sheet and its broader reason for being. We'll also see how you can adapt this same approach, but perhaps through a different lens, to bring purpose to the experiential and service economy business you may operate in. To think about Loren's quote from above, how do we create a sense of purpose that resonates (even if it may not be transformational) to help people understand where they belong at work?

The path these founders have chosen isn't always the easiest. It demands courage to challenge established paradigms, wisdom to navigate competing priorities, and patience to allow purpose-driven initiatives to bear fruit. But as their stories reveal, the rewards – both tangible and intangible – make the journey worthwhile. Welcome to the future of purpose-driven leadership.

Work as vehicle, not a destination

Recently I was meeting a friend for a drink when she asked me how I was and I said, instinctively, absently, 'Busy.' She responded, 'You always say that.' Ouch. Suddenly I saw myself through the fourth wall. At that moment, I wasn't Jessie the friend having a drink, I was Jessica Zwaan, Chief Operating Officer (*this is where I'd insert an emoji of myself eye-rolling*). I felt like I'd trapped my friend in a weak conversation at a networking event (horrible). My natural reaction towards genuine connection, for months of the last few years, seemed to drift miserably into corporate rhetoric. I entered into (seemingly on auto-pilot): busy at work, busy in life, busy when asked, busy, busy, busy. It's an easy mistake to make in a culture that's spent decades conflating our professional identity with our entire sense of self, but it's also a mistake that's quietly destroying both individual fulfilment and organizational culture.

Huw Slater, CEO and founder at Oliva, whose insights on operating principles versus values we'll explore later in this book, offered me one of the more liberating perspectives on work I've happened to encounter, 'We all have our own human journeys that we're going on, right?' he explained during our conversation. 'Work is just a car that you get in, and you get in a car that takes you quickly in the direction you want to go. And when it starts veering off or your personal direction changes... I'm going to hop in a different car.'

The simplicity of this metaphor lies in its insurgent implications. Think about it: when you get in a car, you don't expect to live in it forever. You don't expect it to fulfil every need in your life. You expect it to be reliable, to get you where you're going, and ideally to be a reasonably pleasant experience along the way. The car may be aligned with a purpose you feel strongly about; electric, or a perfectly maintained vintage. You might even grow fond of a particular car, but you don't mistake it for your home, your identity, or your *life's* purpose.

Yet somehow, when it comes to work, we've created this bizarre expectation within the zeitgeist that our jobs should be everything: our passion, our purpose, our community, our identity and one of many (if not our primary) sources of meaning. No wonder so many people feel perpetually disappointed by their careers. We're asking a Honda Civic to be a *house*, a passion and a community.

I learnt this lesson the hard way during my own career journey. SHRM's 'Employee Mental Health in 2024' Research Series found that 44 per cent of 1,405 surveyed US employees feel burnt out at work, 45 per cent feel 'emotionally drained' from their work, and 51 per cent feel 'used up' at the end of the workday.[5] In 2023 I was one of them. I was 33 years old, and at an incredible high point in my career. My first book had been published, I was in my first Chief Operating Officer role of a company I loved, with a team I had passionately built and supported for more than three years. However, I was often working from 6 am through the evening time (never forced or pushed by my board or CEO, but because I genuinely had lost my sense of identity outside of my professional life). Throughout my 20s I had spent my spare time in creative pursuits; writing, music, art. In 2023 I had spent an astonishing amount of time in my apartment, working 50-plus hours a week from home, and I was beginning to lose a bit of myself. The relief I felt when I finally gave myself permission to see work as one important element of my life rather than the defining one was profound. Suddenly, career decisions became clearer, workplace frustrations became more manageable, and paradoxically, I became better at my job because I wasn't asking it to carry the weight of my entire existence.

Huw's analogy is particularly interesting from a leadership perspective: 'If you're the founder, you've created the car, you've created the highway, you've created the destiny, you're probably staying in that car, right? But that's a very select group of people.' This distinction is crucial and often overlooked by founders and executives who can't understand why their employees don't share their level of emotional investment in the company.

Of course the founder is staying in the car: they built it! They chose the destination, designed the route, and have a deep personal stake in reaching that particular endpoint. But expecting everyone else to have that same level of attachment is like expecting passengers on a tour bus to feel as invested in the route as the team who planned it. They might enjoy the ride, they might even prefer your bus to other transportation options, but they're ultimately trying to discover their own experiences, command their own version of their lives, no matter how much you are an influence on that.

This perspective reframes how we think about employee retention, engagement and loyalty. Instead of asking, 'How do we make people never want to leave?' the question becomes 'How do we make our workplace such a good vehicle that people choose to stay for as long as it serves their journey?' It's a subtle but significant shift from possessiveness to partnership.

Bruce Springsteen (stay with me here) captured this beautifully in his song *The River*; not about purpose within work, obviously, but about the gradual realization you're in the wrong place for your life's journey, '*I got a job working construction/For the Johnstown Company/But lately there ain't been much work/On account of the economy/Now all them things that seemed so important/Well mister they vanished right into the air/Now I just act like I don't remember/Mary acts like she don't care*'.[6]

Sometimes the most loving thing you can do for yourself, as well as for others, including your team, is acknowledged when they've outgrown the space you can provide. Sometimes the healthiest organizations are the ones that celebrate people's departures as much as their arrivals, as we explored in Chapter 5.

The companies that truly embrace the car analogy do something counter-intuitive: they explicitly tell people that it's okay to leave, and it's okay to stay for reasons that may not be perfectly aligned with the company's mission and purpose. They invest in their employees' long-term careers, not just their current roles. They celebrate alumni who move on to bigger things. They maintain relationships with former employees who become brand ambassadors, referral sources and sometimes even clients. They understand that in the age of career fluidity, trying to convince or trap people in jobs creates resentment, while giving them permission to grow creates loyalty.

I spoke to an incredible young woman named Liz Hagearty, whose story is remarkable both for her self-awareness, and her bravery.[7] At 21, fresh out of university with a computer science degree, Liz made a plan that would have horrified most career counsellors: she would work as a software engineer for six years, then quit at 27 to pursue a creative gap year. 'I looked around at my co-workers who had started in tech and the ones that never did anything else, they started tech graduating from college. If they get to 30 and they've never done anything else, they're never leaving,' she observed with startling clarity.

This wasn't rebellion or career sabotage. It was strategic self-development. Liz recognized something that most organizations struggle to accept; that holding onto people who have outgrown their roles doesn't just harm the individual, it diminishes the entire team. She saved diligently, building up impressive savings for her creative pursuit and when the time came, she left with grace and purpose.

What happened next validates everything we've discussed about the power of supportive departures. Liz's creative gap year, initially planned for 12 months, stretched to three years as she found unexpected success creating TikTok content for electronic dance music festivals. She went viral, built a following and carved out an entirely new career path that combined her technical background with her creative passions. When she eventually returned to tech (plot twist!), she came back transformed. 'I have so much more humility,' she reflects. 'So much more graciousness. I think in how I approach my work now... It's different than being grateful. I think humility and acceptance, and a desire to be there is more present and less of the focus on me as an individual.'

Liz's story illustrates a fundamental truth that forward-thinking organizations are beginning to understand: sometimes the best way to retain someone's long-term loyalty, and to get the most out of their time in your team, is to gracefully let them go. The car analogy also explains why so many traditional retention strategies backfire. Golden handcuffs, non-compete clauses, and guilt-tripping about 'loyalty' are the equivalent of chaining people to a vehicle they no longer want to ride in. You might keep their bodies in the car, but their hearts and minds are already elsewhere, making them less effective employees and more likely to spread dissatisfaction to others.

The most insightful leaders have realized that different people get in the car for entirely different reasons, and understanding those motivations is the key to creating cultures where people genuinely want to stay, not because they're trapped, but because the journey aligns with their personal destination.

Think about it in terms of the economic structure we have been exploring throughout this book so far. In the *transformation economy*, some employees are genuinely bought into the mission, and into the work creating a fundamental change within themselves as individuals. They're in the car because they believe in the journey's impact on them and/or the world around them. The purpose-driven start-up exec working long weeks, the assistant working with a renowned visual artist, the teacher applying deeply personal approaches to help struggling students, the sustainability consultant who took a pay cut to work for a B-Corp. For these people, work *is* a significant part of their identity and purpose, and that's perfectly valid.

Then there's the *experience economy* group: people who see work as a vehicle for personal and professional growth. They're not necessarily married to your *specific* mission (and my research says that just being 'not evil' is very much good enough for most folks), but they're deeply invested in what the role can teach them, how it can expand their skills, or the doors it might open. These employees ask thoughtful questions in interviews about development opportunities and career trajectories. They're engaged and productive because the experience itself has value, even if they're not planning to retire from your company.

Finally, there's what we might call the *service economy* mindset; people who work to live, not live to work, and there's absolutely nothing wrong with that. These employees see their job as enabling their real life… the parent who wants flexible hours to coach their kid's football team, the artist who needs stable income to fund their creative projects, the graduate student working while completing their degree. They're not disengaged from your company's mission or purpose; they're just optimizing for different purpose-related outcomes.

The breakthrough into something more genuine occurs when leaders understand which type of journey their employees are on and co-create work experiences that honour those different motivations. Instead of trying to convert everyone into transformation economy true believers, they ask better questions: How can we make this role genuinely developmental for a team where our employees are likely to be primarily focused on experience as a driver for their purpose? How can we provide the stability and flexibility that service economy employees need to thrive in their whole lives? How can we support our team's mission-driven employees without burning them out?

I've seen this play out beautifully at companies that have learnt to adapt their approach as we've explored in other chapters. They might offer sabbaticals and passion projects for transformation economy employees, mentorship programmes and stretch assignments for experience seekers, and genuinely flexible arrangements for those balancing work with other priorities. Rather than treating these as different levels of commitment, they recognize them as different but equally valid ways of engaging with work and purpose.

The most successful leaders I've encountered have internalized this truth: they've stopped trying to be everything to everyone and started focusing on being the right vehicle for each person's journey, and for the type of highway they're driving on. They understand that company purpose isn't something you impose on people to convince or motivate; purpose may take different forms, but in any way you do build it, it's something you build together. And paradoxically, when you stop demanding that your company's purpose be someone's driving source of professional meaning, you often create the conditions where it becomes much more meaningful than it would have been otherwise.

The purpose and profit paradox

Let's address the elephant wearing a suit in the boardroom, shall we?

Every time I talk to leaders about building purpose-driven cultures, there's usually that moment when someone clears their throat and asks the question everyone's thinking but nobody wants to be the first to voice: 'This all sounds lovely, Jessica, but does it all fall apart when we need to focus on making money?'

It's a fair question, and frankly, anyone who doesn't ask it probably shouldn't be trusted with a budget. We can wax lyrical about human flourishing and meaningful work all we want, but if the numbers don't add up, you won't have a company left to flourish in. The harsh reality is that businesses need to be profitable to survive, let alone thrive.

What I've discovered through months of research and countless conversations with leaders who've successfully navigated this tension: the question itself is based on a false premise. It assumes that purpose and profit are competing forces, that you have to choose between a positive company purpose and doing well financially. The most successful companies I've studied have cracked a different code entirely: they've discovered that authentic purpose and profitable enterprise aren't just compatible; they're complementary forces that amplify each other.

The real problem: We're rewarding A while hoping for B

The tension between purpose and profit often isn't actually about purpose at all – it's about what Steven Kerr identified in his seminal 1975 paper as 'the folly of rewarding A while hoping for B.'[8] Most organizations say they want purpose-driven cultures while systematically rewarding behaviours that undermine their own purpose, or their team's personal connection with work-purpose entirely.

Consider how many companies operate: They hope for long-term thinking while rewarding quarterly results. They want collaborative teams while promoting based on individual achievements. They post inspiring purpose statements on their websites while measuring success purely through financial metrics that bear no relationship to their stated mission.

It's like the university example Kerr highlighted: 'Society hopes that teachers will not neglect their teaching responsibilities but rewards them almost entirely for research and publications.' Replace 'teaching' with 'purpose-driven culture building' and 'research' with 'short-term financial metrics,' and you've described most modern corporations perfectly.

The insurance company in Kerr's study provides an even more pointed parallel. They hoped for accurate claim processing but systematically rewarded behaviours that led to overpayments because underpayments generated complaints while overpayments were accepted in 'courteous silence'. Their informal motto became 'When in doubt, pay it out!' Meanwhile, they claimed to value fiscal responsibility.

This is exactly what happens with purpose initiatives. Companies install ping-pong tables and meditation apps (easy to measure, generates positive PR) while hoping for genuine engagement and meaning. They implement employee Net Promoter Scores and engagement surveys while continuing to avoid running 360 feedback on managers who achieve targets regardless of how they treat their people. They're paying out for the easy-to-quantify activities while hoping their investment will somehow generate the complex human outcomes they actually want.

The science of purpose at work: What actually drives performance

This isn't correlation masquerading as causation. There's increasingly robust data supporting the business case for purpose-driven cultures. George Serafeim's 2016 Harvard Business School study found that organizations scoring high on purpose and management clarity exhibited superior stock market performance and return on assets.[9] At the individual level, the research is equally compelling. McKinsey found that employees who say they live their purpose at work are five times more likely to report higher resilience, four times more likely to report better health, six times more likely to want to stay at the company, and five times more likely to go above and beyond to make their company successful.[10] This same study highlighted that, 'Research found that 70 per cent of employees said that their sense of purpose is defined by their work.' The same study found that, 'employees at all levels in the organization say that they want purpose in their lives: 89 per cent of our survey respondents agreed, a proportion that tracks closely with academic research.' Within this, only 18 per cent of respondents believed that they get as much purpose from work as they want; 62 per cent said that while they get some purpose from work, they want to get even more! This is really interesting research when it comes to how we can bring purpose into our team's working lives, without 'purpose-washing' or using inauthentic methods.

Recent research on purpose and work-life integration reveals that the benefits extend far beyond the workplace. A longitudinal study tracking employed individuals over 10 years found that people who rated higher in purpose experienced significantly less work-life interference and greater work-life enhancement. They were better at managing competing demands, more likely to see their work and personal lives as mutually reinforcing rather than conflicting, and demonstrated greater resilience when facing professional challenges.[11] This finding demolishes another false choice that organizations often present: the idea that demanding work environments are incompatible with employee wellbeing. People with a strong sense of purpose don't just perform better at work, they're more capable of integrating their professional and personal lives in ways that enhance both domains.

Where most discussions miss the mark

Most conversations about purpose and profit assume every company needs to become a transformation economy business where employees must be personally invested in the mission to be engaged with purpose. This creates the false paradox in the first place. The reality is far more nuanced, and frankly, more achievable for most organizations.

Thinking back to Liz, even though her sense of purpose was more nuanced than a simple company tag line she still said that 'it's really easy to motivate me in that way. So I think that I'm someone who I like, love all hands. I love being bought in on the thing' which shows that even though Liz acknowledged she sees her tech work more as a part of the experiential economy, the way she finds purpose in her work within the corporate world is that, for her, 'purpose comes from like, agency,' Liz's key insight about what drives her sense of purpose at work, 'I feel really high agency when I can voice something I didn't like. And then I actually see changes like, enacted on that.' In short, purpose isn't as simple as a company tag line, and in fact can be found in more tacit dimensions that can be explored and built upon.

Let's go back to our three economic frameworks and how purpose operates differently within each:

- In **transformation economy companies**, purpose, employee's personal evolution, and profit must be tightly aligned because your people are genuinely bought into the journey itself (be it your journey through the work, or the company's impact on your life and vocation). These are your B-Corps, choreographers at theatres, your mission-driven start-ups, resident artists, your organizations tackling climate change or social justice. Here, any disconnect between stated values and business practices creates devastating cognitive dissonance. If you're asking people to work for below-market rates because they believe in the cause, you'd better damn well be living that cause authentically. The purpose-profit alignment isn't optional; it's the foundation of your entire employee value proposition.

- But in **experience economy companies** (which includes most growing businesses) the bar is refreshingly different. Your people aren't necessarily asking you to save the world; they're asking you not to actively harm it while providing them with meaningful professional growth. The purpose threshold here is what I call 'not evil plus positive contribution'. Your employees need to feel that the company does something beneficial for customers or society, but it doesn't have to be their personal passion project. A software company that makes supply chains more efficient, a consulting firm that helps other businesses grow, a financial services company that enables people to buy homes, all of these can create strong purpose alignment without requiring evangelical commitment from employees. Here you can focus on your team's need to get purpose through work via creating an environment that contributes to both their career objectives, immediate quality of life, and longer-term career trajectory.

- **Service economy companies** have perhaps the clearest path to authentic purpose, though it's often overlooked. Here, your company's purpose isn't necessarily the employee's personal mission; it's a vehicle that enables their real purpose outside of work. The parent who can coach their kid's team because you offer genuine flexibility, the artist whose creative work is funded by stable employment, the graduate student who can focus on their studies because your company provides predictable income and supportive management. For these employees, your company's purpose is demonstrated through how you treat them as whole humans with lives and priorities beyond the office.

The Kerr test: Are you measuring what you actually want?

The most effective way to diagnose whether your organization is suffering from purpose-profit misalignment is to apply what I call the Kerr test. Look at what behaviours your reward systems actually incentivize, then ask yourself: Are these the behaviours that would create the culture we claim to want?

> The test is called the Kerr test because it's directly based on Kerr's foundational work identifying this fundamental organizational dysfunction where companies systematically reward behaviours that are completely opposite to what they claim to want.

Take performance reviews. If your stated values include collaboration and long-term thinking, but your review process focuses exclusively on individual achievements and quarterly targets, you're rewarding A while hoping for B. If you claim to value innovation but penalize intelligent failures while rewarding safe, incremental improvements, you're creating the exact opposite of what you say you want.

Or consider how you handle work-life integration. If you say you care about employee wellbeing, but your only promotion candidates are those who sacrifice their personal lives for work, you're sending a clear message about what you actually value, and it's not wellbeing.

The companies that successfully navigate the purpose-profit dynamic have learnt to align their measurement and reward systems with their stated values. They've stopped trying to optimize for everything and started focusing on the metrics that actually drive the outcomes they want. They understand that sustainable competitive advantage comes from building capabilities that can't be easily replicated, and authentic culture is one of those capabilities.

The three-economy solution: Purpose without pretence

This reframing eliminates the paradox entirely more similarly to how we heard from Huw and Liz earlier in this chapter. You don't need every employee to be personally passionate about your *specific* business model to create a purpose-driven and highly aligned culture. You need to understand what type of purpose each group is seeking from work and deliver authentically on that implicit understanding.

For experience economy employees, this might mean being transparent about your business impact, celebrating customer success stories, and ensuring your business practices align with basic ethical standards. You're not asking them to work for the cause, but you're giving them permission to feel good about where they spend their professional energy.

For service economy employees, purpose is often demonstrated through stability, respect and flexibility rather than mission alignment. The purpose you're serving is their ability to have rich, full lives outside of work. This doesn't make them less valuable employees – it makes them employees with clear, realistic expectations about what they need from the employment relationship.

The companies thriving in our current moment have discovered something genuine and powerful: when you match your purpose approach to your employees' actual motivations and stop rewarding contradictory behaviours, both engagement and profitability increase. Not because money doesn't matter, but because authentic purpose creates conditions where people can do their best work, customers receive better service, and sustainable financial performance becomes the natural result.

This doesn't mean every purpose-driven initiative will immediately boost your bottom line. It means building an authentic culture of purpose, one that honours different types of motivation rather than forcing everyone into the same mould, and one that rewards the behaviours you actually want to see reflected. One that creates conditions where sustainable profitability becomes more likely, more resilient, and more fulfilling for everyone involved. And in a world where talent is increasingly mobile and customers are increasingly discerning, that might be the most profitable strategy of all.

Notes and further reading

1 Raconteur (2023) How I became a… corporate wellbeing chief, *Raconteur*, 3 July. www.raconteur.net/talent-culture/how-i-became-a-corporate-wellbeing-chief (archived at https://perma.cc/4HSQ-NZL8)

2 Taylor, N (2024) Loren Shuster, LEGO Group: Children as role models, wisdom in leadership, and purpose in practice, *Lead From Within*, 29 April
3 Oliva (n.d.) About Oliva. https://oliva.health (archived at https://perma.cc/B7DC-D8CG)
4 Wonderbly (n.d.) About (personalized children's and adult books). www.wonderbly.com (archived at https://perma.cc/FS8M-YX2W)
5 Society for Human Resource Management (2024) Here's how bad burnout has become at work, SHRM, 30 April. www.shrm.org/topics-tools/news/inclusion-diversity/burnout-shrm-research-2024 (archived at https://perma.cc/3L83-L3K4)
6 Springsteen, B (1980) *The River*, Columbia Records
7 TikTok (n.d.) Remember when I quit my job? Let's talk about reflections on corporate tech vs freelance creative life. www.tiktok.com/@lizhagearty (archived at https://perma.cc/JKC6-C6QK)
8 Kerr, S (1975) On the folly of rewarding A while hoping for B, *Academy of Management Journal*, 18(4), 769–83. https://web.mit.edu/curhan/www/docs/Articles/15341_Readings/Motivation/Kerr_Folly_of_rewarding_A_while_hoping_for_B.pdf (archived at https://perma.cc/AEA6-5U3Q)
9 Serafeim, G (2016) The role of the corporation in society: An alternative view and opportunities for future research. Harvard Business School Working Paper No. 16-023, Harvard Business School, Boston, MA. www.hbs.edu/faculty/Pages/item.aspx?num=50595 (archived at https://perma.cc/ML8K-H99L)
10 Dhingra, N, Samo, A, Schaninger, B, and Schrimper, M (2021) Help your employees find purpose – or watch them leave, McKinsey & Company, 5 April. www.mckinsey.com/capabilities/people-and-organizational-performance/our-insights/help-your-employees-find-purpose-or-watch-them-leave (archived at https://perma.cc/X5ZR-XJ3E)
11 Sutin, A R (2023) Sense of purpose in life and work-life tension: Perceptions and effects. *Personality and Individual Differences*. Article S2667032123000380. www.sciencedirect.com/science/article/pii/S2667032123000380 (archived at https://perma.cc/QB6C-ENDQ)

9

Crafting the employee experience

In 2019, as WeWork prepared for its highly anticipated IPO, its founder Adam Neumann stood before employees and investors declaring that WeWork's mission was nothing less than 'elevating the world's consciousness'.[1] This wasn't just another real estate company renting office space – oh no, no, *no* – according to its S-1 filing, WeWork was 'a community company committed to maximum global impact'.[2]

From this position of great hubris, the company's valuation soared to $47 billion.[3]

There was one multibillion-dollar problem: WeWork was, at its core, a real estate arbitrage business. They leased buildings long-term, subdivided them, and rented them out short-term at a premium. The disconnect between this reality and their spiritual positioning led to questionable business decisions. Headlines from Forbes to Business Insider accused Neumann of mismanagement and unacceptable behaviour. The inside cover carried a dedication to 'the energy of we – greater than any of us but inside all of us'.[4] The company spent millions on employee summer camps and lavish parties, justified as 'community building' rather than focused on the fundamentals of their real estate operations.[5] According to insiders, the emphasis on being a world-changing movement rather than a disciplined real estate company contributed to undisciplined expansion and unsustainable lease commitments. When the IPO filing revealed the harsh realities of WeWork's finances – massive losses, risky lease obligations, and questionable governance – the company's inflated valuation collapsed.

Here's something that keeps happening in boardrooms across the world: a CEO reads about purpose-driven companies and decides their organization needs a grander mission. Soon, the walls are plastered with inspirational quotes, and every team meeting starts with a reminder about how they're changing the world. In his (really excellent) blog, Andy Whitlock, founder and CEO of The Human Half, a brand strategy consultancy in London, says, 'Brand Purposes. They're either the most important thing your business can have or an exercise in delusional narcissism, depending on who you talk to.'

The WeWork soap opera illustrates a crucial truth about purpose in the workplace: authenticity and good business sense matters more than aspiration... The company's mistake (among many, many mistakes) wasn't in wanting to create an engaging workplace or even in providing attractive amenities.[6] The mistake was in forcing a transformational narrative onto what was essentially an asset and services-based business model. They had fallen into what psychologists would call 'spiritual bypass'; psychologist John Welwood described a 'tendency to use spiritual ideas and practices to sidestep or avoid facing unresolved emotional issues, psychological wounds, and unfinished developmental tasks.'[7]

This pattern repeats itself every day across the business world, though usually less dramatically. Companies rush to adopt whatever purpose-driven philosophy is trending – whether it's becoming a 'mission-driven organization' or promising to change the world through their products – without considering if these approaches align with their fundamental business model and value creation method. Whitlock offers a particularly useful metaphor: 'You want to buy a suit that you can grow into, but not one that you look ridiculous in.' Charging forward to adopt a grandiose purpose statement (even if your CEO or founder believes it with all of their being) forms the organizational equivalent of wearing clothes that don't fit: uncomfortable and obvious to everyone.

The mistake many companies make isn't aiming too low, nor *necessarily* too high, it's pretending to be something they're not. A particularly interesting thread on Reddit, titled 'What is the logic behind company mission statements and values?' offers a clear look into the dichotomy of how these statements are viewed. One user posits, 'It's supposed to align how they want to make money with how they wrangle the troops. The problem with most listed company is that the owners, executives and troops have irreconcilable conflict of interest, and the best they could manage with short-term incentives is some consultant driven mumbo-jumbo that allays the board, gets execs their bonus, and the troops half a day off work and some free lunch.'[8]

While another, less critical, reflected, 'It's to try to align people around a reasonably inspiring statement that is easy to understand and apply, and with values that articulate the types of behaviour the business wants to see. They're not magic, but they can help a bit.'

What's fascinating is that this pattern often intensifies the further a company gets from having a naturally compelling purpose. As one senior staffer at a post-IPO tech confided to me, 'I literally don't think about our purpose statement. I never think about it. Every time someone tells me to include it in my work, we nod and roll our eyes and go away. I come to work because I want to make my parents proud and because the work is interesting.' This candid admission reveals the gulf between corporate purpose statements and the actual human motivations that drive people.

When a company in the service economy tries to force fit a transformational purpose, they create an 'authenticity gap'. Employees can smell this from a mile away. They know they're processing insurance claims or stocking shelves, and no number of inspirational posters will convince them they're saving the world. Further, as seen in online forums discussing the 'corporate w*nk' of company purposes, it's clear that once a gap forms, it can be toxic, but they can also motivate. Within the Reddit post mentioned previously we hear, 'Man this post hit a nerve for me, because I care passionately. I work in start-ups where every person has an impact, so I think that amplifies it a bit. Our specific mission statement is nothing special, but our customers are mostly small businesses who rely on our software to earn a living, so it matters. Also I can't lie its mostly ego/pride that makes me want to build something I'm proud of.'

Let's imagine a relatively non-aspirational cloud accounting software company. Their marketing might proclaim they're 'revolutionizing global finance' or 'transforming the future of business', but at their core, they're making bookkeeping more efficient. And that's perfectly fine – in fact, it's valuable and necessary work. The problem isn't with their function; it's with their fiction.

It's like what happens when you ask someone why they chose their profession. Few people will launch into grandiose statements about transforming humanity. Instead, you'll hear honest stories about practical decisions, personal circumstances and individual aspirations. These authentic narratives – even if they're not world-changing – have a power that manufactured purpose statements never will.

The solution isn't to abandon purpose altogether, but to rightsize it. Just as a local deli doesn't need to claim it's 'revolutionizing human nutrition' to be a valued part of its community, companies need to find authentic ways to articulate their value without overreaching. Sometimes, making someone's day a little easier, doing unglamorous work really well, or simply providing stable employment in your community is purpose enough. It's what I call 'honest purpose' – the kind that fits so naturally you don't have to keep adjusting it like an ill-fitting suit.

But how do we create something aspirational and true for our teams to look towards? As we know from the previous chapter, humans need some sense of forward momentum for their work – some belief that tomorrow could be better than today, and what they are doing has dignity and purpose. But overreach seems easy without the right tools to help us create useful purpose statements.

All is not lost

Every type of business can create meaningful engagement with their employees. The key isn't to force fit a transformational purpose where it doesn't belong, but to understand which type of economy your organization operates in and align your employee value proposition accordingly. Just as Walmart doesn't try to be Patagonia, and a local accounting firm doesn't try to be a humanitarian organization, your approach to purpose and engagement should be authentic to your organization's role in the economy. 'Like most things, we can reach a sensible conclusion by removing the nonsense and talking like normal people,' says Andy. 'For me, I don't like the word purpose because it's just ruined and it's too big. I think it's just about having a point. If you work for a cloud software company and you are enabling people in ways that weren't otherwise possible, even if they're quite ordinary ways... that's great. Be proud about that. You don't need to pretend you're doing something else.'

In this chapter, we'll explore our three distinct economic models – service, experiential and transformational – and how each demands a different approach to purpose and employee engagement. We'll learn why pretending to be something you're not, isn't just ineffective – it's counterproductive. Most importantly, we'll discover how to create authentic engagement regardless of your organization's economic model, avoiding the pitfalls that trapped companies like WeWork while building something genuinely meaningful for employees.

Concentric circles

When developing the purpose narrative within your employee value proposition (EVP), the first step is often the hardest: being brutally honest about what you actually are. As brand strategist Andy Whitlock puts it, it's about understanding where your 'centre of gravity' lies – are you truly centred on your customers and employees, or are you stuck in your own internal narrative? Andy says, 'The greatest companies in the world really have their whole centre of gravity on the customer. They're always thinking what's going to be good for the customer, what do they need? There's a humility.'

When deciding your company's purpose, Andy makes a salient point that in his research; he's spoken with dozens of HR leaders, CEOs and company founders about purpose. A common thread emerges in these conversations: they're struggling to articulate something that feels both authentic and inspiring. Time and again, I too hear variations of: 'We know there's something meaningful here, but we can't quite put our finger on it. And now that we're scaling, that vagueness is becoming a real problem.'

In the early stages, purpose often exists as an unspoken understanding, an intuitive force guiding decisions. The founder and their initial team operate from a shared, implicit sense of what matters to get to their next goal. This works well enough when you're small – the purpose naturally infuses decisions and culture through daily interactions and shared experiences. But as your company grows, this implicit understanding starts to break down. New employees don't have access to that original context. They need something more concrete, more explicitly stated. That's when the lack of a clear, articulated purpose becomes a genuine obstacle to growth and alignment.

This is what leads us to create purpose statements, or rather, distil what is already in existence, and make it understandable, memorable, and useful for our teams. Andy says, 'Finding your "purpose" (or mission if you prefer), is a bit like therapy. It involves unpacking lots of internal thoughts and disparate behaviour until you recognize which things matter and why.'

The positioning triangle test

One practical framework emerges from Whitlock's approach to positioning: imagine a triangle formed by your company, your customers (in this case, potential employees), and your competition. Your value and purpose statements should live at the intersection of:

- What would your customers say you're genuinely good at?
- What do your current and potential employees actually care about?
- What makes you different from other companies?

The key word here is 'genuinely'. If you find yourself reaching for grandiose statements about changing the world through cloud computing, you're probably straying too far from your centre. Instead, ask yourself: What real,

FIGURE 9.1 Purpose triangle

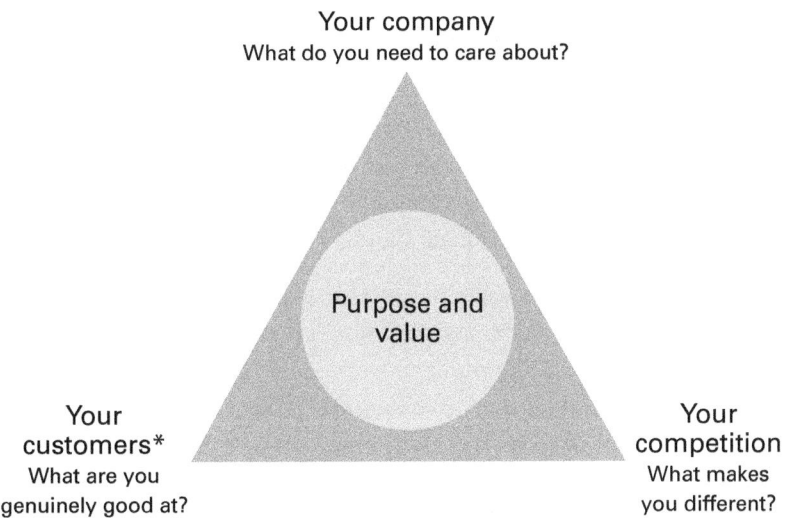

*Your employees, in a 'people ops as a product' mindset

tangible value do we offer employees and customers? What authentic story can we tell about working here?

Your work should be aspirational enough to inspire growth but not so overreaching that it becomes uncomfortable and obvious to everyone. For most companies, this means finding meaning in the practical value they provide rather than trying to force fit a transformational narrative.

For example, instead of claiming to 'revolutionize human potential through innovative workplace solutions', a company might simply say: 'We help make work better for people by taking the frustration out of everyday tasks. Join us in creating tools that give people more time to focus on what matters.'

I don't know about you, but for me this second statement resonates in a fundamentally different way. It's not just a matter of tone or humility – it creates a genuine connection between what the company actually does and the human experience of those who interact with it.

The approach works because it is tangible, respectful and measurable:

- **It speaks to tangible experience.** Everyone has felt the drain of tedious, frustrating tasks eating away at their workday. When a company acknowledges this lived reality, employees and customers immediately recognize the authenticity. They don't have to mentally translate grandiose claims into practical reality – the connection is immediate and visceral.
- **It respects intelligence.** Overly aspirational language can feel manipulative, as though the company is trying to disguise mundane work under a

veneer of world-changing importance. The more honest statement respects people's ability to find meaning in improving everyday experiences without requiring cosmic significance.

- **It creates measurable purpose.** 'Making work better' and 'taking frustration out of everyday tasks' can be directly observed and measured, while 'revolutionizing human potential' remains forever abstract and unverifiable. This concreteness means employees can see their purpose in action, creating powerful reinforcement loops.

This aligns perfectly with what Aaron Hurst discovered in his research on individual purpose.[9] As he explains, 'There's a lot of talk about purpose… And it puts a lot of pressure on us to figure out what is our purpose, a sort of grandiose idea. And it's scary to enter that. What we've found, actually, in studying individual purpose is that it's much simpler than that.'

Hurst's research revealed that people find meaning in different ways, particularly in how they experience the elevation of meaning in their work. 'For about a third of the population,' he notes, 'they get the most meaning at work when they can directly see their work impacting other people. They need to have that visceral sense that their work actually made an impact in someone's life.'

It connects to different sources of purpose. A more honest, grounded purpose statement acknowledges the various ways people find meaning. As Hurst describes, 'We then have about a third of the workforce who gain much more meaning from working at an organizational level. They say, it's great to help people, but, ultimately, I want to build a more sustainable impact by helping build teams, to build organizations, to build institutions that can make a longer, sustained impact on the world.'

A well-crafted, right-sized purpose can speak to both groups – those who need to see direct impact and those who find meaning in building systems that create broader change.

It acknowledges the dignity in everyday improvements. There's profound worth in making people's daily experiences better, less frustrating, more efficient. By explicitly valuing these incremental improvements, the company validates the meaningful contribution its employees make without overreaching.

When employees hear this more grounded purpose, they can immediately picture how their work contributes. The developer debugging code sees how fixing that glitch removes frustration. The customer service representative understands how solving problems gives customers back precious time. The designer recognizes how thoughtful interfaces make work flow more naturally.

This connection to daily reality doesn't diminish motivation but rather enhances it. Research by Teresa Amabile and Steven Kramer found that the

CRAFTING THE EMPLOYEE EXPERIENCE

most powerful motivator isn't grand visions but 'the progress principle' where you are able to see tangible forward movement on meaningful work. A purpose statement that directly connects to observable improvements taps into this powerful intrinsic motivator.[10]

The irony here is that by aiming for something less grand, these purpose statements end up reaching higher. They create authentic connections precisely because they don't overreach. They find the genuine thread of meaning that already exists in the work rather than manufacturing an artificial narrative. And in doing so, they respect both the organization's true contribution and the people who make it possible.

The reality-ambition gap: A framework for authentic company messaging

Andy Whitlock describes a powerful visual model: two concentric circles. The inner circle represents reality – the truth of what your company is and does. The outer circle represents your public-facing ambitions and messaging. The relationship between these circles tells us everything about authenticity in corporate communications.

FIGURE 9.2 Reality-ambition gap

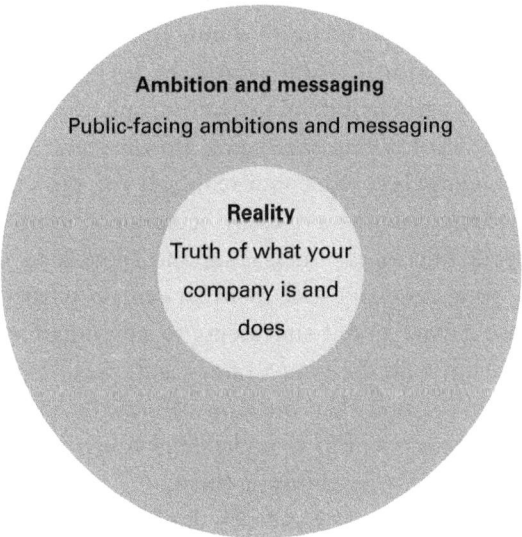

To turn this into a practical framework for developing your company's messaging:

STEP 1: DRAW YOUR INNER CIRCLE (REALITY)
Start by being ruthlessly honest about what your company actually is today:

- What do you actually do for customers? (Not the grand vision, but the day-to-day reality)
- What genuine impact do you have? (Not the pitch deck version, but the tangible effects)
- What truly makes you different? (Crucially, not what you wish made you different, but what actually does)

STEP 2: MAP YOUR OUTER CIRCLE (AMBITION)
Now consider where you want to go:

- What's the next achievable level of impact?
- What realistic improvements are you working towards?
- What credible ambitions do you have?
- What messages would feel authentic to your best employees?

STEP 3: MIND THE GAP
The space between your circles is crucial. As Whitlock notes, 'If there is even a seed of something thoughtful and meaningful, then it's very easy to just grab that and work with it.' Your goal is to keep these circles as close together as possible while maintaining healthy ambition.

Here's a crucial test for your messaging: imagine your outer circle (your aspirational messaging) becoming your reality. If you can't honestly see that happening within five years, you're likely being too ambitious.

Then, take your outer circle messaging and show it to someone who's never heard of your company. Ask them to explain what you do. If they struggle to connect your grand statements to any tangible reality, you've fallen into what Andy calls the 'your strategy is showing' trap, where people can 'smell the conversation that went on behind the scenes'. When your messaging requires a decoder ring to understand your actual business, you're not inspiring people… you're confusing them.

The most powerful company narratives don't require translation. They're like a clear window into your future, not a maze of aspirational buzzwords. After all, if someone can't understand what you do today, why would they believe in where you're going tomorrow?

- Warning signs:
  - If your outer circle is vastly larger than your inner circle, you're likely in 'spiritual bypass' territory
  - If your circles are completely divorced from each other, you've lost authenticity
  - If your outer circle is smaller than your inner circle, you're underselling your true value
- The sweet spot:
  - The best messaging happens when these circles are *nearly* touching, with just enough space between them to create healthy tension. Your outer circle should feel like a natural evolution of your inner circle, not a fantasy version of a different company entirely.
- Poor alignment (large gap):
  - Inner circle: We make accounting software for small businesses
  - Outer circle: We're revolutionizing global commerce through transformative technology

FIGURE 9.3 Reality-ambition gap (large gap)

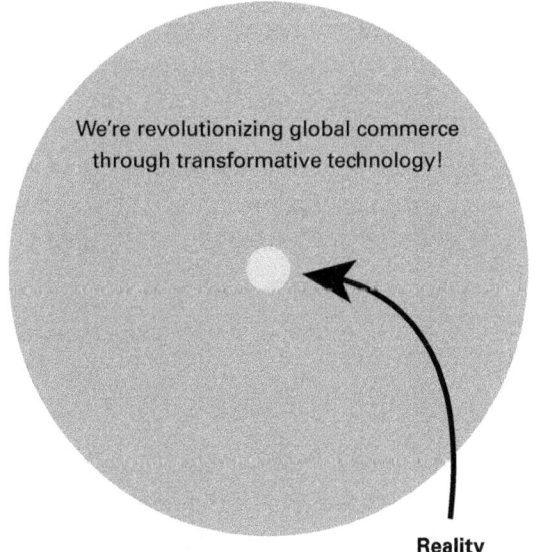

FIGURE 9.4 Reality-ambition gap (small gap)

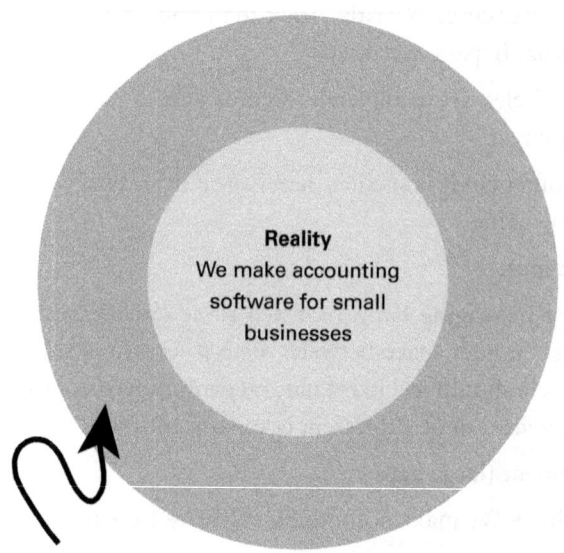

We're giving small business owners their time back by making accounting painless

- **Good alignment (small gap):**
  o Inner circle: We make accounting software for small businesses
  o Outer circle: We're giving small business owners their time back by making accounting painless

Remember, as Whitlock says about building credible messaging: 'You just need there to be a credible thread between the reality and the near future that you're trying to aim for.' This framework helps you find and maintain that thread.

But we can become even more specific.

The service economy: Honest transactions

Service economy organizations focus on efficient delivery of products or services where the primary value proposition is reliability and cost-effectiveness. Think customer service centres, manufacturing facilities, logistics companies, and many traditional retail operations. These organizations succeed through consistency, standardization and operational excellence.

In these environments, attempting to create a deeply purposeful or transformational employee experience often rings hollow and can even breed cynicism. Instead, service economy organizations should focus on:

- Competitive compensation and clear, fair benefits
- Strong compliance and ethical practices
- Professional respect and basic dignity
- Clear boundaries between work and personal life
- Support for employees to find purpose outside of work
- Transparent career progression paths
- Efficient, well-organized work processes

The goal isn't to make work transformational but to make it sustainable and dignified. By being honest about the transactional nature of the relationship while ensuring fairness and respect, these organizations can build long-term loyalty without pretence.

The experiential economy: Engaging excellence

Experiential economy organizations create value through innovation, creativity and complex problem-solving. This includes most technology companies, professional services firms, creative agencies, and similar knowledge-work organizations. These companies succeed through employee engagement and intellectual capital rather than pure operational efficiency.

These organizations should focus on creating exceptional work experiences through four key elements:

1 Connection and impact
    o Direct interaction with customers and community
    o Visible impact of work on others
    o Strong team relationships and collaboration
    o Clear line of sight to how individual work affects the whole
    o As Dr Ben-Shahar notes, 'The No. 1 predictor of happiness is the quality time we spend with people we care about and who care about us. In other words, relationships.'
2 Autonomy and agency
    o Freedom to choose how work gets done
    o Control over schedule and work environment

- Ability to influence company direction
- Ownership of projects and outcomes

3 Intellectual challenge
- Complex problem-solving opportunities
- Creative freedom
- Learning and growth opportunities
- Innovation encouragement

4 Basic purpose alignment
- Company should not be actively harmful
- Basic alignment with employee values
- Ethical business practices
- Positive contribution to society

The key is that these organizations don't need to promise world-changing transformation – they just need to create engaging, meaningful work experiences that challenge and fulfil employees professionally.

The transformation economy: Purpose-driven impact

Finally, transformation economy organizations exist primarily to create significant positive change in the world and within their teams through their work experiences. This includes many creative pursuits, non-profits, social enterprises, healthcare organizations, educational institutions, and companies with genuine social or environmental missions at their core.

These organizations can and should lean heavily into purpose as a primary motivator because:

- Their mission is genuinely transformational
- The work directly impacts important human transformation or development within its day-to-day
- Employees typically choose these organizations specifically for their mission or because it's their 'calling'
- The organization's success is measured by impact as well as finances

For these organizations, purpose isn't just a nice-to-have – it's the fundamental reason for their existence and their primary tool for attracting and retaining talent.

Bridging the purpose gap: When reality and aspiration have drifted

Many leaders reading this may recognize they're already facing a purpose gap. Perhaps your company's stated mission feels increasingly disconnected from daily operations, or employees have grown cynical about corporate values that seem like empty words. This situation requires a careful, thoughtful approach rather than simply creating yet another revised statement.

Acknowledging the gap without defensiveness

The first step towards healing a purpose misalignment is simply acknowledging it exists. This can be challenging for leaders who may have personally championed the current purpose or feel responsible for the disconnect. As Paul Polman, former CEO of Unilever, noted in his reflections on purpose-driven leadership, defensiveness about misalignment only widens the credibility gap. This gap arose from the perception that his vision for a more sustainable and responsible business model was not always reflected in Unilever's actions. He acknowledged this gap and actively worked to bridge it by prioritizing sustainability initiatives and engaging with various stakeholders.[11]

Instead, create safe spaces for honest discussion about where your stated purpose and actual operations have drifted apart. This might include anonymous surveys, facilitated discussions, or bringing in trusted external advisers who can gather unfiltered feedback without hierarchical pressure. Paul Polman said to Forbes, 'It is key to keep in mind that everyone can be a leader, and that everyone can make a difference. Being a good leader starts with a firm commitment to your purpose. It is not enough to just say it, you have to act on it, too. Walking the talk, if you like. It is in fact an exciting time to be part of a fast-changing world of business, and instilling your own purpose in what you do is becoming more and more important.' If you are able to create a culture where everyone in your team can both connect to and interrogate your purpose, your team requires, 'those who can be total system thinkers. We're living in a complex world, and we cannot operate in silos.'

Diagnosis before prescription

Before rushing to 'fix' your purpose statement, take time to understand the nature and causes of the misalignment. Is it:

- A communication gap, where your actual operations align with your purpose, but employees don't see the connection?

- An implementation gap, where middle management hasn't been equipped to translate purpose into action?
- A leadership credibility gap, where executive behaviour contradicts stated values?
- A fundamental business model disconnect, where your purpose simply doesn't align with your economic reality?

Each of these gaps requires a different approach. For example, a communication gap might be addressed through better storytelling and examples, while a business model disconnect may require a more fundamental rethinking of your purpose statement itself.

The purpose reconciliation process

When addressing entrenched purpose scepticism, consider a structured reconciliation process:

1 **Listen deeply:** Create multiple channels for employees to express their perspectives on the gap between stated purpose and lived experience. Invite them to think of the system and understand how their concerns may factor into the wider network of stakeholders, customers and ownership.
2 **Share the diagnosis:** Transparently communicate what you've learnt about the nature and causes of the gap.
3 **Co-create solutions:** Involve representatives from across the organization in developing approaches to close the gap.
4 **Make visible changes:** Identify and implement immediate, visible actions that demonstrate commitment to alignment.
5 **Create accountability mechanisms:** Establish clear metrics and feedback channels to monitor progress.
6 **Rebuild trust incrementally:** Recognize that restoring faith in purpose takes consistent action over time, not just revised statements.

When rationalization is needed

Sometimes, the challenge isn't just practical implementation but fundamental disagreement about interpretation. Different stakeholders may have dramatically different understandings of what your purpose actually means in practice. This interpretive conflict can be more challenging than simple implementation issues because it strikes at the very heart of organizational identity.

Real-world examples show how even purpose-driven companies like Patagonia face internal conflicts over how their mission should be interpreted and applied. Patagonia's mission statement evolved to 'We're in business to save our home planet' in 2018, creating a powerful but broad purpose that required translation into specific actions as the founder believed the company needed to address environmental issues with even more urgency.[12]

Research on organizational conflicts reveals that these purpose interpretation challenges are common. A documented tension in purpose-driven organizations is the balance between profitability and environmental commitments. For Patagonia, this manifested in what one study calls 'a clear conflict of goals, which show the problems of having an environmental sustainability mission at the same time they are pursuing ambitious plans to grow and expand.'[13]

When facing such fundamental interpretation differences, companies like Patagonia have developed structured approaches that can guide other organizations.

Empower stakeholders through formal structures

Rather than allowing different interpretations to create dysfunction, Patagonia formalized stakeholder input through clear decision-making structures. The company makes supply chain decisions based on meetings with staff representing four major concerns: business needs, quality standards, environmental implications, and labour/community treatment. As one executive noted, 'Each one of those stakeholders has a veto.'[14] This approach ensures multiple perspectives have real power in decision-making.

Create accountability through transparent assessment

Concrete measurement helps reveal different interpretations and resolve conflicts. Patagonia dedicated a team to report regularly on progress towards stated benefit purposes, noting that 'it takes some of the subjectivity out of it' because 'you can't argue with a report card that says you've gotten Ds for three years in a row.'

The lessons from companies like Patagonia is that purpose conflicts shouldn't be suppressed but rather structured and channelled productively.

By creating formal systems to engage different interpretations, organizations can harness the creative tension between perspectives to drive innovation and deeper engagement with their core purpose. This approach recognizes that organizational purpose, like many meaningful concepts, has an essentially contested nature – and that the dialogue between different understandings often leads to more robust implementation than forced consensus ever could.

In these cases, if you are inspired by Patagonia but want to start smaller, try a structured dialogue approach with your team or leaders:

1 **Map the interpretations:** Explicitly document the different ways key stakeholders understand your purpose and make notes of places where there are conflicts or inconsistencies.
2 **Identify shared elements:** Look for common ground and overlapping interpretations, and be deeply curious about where the 'truth' may lie.
3 **Clarify boundaries:** Determine which interpretations simply cannot be reconciled with your business model or values.
4 **Develop guiding principles:** Create decision frameworks that help translate purpose into consistent action despite different perspectives.
5 **Allow for reasonable pluralism:** Accept that some degree of varied interpretation is healthy and can actually strengthen your purpose by making it relevant across different contexts.

The courage to rebuild

In some cases, the purpose gap may be so significant that incremental approaches won't suffice. If your company's stated purpose fundamentally misrepresents your value creation model or has been so undermined by contradictory actions that it cannot be rehabilitated, you may need to take a more dramatic approach.

This doesn't mean abandoning purpose altogether, but rather having the courage to rebuild from a foundation of honesty. The resulting purpose statement may be less lofty but, hopefully, infinitely more credible – and ultimately more engaging because employees can see themselves in it.

Resolving a purpose gap isn't about crafting more inspiring language – it's about closing the distance between what you say and what you do. Organizations that successfully navigate this challenge emerge with something far more valuable than a perfect purpose statement: they develop the muscle of integrity that builds lasting trust with both employees and customers.

The power of rightsizing purpose

This framework isn't about limiting ambition – it's about creating authentic, sustainable relationships with employees. A service economy organization that's honest about its transactional nature while ensuring fairness and respect will build more trust than one that pretends to be transformational. An experiential economy organization that focuses on creating engaging work rather than changing the world will maintain credibility even in tough times.

The goal isn't to minimize purpose but to rightsize it – to promise what you can genuinely deliver and then deliver it consistently. This creates the foundation for long-term engagement and success, regardless of which economy you operate in.

When organizations align their purpose proposition with their economic reality, they create the conditions for sustainable success. Employees know what to expect and can make informed choices about where to invest their time and talent. Organizations can focus their resources on what really matters in their context rather than trying to be all things to all people.

The future of work isn't about every company becoming unrelentingly purpose-driven – it's about every company finding its authentic place in the purpose spectrum and delivering on that promise consistently.

In a world increasingly sceptical of corporate motives, the organizations that will thrive are those that match their purpose rhetoric with authentic action. By rightsizing purpose, implementing it thoughtfully, measuring it consistently, and evolving it appropriately, leaders create sustainable engagement that withstands both market pressures and employee cynicism.

The goal isn't a perfect purpose statement – it's purpose alignment that creates both meaning for employees and value for customers for the sake of it. When purpose flows naturally from who you truly are as an organization rather than who you wish you were, you create the foundation for lasting impact regardless of which economic model you operate within.

As Andy Whitlock so aptly puts it, you're not looking for a purpose that turns heads, you're looking for one that fits so naturally you forget you're wearing it.

Notes and further reading

1 Lash, H (2019) WeWork's IPO filing spells rough landing for CEO Neumann, Reuters, 15 September. www.reuters.com/article/world/wework-ipo-spells-rough-landing-for-ceo-neumann-idUSKBN1W009S/ (archived at https://perma.cc/58JP-9H3W)

2. Ghosh, S and Wolverton, T (2019) WeWork's S-1: We are a community company committed to maximum global impact. Our mission is to elevate the world's consciousness, *Business Insider*, 14 August. www.businessinsider.com/wework-s-1-prospectus-ipo-revenue-cash-flow-2019-8 (archived at https://perma.cc/VU7E-H53M)
3. Campbell, D (2019) How WeWork went from $47 billion valuation to…, *Business Insider*, 23 November. www.businessinsider.com/weworks-nightmare-ipo (archived at https://perma.cc/SMP2-7A6W)
4. Lopatto, E (2019) WeWork isn't a tech company; it's a soap opera, The Verge, 15 August. www.theverge.com/2019/8/15/20806366/we-company-wework-ipo-adam-neumann (archived at https://perma.cc/M7SM-TMYX)
5. Kosoff, M (2018) WeWork throws a party as it burns through cash, *Vanity Fair*, 24 August. www.vanityfair.com/news/2018/08/wework-summer-camp-party (archived at https://perma.cc/U6VS-3NVA)
6. Zeitlin, M (2019) Why WeWork went wrong, *The Guardian*, 20 December. www.theguardian.com/business/2019/dec/20/why-wework-went-wrong (archived at https://perma.cc/M6FG-P8KA)
7. Welwood, J (1984) Principles of inner work: Psychological and spiritual, Center for Inner Work, San Francisco, CA
8. Reddit (2024) What is the logic behind company mission statements and values? r/australian. www.reddit.com/r/australian/comments/1f7srnw/what_is_the_logic_behind_company_mission/ (archived at https://perma.cc/67PH-VH9T)
9. Hurst, A (n.d.) How to find a meaningful job, or find purpose in the job you do… YouTube. www.youtube.com/watch?v=H54vh7UI3_I (archived at https://perma.cc/3TDZ-LPGQ)
10. Amabile, T and Kramer, S (2011) The Progress Principle: Using small wins to ignite joy, engagement, and creativity at work, Harvard Business Review Press, Boston
11. Pryer, I (2012) Paul Polman (Unilever CEO) on cultural change, leadership, Asia and corporate social responsibility, tutor2u blog, 27 April. www.tutor2u.net/business/blog/paul-polman-unilever-ceo-on-cultural-change-leadership-asia-and-corporate-s (archived at https://perma.cc/Z8UR-9ZQF)
12. DEAL (2024) Patagonia: Doughnut design case study. DEAL – Doughnut Economics Action Lab, 31 October. https://doughnuteconomics.org/stories/patagonia-doughnut-design-case-study (archived at https://perma.cc/948U-G42L)
13. Studypool (n.d.) Patagonia case study, Studypool discussion, MGMT 301 Dominican University. www.studypool.com/discuss/26295362/patagonia-case-study-4 (archived at https://perma.cc/UF4S-86F2)
14. Kenney, A (2018) Patagonia: A case study in managing a mission, *Journal of Accountancy*, 1 July. www.journalofaccountancy.com/issues/2018/jul/patagonia-benefit-corporation/ (archived at https://perma.cc/2XDE-T97D)

10

Aligning values and actions

Picture the last time you roamed the halls (real or virtual) of your organization. How many of the employees you saw or spoke with that day would you guess truly believe in your organization's values and purpose statements? Not just recognize them, or could recite them if pressed, but genuinely believe they matter?

Here's an uncomfortable experiment: pull up your company's values right now. Then open five company websites – your competitors and companies in similar industries, but it may not matter how similar you are. I'm willing to bet you'll find at least three examples where you could swap all or part of their values with yours, and your team may not notice the nuanced differences.

Integrity. Innovation. Passion. Teamwork. Respect. These words appear on so many corporate walls and websites that they've become the business equivalent of elevator music, technically present, but subtle background noise that everyone has learnt to ignore. This homogeneity in values, and the struggles companies have crafting genuine purpose statements, as we explored within Andy Whitlock's interview, has led to Gallup describing leaders who, 'objectively evaluate their organization's values discover[ing] that their operating philosophy has evolved and their values are no longer relevant.'[1]

The fundamentally most important question isn't whether your employees can remember your values. It's whether they believe those values represent anything real, anything that actually influences how decisions get made when things get difficult. And if Nate Dvorak and Niraj Patel's research is any indication, the answer is probably more sobering than you'd like: only 27 per cent of employees believe in their company's values, while just 23 per cent apply them to their daily work decisions.[2] This disconnect represents a critical implementation gap.

This isn't just a communication problem or an engagement issue. This disconnect represents a critical undermining of what your company claims to stand for. Even when organizations get their purpose statements and values right, they often struggle with translating them into daily operations. When carefully crafted values stay confined to presentations and company websites, they're not just meaningless, but they may also be actively harmful, creating confusion or cynicism where there could have been genuine alignment.

You might wonder why a book about purpose is spending time dissecting values statements, and it is because values are often the primary vehicle through which organizations attempt to operationalize their team's relationship with purpose. They're meant to be the bridge between lofty purpose statements and daily decision-making. When companies struggle to make their purpose feel real and actionable, they typically turn to values as the solution. 'Our purpose is to democratize education, and our values of integrity, innovation, and inclusion guide how we do that.' The problem is that this bridge is fundamentally broken. If we want to understand why so many purpose-driven initiatives fail to translate into authentic cultural change, we need to understand why the traditional values approach creates more cynicism than alignment. Only then can we explore what actually works.

The values delusion: Why traditional approaches fail

The ubiquity and repetition of corporate values is well documented. Research by the Values Institute reveals that company values worldwide cluster around four predictable themes: integrity, goal-orientation, building a better world, and people-centric values.[3] Integrity alone shows up on corporate walls seemingly everywhere, encompassing commitment, honesty, respect, trust and personal responsibility. The result is a global epidemic of corporate sameness where you could swap values lists between a tech start-up in Silicon Valley and a manufacturing company in Munich. But does that matter? Surely there are only so many values from which we can choose.

Well, as one Reddit user astutely observed: 'The problem is slogans aren't a determining factor: Behaviour is Culture. In other words, you do what you are. This is mighty inconvenient when words mismatch deeds and people are trying to spin these – how should I put it – counter-factual inconsistencies.'[4]

This hints at the fundamental problem with traditional company values: they're frequently impossibly vague, inherently personal, and more or less completely unactionable in times of conflict or disagreement. Take integrity, probably the most popular corporate value in the Western world. What does that actually mean on a Tuesday afternoon when your biggest client is demanding something that makes you uncomfortable? Does integrity mean losing the client to preserve principle? Does it mean finding a creative middle ground? Does it mean having an honest conversation about your concerns? The value itself provides zero guidance for the actual decision.

This is what I call the values delusion: the belief that declaring shared principles will somehow magically align behaviour across an organization. It's like assuming that because everyone agrees pizza is delicious, they'll all want the same toppings. Values are deeply personal constructs shaped by our upbringing, experiences, and individual moral frameworks. My version of 'respect' might emphasize direct feedback and honest communication, while yours might prioritize harmony and conflict avoidance. Neither is wrong, but they're fundamentally different approaches to the same stated value.

The cynical reality behind this delusion was perfectly captured by another Reddit commenter: 'Because they all go to the same seminars or hire the same consultants who say "you should have a list of core values". I have sat through those seminars at almost every job I have worked since 1980. Every company develops them with the best of intentions. Very few ever put them into action, or, if they do, continue to follow them when times get tough.'[5]

The corporate scandals documented by the Values Institute perfectly illustrate this disconnect in action. Wells Fargo promoted 'trust' and 'customer service' while employees created millions of unauthorized accounts to meet sales goals. Enron championed communication, respect and integrity, while engaging in massive accounting fraud. Volkswagen celebrated responsibility, while deliberately programming diesel engines to cheat emissions tests. These weren't failures of individual character – they were the inevitable result of reward systems that contradicted stated values.[6]

The really insidious part is that values-based systems often become performative rather than operational. Employees learn to speak the values language, peppering their presentations with references to 'living our values' and 'demonstrating excellence', while making decisions based entirely on the *actual* incentive structures. Values become corporate virtue signalling, a way to *seem* principled without the harder work of actually living by those standards.

Values-based hiring suffers from the same fundamental flaw. I've watched countless interview panels confidently assess 'cultural fit' based on candidates' ability to articulate alignment with company values. But most intelligent people can figure out what you want to hear about integrity, collaboration and customer focus. What they can't always figure out, outside of a sanitized interview process, is how those values actually translate into daily decision-making when the pressure is on.

The static nature of traditional values makes them even less useful over time. Companies frame their values as timeless principles, unchanged since the founder's original vision, but business reality is constantly evolving. The 'customer first' mentality that worked when you had 50 clients might be operationally impossible when you have 50,000. The 'move fast and break things' approach that drove start-up success might be actively dangerous when you're handling sensitive data for major corporations. But because values are treated as sacred and unchangeable, organizations find themselves trapped by principles that no longer serve their actual needs.

Perhaps most damaging is the cynicism that values theatre creates among employees. As the Values Institute research shows, when people consistently observe gaps between stated values and actual behaviour, they stop believing that leadership means what they say about many things across your organization. It's not just that they dismiss the values: they start questioning the authenticity of every communication from leadership. The beautiful diversity and inclusion statement rings hollow when employees notice that every senior hire looks remarkably similar to the existing executive team. The work-life balance messaging feels like mockery when managers consistently schedule 'urgent' meetings during family time.

As one particularly insightful Reddit user on the subreddit No StupidQuestions put it: 'What you're referring to is lazy corporate management trying to force fit something that can only happen with actions, not words. They want all the benefits without the work and costs associated with it. …Nobody buys it. It's stupid.'[7]

The result is a workforce that has learnt to decode what companies actually value by watching what gets rewarded, promoted and celebrated, not what gets printed on coffee mugs. They develop a sophisticated understanding of the real operating system while maintaining the fiction of believing in the stated one. It's an exhausting dance that benefits no one and serves as a constant reminder that authenticity is apparently just a bit too much to ask for at work.

This is why traditional values approaches don't just fail when they do, they actively undermine the trust and alignment they're supposed to create. They turn culture into performance art, where everyone knows their lines, but nobody believes the narrative. The good news is that there's a better way, one that trades the comfortable fiction of shared values for the uncomfortable truth of shared agreements about how we actually make decisions when it matters.

From values to operating principles

Just when I was beginning to think that the values-purpose implementation gap was a near unsolvable problem, I encountered an approach so elegantly simple that it made me wonder why more organizations hadn't implemented it (or perhaps, why I'd never heard of it!). Huw Slater, CEO and founder at Oliva who we heard from previously, the workplace mental health platform, had completely reframed the entire conversation in a way that cut through decades of corporate jargon with surgical precision.

'What we have at Oliva are, we don't have values, we have agreements, operating principles, right?' Huw explained during our conversation. 'What that helps us do in the interview is, say, put questions around that.'

At first, this might sound like semantic hair-splitting. Aren't agreements just values by another name? But the more Huw described his philosophy, the more I realized he'd identified something fundamental that most organizations completely miss. The difference between values and operating principles isn't just linguistic; it's operational, psychological and ultimately an agent for meaningful alignment.

'Values are tricky because I have my core values, and they might not 100 per cent overlap with a company's core values. That's okay,' Huw continued. 'But we do need to agree on the way I'm going to make decisions, right? That's why they're agreements.'

This distinction is interesting to me because it acknowledges a reality that traditional values approaches desperately try to ignore; you can't change people's fundamental moral frameworks, nor should you try. My personal values around integrity, relationships and social justice are mine, shaped by decades of experience and reflection. Expecting those to perfectly align with any company's stated values is both unrealistic and invasive. But what we can do, what we must do, is agree on how we'll make decisions together when we're working towards shared goals.

The thing I love the most about Oliva's approach lies in its practical focus: 'They have to be decision-making tools. You have to update them. Otherwise, as you pivot or the direction changes slightly, the goals change.' Unlike traditional values, which many companies treat as sacred and unchanging, operating principles are designed to evolve. They're not moral pronouncements carved in stone; they're functional agreements that can be modified as circumstances change.

Think about how this reframes how you're using values in your work. Instead of asking 'Do you have examples where you've worked on a project with a focus on innovation?' during an interview, you might ask 'When faced with a choice between a safe, proven solution and a riskier approach that could yield better results, how would you typically make that decision?' The first question tests someone's personal relationship with innovation. The second reveals actual decision-making patterns and opens a conversation about whether those patterns align with how your organization needs to operate.

This shift from values to operating principles works across all three economic frameworks we've explored, but manifests differently in each:

- In **transformation economy** companies, where employees are genuinely bought into the mission and purpose and see work as a means of personal transformation, operating principles become the tactical expression of shared purpose. A climate tech start-up might have an operating principle like, 'When environmental impact conflicts with short-term profit, we'll choose a path that prioritizes long-term planetary health while ensuring business sustainability.' This isn't a vague value, it's a clear decision-making framework that acknowledges the tension and provides guidance for navigating it.

- For **experience economy** organizations, operating principles focus on learning and growth opportunities. Instead of a generic 'continuous improvement' value, you might have an agreement like 'When choosing between projects, we'll prioritize those that stretch our capabilities, even if they initially slow our delivery speed.' This gives employees permission to take on challenges while setting clear expectations about trade-offs.

- In **service economy** businesses, operating principles often centre around enabling employees' lives outside work while maintaining operational excellence. An agreement might be, 'We'll design our processes to be predictable and efficient, allowing team members to fully disconnect during off-hours while ensuring customer needs are consistently met.' This acknowledges that work is a vehicle for employees' broader life goals while setting clear standards for performance and success.

The practical applications of this approach extend far beyond hiring. Huw described how operating principles transform management conversations: 'I think it's okay to say this is our vision, this is what we believe in as a company. Making decisions with that in mind doesn't mean it has to be your life's purpose.'

This reframing eliminates the emotional manipulation that often characterizes values-based management. Instead of expecting employees to adopt the company's moral framework as their own, leaders can focus on whether people can operate effectively within agreed-upon decision-making parameters. It's the difference between demanding conversion and requesting collaboration.

Performance management becomes more straightforward when you're measuring against specific agreements rather than abstract values. Instead of evaluating whether someone 'values integrity', you can assess whether they followed your agreed-upon decision-making framework when faced with certain dilemmas. Instead of rating 'teamwork', you can review whether they operated according to your collaboration agreements during cross-functional projects.

The evolution from static values to dynamic operating principles also solves an obsolescence problem that plagues traditional approaches. When a startup grows from 20 to 200 employees, their decision-making frameworks need to evolve. Operating principles that worked for a scrappy team making fast decisions might be entirely inappropriate for a more complex organization requiring careful coordination. With Huw's approach, these principles can be updated without the organizational stress of 'changing our values'.

Perhaps most importantly, operating principles create genuine accountability in a way that values never can. When someone violates a vague value like 'respect', there's often endless debate about interpretation and intent. But when someone consistently ignores agreed-upon decision-making frameworks, the conversation becomes much more straightforward. You're not questioning their character or moral fibre; you're addressing their adherence to mutually agreed-upon operational standards.

From where I am sitting, the psychological shift this creates is material. Employees stop feeling judged against abstract moral standards and start feeling empowered to make good decisions within clear frameworks. Managers stop trying to be moral arbiters and start focusing on operational effectiveness. Everyone can acknowledge that they're adults with their own values who've chosen to work together according to specific agreements.

'I am wanting to hire people who want to be the best,' Huw explained. 'So I will help you be that. And then in three years, you'll leave; that's okay.' This captures the healthy pragmatism that operating principles enable. You're not trying to convert people to your corporate moral compass; you're creating conditions where they can do excellent work according to shared standards while pursuing their own professional development.

The result, genuine alignment without forced conformity, is something traditional values approaches rarely achieve. People can bring their authentic selves to work because they're not being asked to adopt someone else's value system. They're simply being asked to operate according to agreements they've explicitly accepted. It's the difference between joining a cult and joining a team, and it makes all the difference in building cultures where purpose can actually flourish.

Building decision-making filters that actually work

Values are often the primary vehicle through which organizations attempt to operationalize their team's relationship with purpose – they're meant to be the bridge between lofty purpose statements and daily decision-making. When companies struggle to make their purpose feel real and actionable, they typically turn to values as the solution, creating statements like 'Our purpose is to democratize education, and our values of integrity, innovation and inclusion guide how we do that.' The problem is that this bridge is fundamentally broken, which is why addressing both together in the same implementation wave allows you to fix the disconnect rather than perpetuating the cycle where purpose remains aspirational while values become meaningless wall decorations.

The difference between values and purpose as decoration versus as a decision tool becomes apparent the moment pressure hits. When a client demands something ethically questionable, when budget cuts threaten quality, when short-term gains conflict with long-term values, that's when your team discovers whether your purpose and values statements are real or merely aspirational wall art.

The companies that successfully bridge this gap have learnt to distil their purpose into what I call 'decision filters'. These are simple, practical questions that any employee can apply to any choice they face. These aren't vague exhortations to 'do the right thing' but specific frameworks that acknowledge real tensions and provide guidance for navigating them.

Consider the transformation from 'we value integrity' (meaningless without context) to 'when faced with pressure to compromise quality for speed, we'll choose the option that best serves our customers' long-term needs, even if it costs us short-term efficiency' (a genuine decision-making tool). The first sounds noble but offers very little guidance of substance when you're choosing between rushing a product to market or taking time to fix known issues. The second tells you more acutely how to think through the choice.

The framework for practical purpose

Converting purpose into actionable filters requires the same disciplined approach that Huw applies to operating principles: focus on decisions, not declarations. Start by identifying the most common tensions your organization faces, the moments where people genuinely struggle to know what the 'right' choice looks like. These tension points become the raw material for your decision filters.

The most effective filters I've encountered share three characteristics: they're specific enough to guide actual decisions, simple enough to remember under pressure and honest enough about trade-offs that people trust them when things get difficult. They acknowledge that most meaningful choices aren't between good and evil but between competing goods: quality versus speed, innovation versus stability, individual needs versus collective goals.

Take a software company that transforms their generic 'customer focus' value into two practical questions: 'Does this make our users' lives genuinely better?' and 'Would we be proud to show this work to our families? Why or why not?' Every product decision, from feature prioritization to bug fixes, can get filtered through these criteria. The questions work because they're memorable, applicable, and honest about what the company actually prioritizes when choices must be made.

Integration into daily operations

The real test of decision filters isn't whether they sound good in company meetings, it's whether they become embedded in the actual workflows where choices happen. This means moving far beyond conference room posters to integrate purpose considerations into project management tools, approval processes and team communication channels.

Sophisticated organizations build these filters directly into their operational infrastructure. Project approval templates include sections asking how initiatives align with core decision criteria. Budget reviews require teams to articulate not just what they want to spend money on, but how those expenditures support the organization's fundamental priorities. Performance evaluations assess not just what people accomplished but how those accomplishments reflected the agreed-upon decision-making frameworks.

This systematic integration ensures purpose isn't relegated to special occasions or corporate communications but becomes a practical consideration in how work actually gets done. When teams regularly ask themselves the core questions during planning sessions, when managers reference decision filters during difficult conversations, when hiring discussions include scenarios that test alignment with operational principles, purpose stops being something you talk about and starts being something you practice.

Recognition and reinforcement

Perhaps most critically, organizations must consistently recognize and celebrate decisions that exemplify their filters, especially when those decisions require genuine sacrifice. When teams choose quality over speed because their decision filter prioritizes long-term customer value, when managers support employee development even when it means losing good people to other opportunities, when difficult ethical choices get made according to stated principles rather than expedient alternatives, these moments deserve public acknowledgement.

This recognition creates powerful feedback loops that reinforce the authenticity of decision filters. Employees quickly learn whether the filters represent real priorities or merely corporate theatre based on what gets celebrated when things get tough. When purpose-aligned decisions consistently receive positive reinforcement – even when they cost money or slow progress – it signals that the filters aren't just motivational posters but actual decision-making criteria.

The organizations thriving in our current environment understand that authentic purpose isn't about perfect mission statements or inspiring values lists. It's about creating practical tools that help good people make better decisions when it matters most. When purpose becomes genuinely useful rather than merely aspirational, it stops being a burden and starts being exactly what it should be: a guide for building something worth being part of.

The implementation playbook: Making it stick

The graveyard of corporate purpose initiatives is vast and expensive. Walk through any office building and you'll see the archaeological evidence: faded posters from last year's values roll-out, abandoned digital displays cycling through motivational quotes nobody reads, and conference rooms named after principles that nobody remembers discussing in actual meetings. Research indicates that approximately 70 per cent of organizational change initiatives fail to achieve their intended outcomes, as momentum frequently dissolves within the first 18 months.[8]

This isn't because purpose doesn't matter. It's because most organizations treat purpose implementation more like a marketing campaign rather than an operational transformation. They focus on announcement rather than integration, on inspiration rather than instrumentation. They craft beautiful purpose statements in strategy retreats, then expect them to magically transform daily decision-making without changing any of the systems that actually drive behaviour.

The companies that successfully embed purpose into their operations understand something their peers miss: lasting change requires changing how work gets done, not just how it gets talked about. This means viewing values implementations as an operational challenge that demands the same rigour and persistence as any other business transformation.

Why most purpose initiatives fail within 18 months

The predictable failure pattern looks remarkably similar across industries and company sizes. Month one brings excitement and energy as leadership unveils the new values and purpose with fanfare. Months two through six, see initial implementation efforts, with training sessions, town halls, and communication campaigns. By month 12, momentum has visibly slowed as competing priorities crowd out purpose initiatives. By month 18, the purpose statement has become wallpaper, present but ignored.

The fundamental error lies in treating purpose as a communication problem rather than a systems problem. Most organizations invest heavily in crafting the perfect message and launching it with maximum impact, then assume that clarity and inspiration will drive adoption. But purpose isn't a product to be sold to employees; it's a new way of operating that must be built into the infrastructure of how decisions get made.

Consider the typical purpose roll-out: senior leaders spend months in workshops developing the statement, then task HR with 'cascading' it through the organization. Training sessions teach people what the purpose means. Managers receive talking points for team meetings. Posters appear on walls and screensavers updated with purpose messaging. Then everyone sits back and waits for behaviour to change.

But behavioural change doesn't happen through messaging; it happens through altered incentives, revised processes and consistently modelled expectations. If your performance review criteria haven't changed, if your budget approval process still ignores purpose considerations, if your promotion patterns remain unchanged, then your purpose statement is just expensive decoration.

A call to action:
Audit your own values vs operating principles

Take a moment to examine your own organization's stated values and purpose. Now ask yourself: if you removed all the posters, deleted all the corporate communications, and eliminated all the formal statements, would an outside observer be able to identify your organization's purpose by watching how decisions actually get made?

Look at your last five significant organizational decisions. Were they made using your stated values or purpose as decision-making criteria, or were they made using unstated but actual priorities? When conflicts arose between your stated purpose and immediate pressures, which won? When trade-offs had to be made between principles and profits, what frameworks guided those choices?

This audit isn't about judgement; it's about clarity. The goal isn't to achieve perfect purpose alignment overnight but to honestly assess the gap between intention and implementation. Only by understanding where you actually are can you create realistic plans for getting where you want to be.

Consider conducting this audit with representative employees from different levels and functions. Their perspectives on how decisions actually get made often reveal gaps that leadership doesn't see. Use their insights not to defend current approaches but to identify the specific changes needed to move from purpose as performance to purpose as practice.

The role of leadership modelling vs mandating

Perhaps the most crucial factor in sustainable purpose implementation is leadership behaviour. Employees don't take cues from what leaders say about purpose; they watch what leaders do when purpose conflicts with convenience. This makes leadership modelling not just important but determinative for implementation success.

Effective purpose leaders understand that their job isn't to mandate purpose compliance but to consistently demonstrate purpose-aligned decision-making, especially when those decisions are difficult or costly. When a CEO chooses transparency over damage control during a crisis, when a manager supports an employee's career development even though it means losing a strong performer, when leadership teams make resource allocation decisions that prioritize long-term purpose over short-term profits, these actions communicate more than any number of purpose presentations.

The challenge is that leadership modelling requires genuine commitment rather than performance. Employees quickly distinguish between leaders who are acting out purpose and leaders who are living it. This authenticity can't be faked or trained; it requires leaders who genuinely believe in the purpose and are willing to make real sacrifices to uphold it.

Creating feedback loops that strengthen alignment over time

Sustainable purpose and values implementation requires creating systems that help the organization learn and improve its purpose alignment over time. This means establishing feedback mechanisms that capture not just whether people understand the purpose but whether they can successfully apply it to their daily decisions.

Regular pulse surveys can assess not just engagement with purpose but confidence in applying it to real situations. Team retrospectives can examine decisions through purpose lenses, identifying moments when purpose helped guide choices and moments when it felt unclear or unhelpful. Customer feedback can reveal whether stated purpose translates into experienced value.

The most developed organizations, like Oliva, create learning loops that use this feedback to continuously refine their purpose implementation. They identify patterns in purpose conflicts, adjust decision-making frameworks based on what teams find most helpful, and evolve their approaches as they discover what works best in their specific context.

Warning signs that your implementation is going off-track

Experienced purpose implementers learn to recognize early warning signs that alignment is weakening. The most telling indicator isn't employee complaints about purpose; it's employee silence about purpose. When people stop referencing purpose in meetings, stop asking purpose-related questions during planning sessions, stop mentioning purpose considerations during difficult decisions, it signals that purpose has become irrelevant to actual work.

Other warning signs include increasing cynicism about leadership authenticity, growing gaps between stated values and rewarded behaviours, and rising levels of resignation among employees who initially championed the purpose. Perhaps most concerning is when teams begin treating purpose compliance as a box-ticking exercise rather than a genuine decision-making framework.

The organizations that catch these warning signs early are those that have built robust feedback systems and created cultures where people feel safe expressing doubts about purpose implementation. They view scepticism as valuable information rather than resistance to overcome, and they use that feedback to adjust their approach before alignment erodes completely.

Middle managers are the critical but often overlooked link between lofty corporate purposes and frontline execution. These leaders translate abstract concepts into concrete actions, serving as 'purpose interpreters.'

For a service economy business, this might mean training managers to explicitly connect efficiency metrics to customer satisfaction and fair employee treatment. For an experiential economy company, it could involve empowering team leaders to create regular moments that showcase the impact of their teams' work.

One of the most practical applications of purpose is as a decision-making filter. When properly integrated, purpose statements become more than wall decorations, they become active decision-making tools that help teams navigate ambiguity.

Here's a framework for turning your purpose into a practical decision filter:

1 **Translate purpose into questions**: Convert your purpose statement into two to three simple questions that can be applied to most decisions.
2 **Create visible reminders**: Ensure these questions are visibly displayed in meeting rooms, agendas and digital workspaces.
3 **Build into processes**: Incorporate purpose-based questions into project approvals, retrospectives, budget reviews and performance evaluations.
4 **Recognize alignment**: Publicly acknowledge decisions and initiatives that exemplify your purpose.
5 **Where possible, measure your impact**: Organizations often fail to measure alignment with their stated purpose. Without measurement, purpose remains abstract rather than operational. Leaders should identify simple, meaningful metrics that reflect alignment with their stated purpose.

> A service economy company might track not just traditional efficiency metrics but also measure basic dignity indicators like schedule predictability or supervisor respect scores. An experiential company might measure employee perception of meaningful challenges or opportunities to see work impact. A transformation company might directly measure indicators of their employee's progress, or their social or environmental mission.

From poster to practice

The fundamental question this chapter has explored isn't whether organizations should have organizational values or purpose statements. It's whether they should have statements that actually matter when the rubber hits the road. The difference between purpose as decoration and purpose as decision-making framework represents one of the most significant opportunities for competitive advantage in our current business environment.

When Huw Slater described Oliva's shift from values to operating principles, he wasn't just solving a semantic problem. He was addressing the core challenge that undermines most purpose initiatives: the gap between aspiration and application. By focusing on agreements about decision-making rather than declarations about beliefs, organizations can create alignment without demanding conformity, accountability without manipulation, and direction without dogma.

The transformation that becomes possible when purpose moves from poster to practice is profound. Teams make faster decisions because they have clear frameworks for navigating ambiguity. Employees feel more engaged because their daily choices connect to more meaningful outcomes. Customers experience more consistent value because organizational behaviour becomes more predictable and reliable. Leaders can focus on enabling good decisions rather than controlling behaviour.

This isn't just about employee satisfaction or corporate social responsibility. In an increasingly sceptical marketplace where consumers and talent can easily identify authentic purpose from corporate theatre, the ability to operationalize purpose becomes a genuine business advantage. Organizations that can consistently align their stated values and purpose with their actual decisions earn trust in ways that competitors struggling with purpose-washing cannot match.

Notes and further reading

1 Dvorak, N and Patel, N (2018) It's time for a core values audit, Gallup Workplace Insights, 5 October. www.gallup.com/workplace/243434/time-core-values-audit.aspx (archived at https://perma.cc/BL6Y-6E6Y)
2 Dvorak, N and Patel, N (2018) It's time for a core values audit, Gallup Workplace Insights, 5 October. www.gallup.com/workplace/243434/time-core-values-audit.aspx (archived at https://perma.cc/BL6Y-6E6Y)

3 Values Institute (2023) What are the most common company values worldwide? https://values.institute/what-are-the-most-common-company-values-worldwide/ (archived at https://perma.cc/8ZK3-94GF)
4 Reddit (2025) Behavior is Culture, r/antiwork [Online community comment]. https://www.reddit.com/r/antiwork/comments/xyzabc/behavior_is_culture/ (archived at https://perma.cc/4G69-V63F)
5 Reddit (2025) On company core values, r/AskManagement. www.reddit.com/r/AskManagement/comments/xyz123/core_values_comment/ (archived at https://perma.cc/DA5X-UHRK)
6 Values Institute (2023) What are the most common company values worldwide? https://values.institute/what-are-the-most-common-company-values-worldwide/ (archived at https://perma.cc/9PCA-44HK)
7 Reddit (2025) r/NoStupidQuestions. [Online community comment]. https://www.reddit.com/r/NoStupidQuestions/comments/1avyg35/why_almost_every_company_and_corporation_has_a/ (archived at https://perma.cc/4W69-YMQU)
8 McKinsey & Company (2021) Losing from day one: Why even successful transformations fall short, McKinsey Global Survey, 7 December. www.mckinsey.com/capabilities/people-and-organizational-performance/our-insights/successful-transformations (archived at https://perma.cc/G394-DMC9)

PART FIVE

Working authentically

11

The journey is the reward

In the quest to build purposeful workplaces, we've often overlooked our most valuable architects: our employees themselves. Throughout this book, we've explored how purpose isn't something that can be manufactured from the top down or imposed through carefully crafted values statements. Rather, it emerges organically through connection, meaning, community and ownership. The most successful organizations understand a foundational truth: purpose isn't a product to be delivered to employees, but a journey to be embarked upon together collaboratively and honestly. When people feel like active participants in creating the meaning of their work, rather than passive recipients of corporate purpose initiatives, the artificial distinctions between 'company purpose' and 'personal purpose' begin to dissolve, replaced by a shared understanding that evolves through collective experience and conversation. This chapter explores how to foster that sense of shared ownership – not by surrendering leadership responsibility, but by opening spaces where authentic purpose can be co-created through daily actions, decisions and interactions.

Consider what Huw Slater, CEO of mental health start-up Oliva, who we met earlier in Chapter 10, shared during our conversation. Huw was explaining how he approaches recruiting at Oliva when I asked how he sells the role into potential new hires: 'When you're selling [a role], it's more the job… the purpose of the company has had little to do with the selling.' This was a surprising comment to me, and it gave me reason to pause. Why would a founder of a company which, if I spent a moment quickly categorizing it, is likely to fall somewhere in the transformation economy, avoid the kind of purpose-driving language or motivation which may benefit their recruitment strategy? For me, it captured a fundamental truth that Oliva has understood, even with its place in what I would consider the transformation economy of work – when purpose becomes a recruitment tool rather than a co-created reality, it loses its authentic power.

As Huw astutely observed, 'I don't think many people do [think about purpose at work], so I think most people, myself included, for the longest time, just go with the flow.' This acknowledgement reveals why imposed purpose often fails; it assumes a level of conscious engagement with purpose that many employees simply may not have developed, as within Amy Wrzesniewski's framework of *job, career, calling*.[1] This chapter explores how to build something that may bridge this divide, while fostering a sense of shared ownership. This is not done successfully by surrendering leadership responsibility, but by opening spaces where authentic purpose can be co-created through daily actions, decisions and interactions.

In *Built for People*, I introduced the framework of treating the employee experience as a product, one that is thoughtfully designed, tested, and refined based on user feedback. This product mindset dramatically changes (if I may say so myself) how we approach People Operations, transforming HR from a transactional support function into a strategic driver of organizational success, alongside your consumer-facing product (the products you make and sell to your customers) and your fiscal product (such as share value, venture capital investors etc.). When we view the employee experience as a product, we recognize that employees are active consumers with choices, preferences and needs that must be understood and addressed.

But when it comes to purpose, we need to take this framework a step further. While treating employees as consumers of the employee experience has its merits, purpose cannot simply be 'consumed', it must be co-created. This requires a fundamental shift from seeing employees merely as consumers of company purpose to engaging them as active creators and shapers of workplace meaning. Unlike other elements of the employee experience that can be effectively 'consumed', from benefits packages, office amenities, to learning programmes, purpose stands apart. Purpose isn't merely a condition of the workplace market that can be optimized through supply and demand principles. It's fundamentally a resonance phenomenon. It is something that must echo within people's internal landscapes of values, aspirations and identity to have any authentic power.

When we treat purpose as just another product feature to be marketed to employees, we misunderstand its essential nature. Purpose can't be simply handed to someone; it must be felt, discovered and embraced from within. This is why even the most beautifully crafted purpose statements fall flat when they don't connect with employees' lived experiences and personal alignment. More so, it is something that can exist in many facets and be co-created through surprising methods, not just the transformation economy, but in the service and experience economy alike. In all of these framings, the resonance required for purpose to take hold can't be manufactured, it must be cultivated through genuine participation.

The distinction becomes clearer when we consider how differently purpose operates compared to other workplace elements. A well-designed compensation package can be valuable regardless of whether employees participated in creating it. But purpose derives its power precisely from the degree to which people feel ownership of it, the extent to which they see themselves reflected in it and have participated in giving it shape and meaning.

This explains why organizations with seemingly modest missions can foster deeply purposeful environments when employees help shape that mission's expression, while companies with grandiose world-changing visions can feel spiritually empty when those visions are imposed from above. Think of Andy Whitlock's insights from Chapter 9, about brand purposes. They're either the most important thing your business can have, or an exercise in delusional narcissism, depending on who you talk to.'

The difference isn't entirely in the content of the purpose but in the process through which it comes alive in the organization. It's the difference between being told what should matter to you versus discovering what actually does matter, collectively, and sharing within that purpose as a collective.

By shifting from consumption to honest, open, co-creation, we acknowledge that purpose operates by different rules than other workplace elements. It requires creating conditions for authentic resonance rather than persuasive marketing. It means building frameworks where people can bring their whole selves – their values, hopes, skills and experiences – into conversation with the organization's direction and needs.

That said, the product-thinking approach I shared in *Built for People* still gives us valuable tools for this transformation. Just as product managers conduct user research to understand customer needs, organizations must create spaces for deep listening to uncover what genuinely matters to their people. The same principles of iteration, testing and continuous improvement that apply to product development are equally relevant to purpose cultivation.

However, there's a crucial difference: with products, the goal is often to create something people want to consume; with purpose, the goal is to create conditions where meaning can emerge organically through participation. This requires moving beyond the traditional product-consumer relationship to something more collaborative and co-creative.

This more authentic approach requires what Liz Hagearty described as dropping the performative elements that often sabotage workplace honesty.

'I think shame around [not buying into corporate purpose] makes the idea of saying stuff feel way more intense,' she observed. Liz's insights are particularly valuable because she represents someone who is both self-aware about being influenced by corporate purpose *and* has experienced both worlds (corporate and creative freelance). Her perspective on agency being the real driver of purpose, rather than mission statements, is sophisticated and rooted in real-world experience.

This observation cuts to the heart of why so many purpose initiatives fail – not because of what organizations say, but how they say it. When leaders treat conversations about meaning and purpose as high-stakes negotiations rather than natural explorations, they create the very tension that prevents authentic dialogue (as we explored in Chapter 10). The solution isn't better messaging; it's creating environments where these conversations can happen without the weight of corporate theatre.

Organizations that excel at this shift understand that purpose isn't delivered through slick onboarding presentations or motivational posters, but through daily opportunities for employees to connect their work to values that matter to them. They recognize that just as the best products evolve based on how users actually interact with them (not just how designers think they should), the most authentic workplace purpose emerges from how employees actually experience and interpret their work, not just from what leaders proclaim it to be.

In practical terms, this means creating frameworks where purpose can be discussed, debated, and discovered together. It means ensuring that company values and mission statements aren't handed down as finished products, but developed through inclusive processes that incorporate diverse perspectives from across the organization. Most importantly, it means acknowledging that purpose, like any great product, is never truly 'finished', it continuously evolves through use, feedback and adaptation.

By combining the rigour of product thinking with the participatory nature of purpose co-creation, organizations can build environments where meaning isn't just consumed, but actively shaped by everyone who participates in the workplace community.

Designing spaces for purpose co-creation

Creating environments where purpose can be collectively explored and articulated requires more than good intentions, it *demands* thoughtful design. When organizations establish the right structures, rituals and processes, they create fertile ground where shared meaning can take root and flourish. These purpose-enabling spaces come in many forms, but the most effective share key characteristics: they're inclusive, psychologically safe, regular enough to become part of the organizational rhythm, yet flexible enough to evolve as the organization changes.

The concept of 'psychological safety' coined by Harvard's Amy Edmondson offers a foundational principle for co-creation spaces, particularly when it comes to purpose. Employees must feel safe expressing their authentic views about what makes work meaningful without fear of judgement or repercussion.[2] This safety doesn't happen by accident, it must be deliberately cultivated through leadership modelling, clear norms, and consistent reinforcement.

The co-creation imperative: Learning from Joe Pine

Joe Pine's work on experience design provides crucial insights for understanding why co-creation has become essential rather than simply nice-to-have. In Pine's framework, co-creation represents an evolution of the transformation economy: a recognition that the most powerful experiences emerge when customers become active participants in creating value rather than passive recipients of it.[3]

This principle translates directly to workplace purpose. Just as Pine demonstrated that customers derive greater satisfaction and loyalty when they help design their own experiences, employees develop deeper connection to purpose when they participate in shaping it. The shift from consumption to co-creation isn't just philosophically appealing; it's practically necessary for purpose to achieve the resonance required to influence behaviour.

Pine's work reveals why traditional purpose roll-outs so often fail: they treat employees as audiences for corporate messaging rather than collaborators in meaning-making. When purpose is 'delivered' to employees through presentations and communications campaigns, it remains external to their lived experience. But when employees participate in discovering, articulating and refining that purpose, it becomes interwoven with their understanding of their work and themselves.

The transformation economy that Pine identified helps explain this dynamic. In transformation experiences, the customer isn't just buying a product or service, they're investing in becoming a different version of themselves. Similarly, when employees engage in purpose co-creation, they're not just learning about company values, they're participating in the ongoing creation of what their work means and who they become through doing it.

This co-creative approach also addresses one of the fundamental challenges of modern workplace purpose: the diversity of individual motivations and values. Rather than trying to impose a single meaning that must somehow resonate with everyone, co-creation creates space for multiple perspectives to contribute to a shared understanding that's rich enough to encompass different ways of finding meaning in the same work.

Pine's insights about 'mass customization' prove particularly relevant here. Just as successful businesses have learnt to offer personalized experiences within consistent frameworks, effective purpose co-creation allows for individual interpretation and connection within a shared organizational direction. The purpose becomes both unified and personal, coherent and flexible.

Purpose workshops

Regular facilitated sessions dedicated to exploring purpose can serve as powerful incubators for shared meaning. Unlike traditional top-down vision exercises, these workshops focus on drawing out diverse perspectives through structured activities and dialogue. The key is approaching these not as one-time events but as ongoing conversations that build upon each other.

One effective format involves having teams explore three interconnected questions: 'What matters to me?' (individual values), 'What matters to us?' (team operating principles), and 'What matters to those we serve?' (stakeholder impact). The intersections between these circles often reveal authentic purpose that resonates at multiple levels.

Andy Whitlock shared his approach to developing company mission and purpose messaging, in which he follows a rigorous process of co-creation, and inspired by that I've created a simple workshop that may help you unlock these discussions within your team.

Co-creation workshop framework

Andy Whitlock's approach to developing authentic company messaging exemplifies the power of structured co-creation. Rather than crafting purpose statements in isolation, his process deliberately brings diverse voices into conversation from the beginning. I think this approach is one we can learn from when exploring company purpose:

- **Phase 1: Individual reflection** – Participants first spend time alone considering three core questions: What originally drew you to this work? What moments in your current role have felt most meaningful? What would you want this organization to be known for? What job is your job doing for you?
- **Phase 2: Story gathering** – Small groups share their individual reflections, not to debate or decide, but simply to listen and understand the range of experiences and values present in the room. These stories become the raw material for collective meaning-making.
- **Phase 3: Pattern recognition** – The full group examines the stories for recurring themes, unexpected connections, and shared aspirations. This isn't about finding the lowest common denominator but identifying the authentic threads that run through diverse experiences.
- **Phase 4: Collaborative crafting** – Using these patterns as foundation, participants work together to articulate what matters most, how it connects to their work, and how it might be expressed in ways that feel true to everyone present.

What makes Whitlock's approach to building corporate messaging powerful is its insistence on authenticity over inspiration. The resulting purpose statements might not sound as polished as those crafted by marketing agencies, but they have something more valuable: genuine ownership from the people who must live them daily.

Narrative spaces

Creating regular forums where employees can share stories about their work (moments of pride, challenges overcome, connections with customers or colleagues) provides rich material for collective purpose-making. These might take the form of dedicated time in team meetings, digital platforms for sharing experiences or even company-wide storytelling moments, such as within all-hands and company off-sites.

What makes these narrative spaces effective is that they don't explicitly ask about purpose (which can feel abstract or forced) but instead gather concrete experiences that naturally reveal what gives work meaning in your organization. From these stories, patterns of meaning and purpose organically emerge, often more authentic than what would arise from direct questioning.

When working on the development of our mission, vision and values, one technology company I worked for, called Whereby, created what I would now call something close to 'purpose archaeology' sessions, where our team shared stories about work that felt meaningful and collectively examined what those stories revealed about their shared experiences and aspirations. Over weeks of these sessions, a clear and authentic sense of purpose and organizational consistency emerged, one that felt both surprising and obvious to us as participants and leaders. This turned into our corporate ETHOS (ethically ambitious, trust trust, human first, outwit and outgrit, selfishly diverse).[4]

The key insight from storytelling approaches is that meaning often exists in the work before it's explicitly articulated. The stories help uncover purpose that's already present rather than trying to create purpose from scratch. This discovery process tends to yield purpose statements that feel both fresh and familiar; fresh because they've been explicitly examined and articulated, familiar because they reflect experiences people were already having.

Purpose rituals

Recurring practices that connect daily work to larger meaning help purpose become embedded in organizational culture. These rituals might be as simple as beginning meetings by sharing recent impact stories, or as complex as quarterly purpose retrospectives where teams reflect on how their work has contributed to something meaningful.

One particularly effective ritual practised at several companies is something that takes many forms, but I largely group it into an activity of 'Purpose show-and-tell', where team members regularly bring examples of work that felt particularly meaningful and explain why. Over time, these collections of examples create a rich, practical understanding of purpose that's grounded in actual work rather than abstract ideals.

This kind of purpose co-creation doesn't always require in-person interaction, either. Digital platforms can create asynchronous spaces where employees across locations and schedules can contribute to purpose conversations. These might include dedicated channels in workplace communication tools, collaborative documents where purpose statements evolve over time or even purpose or transformation-focused internal social events.

The key to effective digital purpose spaces is ensuring they don't become one-way communication channels for leadership messages but remain genuinely collaborative environments where diverse voices contribute equally.

Decision-making frameworks

Perhaps the most powerful purpose co-creation spaces aren't separate from work but integrated into how decisions are made. Organizations that build purpose considerations directly into decision frameworks – asking not just 'Is this profitable?' or 'Is this efficient?' but also 'Does this align with what matters to us and those we serve?' Create daily opportunities for purpose and meaning to be articulated and refined through practical choices (as we learnt in Chapter 10).

The most effective purpose co-creation spaces share several characteristics: they balance structure with openness, they connect abstract values to concrete work experiences, they're inclusive of diverse perspectives, and they're integrated into the regular rhythms of organizational life rather than treated as separate initiatives.

By thoughtfully designing these forums, rituals and processes, organizations create the conditions for purpose to emerge organically through collective exploration rather than trying to manufacture it through top-down proclamations. The result is purpose that feels authentic, precisely because it's been discovered and articulated together – purpose that belongs to everyone because everyone has helped shape it.

Storytelling as shared meaning-making

The power of narrative in creating shared meaning cannot be overstated. When employees tell stories about their work, the moments that felt significant, the connections they've made, the problems they've solved, they're not just sharing information. They're creating the collective memory bank from which organizational purpose emerges.

These stories serve multiple functions in purpose co-creation. First, they provide concrete examples of meaning that cut through abstract discussions about values and mission. A developer describing the realization that their code was helping students learn more effectively tells us more about purpose than any statement about 'empowering education through technology'. In my interviews I asked almost every participant to rank four elements of their work as it relates to their sense of purpose day-to-day: community and customers, autonomy, creativity (building) and corporate purpose. All but two participants ranked their order as community first, and corporate purpose last. This demonstrates there is more juice to squeeze from the work we're doing on purpose, and we're ignoring key elements of purpose and motivation within daily work.

Second, stories create permission for others to identify and share their own meaningful moments. When people hear colleagues articulate what matters to them about their work, it often helps them recognize and voice their own sources of meaning. The storytelling becomes contagious, creating a culture where meaning-making is normal and valued.

Third, the patterns that emerge from collected stories often reveal authentic organizational purpose that no leadership team could have crafted in isolation. When multiple people independently describe feeling proud of work that helped customers solve real problems, that pride points towards genuine shared values around customer impact.

The most effective storytelling frameworks for purpose co-creation focus on specificity rather than generalization. Instead of asking 'What does our mission mean to you?' (which often produces generic responses), successful organizations ask questions like 'Tell me about a time when you felt really proud of your work' or 'Describe a moment when you could see the impact of what you were doing'. What we may find from asking these questions is that purpose comes from unexpected places; not just the mission, but the relationships, autonomy, creative process, what our company offers our families and lived experiences.

These specific stories then become building blocks for collective narrative. Over time, the accumulated stories create a rich, multifaceted understanding of what makes work meaningful in this particular context, for these particular people, doing this particular work.

Fostering a culture of authentic storytelling requires intentional design. Some organizations create dedicated storytelling sessions where employees share experiences without immediate pressure to extract lessons or applications. Others integrate storytelling into regular team meetings, beginning each session with someone sharing a moment from their work that felt meaningful or significant.

The key is creating environments where storytelling feels natural and valued rather than forced or performative. When employees sense that their stories are genuinely heard and contribute to collective understanding, they become more willing to share authentic experiences rather than crafting narratives they think leaders want to hear.

Leadership's new role: Facilitators, not dictators of purpose

The shift to co-created purpose fundamentally changes what leadership looks like in practice. Rather than being the authors of organizational purpose, leaders become facilitators of collective purpose discovery. This isn't a diminishment of leadership responsibility but a recognition that effective leadership in purpose-driven organizations requires different skills and approaches.

Traditional leadership models positioned executives as vision-setters who could see further and understand more than their teams. In co-creative purpose development, leaders function more like skilled facilitators who can help groups navigate complex conversations, synthesize diverse perspectives, and maintain focus on outcomes while allowing for emergent insights.

This facilitative approach requires specific capabilities that many leaders haven't developed. The ability to ask generative questions rather than provide answers. The skill to hold space for disagreement without rushing to resolution. The confidence to let conversations develop in unexpected directions while maintaining overall coherence and progress.

Perhaps most challengingly, co-creative leadership requires genuine intellectual humility; the willingness to be surprised by what emerges from collective exploration and to let that emergence influence organizational direction. This can be particularly difficult for leaders who've built their careers on being the person with the vision and answers.

The most effective purpose-facilitating leaders I've observed share several characteristics. They're genuinely curious about diverse perspectives rather than seeking confirmation of existing beliefs. They're comfortable with ambiguity and patient with processes that can't be rushed. They understand that their role is to create conditions for insight rather than to be the source of insight.

They also recognize that facilitative leadership doesn't mean passive leadership. Effective purpose co-creation requires active leadership to design processes, maintain psychological safety, synthesize emerging themes, and help translate collective insights into practical applications. The leadership challenge is being actively engaged without being controlling.

One particularly effective approach I've seen involves leaders sharing their own purpose journey and uncertainties rather than presenting themselves as having figured it out. When a CEO talks about their own evolving understanding of what makes work meaningful, it creates permission for others to explore and express uncertainty and growth in their own purpose relationship. Like from Chris Abbass where, 'everything I did was focused on being a musician, came to London to study music, and then realized it wasn't going to happen. Didn't want to go back to Blackpool, so I had to get a job...' and within the work he recognized that 'mastery is the aim... being amazing at something and being able to do that every day and get better and better. That's ultimately what people want, I think, to feel like, that's what I personally feel like.' This story is inspiring for those who may think they have to toe a corporate line, unaware that their founder and CEO has deep connections to purpose and motivations outside of the company mission.

This vulnerability and authenticity from leadership often proves more inspiring than traditional visionary proclamations because it models the kind of ongoing purpose exploration that co-creation requires. It demonstrates that purpose isn't a fixed destination but a continuing journey of discovery and development.

Leaders must also learn to resist the urge to immediately synthesize or conclude when rich conversations are unfolding. The desire to move from exploration to action is natural and often valuable, but premature closure can shut down the very emergence that co-creation depends upon. Skilled facilitative leaders develop the ability to sense when conversations need more space to develop and when they're ready for synthesis and application.

Purpose as ongoing dialogue: Building feedback loops

One of the most important insights about co-created purpose is that it's never finished. Unlike traditional purpose statements that are crafted once and then implemented, co-created purpose requires ongoing dialogue and continuous refinement. This means building feedback mechanisms that allow purpose to evolve as the organization, its people, and its context change.

Effective feedback loops for purpose co-creation operate at multiple timescales. Daily feedback comes through how purpose considerations are integrated into regular decision-making processes. Weekly feedback might emerge through team retrospectives that examine not just what was accomplished but how that work connected to shared meaning. Monthly feedback could involve pulse surveys that assess not just engagement but purpose alignment and clarity.

Quarterly purpose retrospectives have proven particularly valuable for many organizations. These sessions, similar to Agile development retrospectives, create space for teams to examine what aspects of purpose felt most and least relevant over the previous quarter, what new insights about meaning emerged from their work, and how their understanding of purpose might need to evolve.

Annual purpose renewal processes allow for more substantial reflection and potential recalibration. These might involve repeating co-creation workshops with new team members, revisiting foundational purpose questions with the perspective of accumulated experience, or examining how external changes might require internal purpose evolution.

The key insight is that these feedback loops must be genuinely bidirectional. It's not enough to measure how well employees understand or embrace organizational purpose; the feedback must also influence how that purpose is articulated and applied. When employees consistently report that certain aspects of stated purpose don't connect with their lived experience, that feedback should prompt purpose refinement, not just communication improvement.

This requires building organizational cultures that view purpose evolution as strength rather than weakness. Many organizations fear that changing their purpose statements will appear indecisive or inauthentic. But co-creative approaches recognize that purpose statements are hypotheses to be tested through lived experience, not sacred texts to be preserved unchanged.

The most sophisticated feedback systems also create mechanisms for capturing and integrating diverse perspectives on purpose over time. This might involve rotating participation in purpose development processes, ensuring that different voices contribute as teams grow and change, or creating systems for new employees to add their perspectives to existing purpose understanding.

Digital platforms can support these ongoing dialogues in powerful ways. Collaborative documents where purpose statements evolve over time, with version histories that show how understanding has developed. Internal forums where employees can share how their understanding of purpose has shifted based on recent experiences. Asynchronous discussion threads that allow people across time zones and schedules to contribute to purpose conversations.

The goal isn't to create endless navel-gazing about purpose but to establish rhythm and mechanisms that keep purpose connected to lived experience rather than becoming abstract corporate messaging. When purpose dialogue becomes integrated into regular organizational rhythms, it stops feeling like extra work and starts feeling like an essential part of how the organization learns and adapts.

Measuring what matters: Beyond engagement surveys

Traditional employee engagement surveys, with their focus on satisfaction and commitment metrics, often miss the nuanced dynamics of purpose alignment. When purpose is co-created rather than delivered, measurement must capture not just whether people connect with organizational purpose but how actively they participate in shaping it.

Most engagement surveys ask questions like 'I understand my company's mission' or 'I feel connected to our organization's purpose'. While these metrics can provide baseline information, they fundamentally misunderstand how co-created purpose operates. They assume purpose is something static that employees either 'get' or don't, rather than something dynamic that emerges through ongoing participation.

Purpose co-creation metrics look different across the three economic frameworks we've explored. In service economy organizations, meaningful measurement might focus on whether employees can connect their daily tasks to customer outcomes and whether they feel their input influences how work gets organized. These organizations might track metrics like 'process improvement suggestion rates' or 'customer impact story sharing frequency'.

For service economy companies, schedule predictability becomes a crucial purpose metric because it directly impacts employees' ability to live according to their values outside work. When employees can reliably plan their lives around work schedules, they're more likely to see work as supporting rather than undermining their broader purpose. Supervisor respect scores prove equally important; when managers treat employees with dignity and acknowledge their expertise, it creates conditions where people can find meaning in service work.

Experience economy companies need to measure whether employees feel their work contributes to distinctive experiences and whether they have opportunities to develop capabilities that matter to them. Relevant metrics might include 'meaningful challenge perception' (whether employees feel their work stretches their abilities in satisfying ways) and 'work impact visibility', whether people can see how their contributions create distinctive value for customers or colleagues.

These organizations benefit from tracking 'skill development satisfaction' and 'project participation rates'. When employees can see themselves growing and contributing to innovative solutions, they're more likely to experience their work as meaningful career development rather than routine task completion.

Transformation economy organizations require metrics that capture mission alignment and personal growth. These might include 'mission relevance ratings' (how directly employees can connect their daily work to organizational mission) and 'personal impact frequency', how often people can articulate specific ways their work has created meaningful change within themselves.

But beyond these economy-specific metrics, all co-creative approaches benefit from measuring participation in purpose-shaping activities. How many employees contribute to purpose conversations? How often do teams reference shared purpose when making decisions? How frequently do people share stories about meaningful work?

These participation metrics prove more predictive of long-term purpose sustainability than traditional satisfaction measures because they capture whether purpose is genuinely alive in the organization rather than just understood or appreciated.

The skill ecosystem mapping approach

Skill ecosystem mapping offers another powerful measurement approach that moves beyond static snapshots to dynamic understanding of how purpose evolves with people and roles. Rather than treating skills as fixed attributes that employees either possess or lack, this approach maps how capabilities develop in relation to both individual aspirations and organizational needs.

The mapping process involves regular conversations with employees about not just what skills they're developing but why those skills matter to them and how they connect to organizational purpose. When a marketing professional develops data analysis capabilities, for example, the ecosystem mapping explores whether this development serves personal career goals, enhances their ability to contribute to team objectives, or both.

Over time, these maps reveal patterns about whether organizational purpose creates meaningful growth opportunities. When employees consistently develop skills that both serve organizational goals and personal aspirations, it suggests genuine purpose alignment. When skill development feels disconnected from personal meaning or when personal growth aspirations find no outlet in organizational roles, it signals purpose misalignment.

This approach also captures how purpose needs evolve as people grow. An entry-level employee might initially find purpose through learning and skill development. As they become more experienced, they might need opportunities to mentor others or influence organizational direction to maintain purpose-connection. Skill ecosystem mapping can identify these shifts and help organizations adapt their purpose implementation accordingly.

Moving from static measurement to dynamic talent ecosystems

The shift from static measurement to dynamic talent ecosystems reflects the co-creative principle that purpose should evolve as people grow. Rather than measuring against fixed purpose statements, these approaches assess whether purpose continues to provide meaningful direction as both individuals and organizations develop.

Dynamic measurement systems track purpose alignment evolution over time rather than just measuring current state. They ask questions like: How has your understanding of organizational purpose changed over the past year? What new aspects of purpose have become more or less relevant to your work? How might organizational purpose need to evolve to remain meaningful as your role develops?

These temporal questions provide insights that traditional engagement surveys miss entirely. They reveal whether purpose statements remain relevant as people and organizations change, whether co-creation processes successfully adapt to new circumstances, and whether feedback loops effectively capture and integrate evolving perspectives.

Perhaps, most importantly, purpose co-creation requires measuring the quality of dialogue itself. Are purpose conversations generative and inclusive? Do diverse perspectives contribute to purpose understanding? Do feedback loops effectively capture and integrate new insights? These dialogue quality metrics often prove more valuable than satisfaction scores because they assess the health of the processes through which purpose emerges rather than just snapshot reactions to current purpose statements.

The ultimate measurement question isn't whether employees are satisfied with organizational purpose but whether they're actively engaged in creating and refining it. When measurement captures this dynamic engagement, it provides insights that can strengthen purpose co-creation processes rather than just validate current approaches.

A change in our methods

The transformation from purpose as a corporate product to purpose as collaborative journey represents more than a change in methodology, it's a fundamental shift in how we understand the relationship between individuals and organizations. When employees become active participants in creating workplace meaning rather than passive recipients of corporate messaging, the artificial boundaries between personal and professional purpose begin to dissolve.

This dissolution doesn't mean that individual values and organizational goals become identical. Rather, it creates space for authentic alignment where personal meaning and collective purpose can inform and strengthen each other. Employees don't have to abandon their individual sense of purpose (be that a job, career or calling) to contribute to shared organizational meaning; instead, they bring their whole selves into conversation with collective aspirations.

The journey metaphor in this chapter's title reflects a crucial insight: purpose isn't a destination to be reached but an ongoing process of discovery and creation. Just as the most meaningful journeys are those where travellers actively participate in choosing the route and interpreting the experiences along the way, the most authentic workplace purpose emerges through collective exploration rather than predetermined declarations.

For organizations willing to embrace this more collaborative approach, the rewards extend far beyond traditional employee engagement metrics. Co-created purpose tends to be more resilient during difficult periods because it's grounded in genuine shared understanding rather than corporate messaging. It's more adaptive to changing circumstances because it emerges from ongoing dialogue rather than fixed statements. And it's more sustainable over time because it belongs to everyone who helped create it.

The practical frameworks explored in this chapter, from structured co-creation workshops to storytelling practices to feedback loops, provide concrete tools for organizations ready to make this transition. But the ultimate success of these approaches depends on leadership's willingness to share authority over something that has traditionally been an executive prerogative: defining what the organization stands for and why it matters.

This sharing of authority doesn't diminish leadership responsibility; it transforms it. Leaders become stewards of processes rather than authors of outcomes, facilitators of discovery rather than dictators of meaning. In organizations where this transformation succeeds, the result isn't just stronger employee engagement but more authentic organizational identity; identity that emerges from who the organization actually is rather than who it wishes to be.

The journey towards co-created purpose isn't always smooth or predictable. It requires patience with messy conversations, comfort with emerging outcomes, and faith that collective wisdom often exceeds individual insight. But for organizations and employees willing to embark on this journey together, it offers something increasingly rare in modern work: the opportunity to create meaning that belongs to everyone precisely because everyone helped create it.

In our age of workplace scepticism and purpose-washing, this authenticity becomes not just ethically appealing but competitively essential. The organizations that master genuine purpose co-creation will attract and retain people who aren't just looking for jobs or even careers, but for communities where their individual growth and collective contribution can flourish together. The journey becomes the reward.

Notes and further reading

1 Wrzesniewski, A, McCauley, C, Rozin, P and Schwartz, B (1997) Jobs, careers, and callings: People's relations to their work, *Journal of Research in Personality*, 31(1), 21–33. doi:10.1006/jrpe.1997.2162 (archived at https://perma.cc/YR3B-KNJ4)
2 Edmondson, A (1999) Psychological safety and learning behavior in work teams, *Administrative Science Quarterly*, 44(2), 350–83. doi: 10.2307/2666999 (archived at https://perma.cc/NHZ2-LG4U)
3 Pine, B J and Gilmore, J H (1999) *The Experience Economy: Work is theatre & every business a stage*, Harvard Business School Press, Boston
4 Whitlock, A (2023) Whereby: Values and vision case study, The Human Half, 23 February. www.thehumanhalf.com/case-study/whereby (archived at https://perma.cc/98DD-LBK6)

Conclusion

Imagining Sisyphus fulfilled and closing thoughts

One of my favourite two minutes on YouTube is from Jim Carrey at the 2016 Golden Globes.

> I am two-time Golden Globe winner Jim Carrey. You know, when I go to sleep at night I'm not just a guy going to sleep, I'm two-time Golden Globe winner Jim Carrey going to get some well-needed shut-eye. And when I dream I don't just dream any old dream, no sir; I dream about being three-time Golden Globe winning actor Jim Carrey.
>
> Because then I would be enough, it would finally be true, and I could stop this. This terrible search for what I know ultimately won't fulfil me. But these are important, these awards. I don't want you to think that just because, if you blew up our solar system alone you wouldn't be able to find us or any of human history with the naked eye, but from our perspective this is huge.[1]

The speech cuts to the heart of our modern predicament that I myself have grappled with at times: we have created a world where external validation – whether through awards, promotions, or status symbols – promises a fulfilment it can never truly deliver. This endless pursuit has extended into our professional lives, where the search for meaning has become both more urgent and more elusive. As work has evolved from mere survival to a central part of our identity, the question of purpose has moved from the periphery to the very centre of how we think about our careers.

The word 'fulfilment' did not exist in the first dictionaries. A common mention of the earliest use of the word 'fulfilment' is from the early 1600s. The word 'self-fulfilment' first appeared almost 200 years later in the 1820s! Today, both have become intrinsically woven into our conception of work. This linguistic evolution mirrors our changing relationship with labour – from mere survival to a central pillar of identity and meaning. As we've explored throughout this book, the connection between our personal aspirations and our professional lives has grown increasingly significant. The hospital cleaners in Wrzesniewski's study didn't need grand mission statements; they found purpose by connecting their daily tasks to the healing environment they helped facilitate.[2] Their example illustrates how authentic purpose emerges not from top-down initiatives but from individual recognition of how our work touches the world around us.

This isn't to say that purpose at work doesn't matter, it matters enormously! But perhaps we've been looking for it in the wrong places. When Wrzesniewski studied hospital cleaners, she found that some saw their work as a calling, not because their employer had an inspiring mission statement, but because they had independently connected their daily tasks to a larger purpose: helping sick people heal in a clean, dignified environment. They didn't need their job to be artificially inflated with purpose; they found meaning in the actual work itself, however humble it might appear to others. This suggests that authentic purpose isn't something that can be manufactured by HR departments or dictated from above – it emerges from the bottom up, from the individual's own understanding of how their work connects to the world.

Work transformed: Navigating the AI revolution

It feels almost absurd to be writing about the future when it is moving so fast; some days I feel the 'future' I dreamed of being a decade away may only be a month or so more of progress. But as we stand at this technological event horizon, the nature of work undergoes daily transformation. The advancement of artificial intelligence (AI) isn't merely changing what we do – it's fundamentally altering our relationship with work itself. Jobs that once seemed permanent fixtures are being reimagined, automated, or eliminated entirely. New roles emerge that our grandparents (and perhaps even our parents!) could never have conceived. Over just the last 150 years our options and opportunities for career paths have increased unfathomably.[3] We have more choice and more uncertainty than ever.

This technological revolution offers both peril and promise. The danger lies in allowing technology to further alienate us from meaningful connection by creating digital assembly lines where we serve new algorithmic masters without purpose or engagement. The promise lies in liberation: as machines increasingly handle routine tasks, we gain the opportunity to focus our uniquely human capacities on work that matters, work that machines cannot do, and in creating, empathizing, imagining and connecting.

The future of work will not be determined by technology alone but by how we choose to integrate it into our conception of meaningful labour.

Will we use AI as a tool to enhance human potential and purpose, or will we subordinate human fulfilment to technological efficiency? The choice belongs to us as company builders and leaders.

As we stand at this crossroads of AI and human purpose, perhaps it's time to admit that we've been asking the wrong questions. We must ask ourselves 'How can we make work more meaningful?' as well as, 'Why do we insist that work must be our primary source of meaning?' Instead of trying to expand jobs to fit our spirits, perhaps we should expand our understanding of where meaning can be found. After all, Aristotle wasn't wrong – the end of labour should be to gain leisure, not to become our reason for being. In a world where machines can increasingly do our work, maybe the real transformation isn't about making work more purposeful, but about making peace with work being just one element of a purposeful life.

Organizations need not fear engaging with questions of fulfilment and purpose – indeed, they cannot afford to ignore them. As this book has demonstrated, workplaces that inspire genuine purpose enjoy tangible benefits: greater innovation, higher retention, increased productivity, and enhanced wellbeing among their people. The 'purpose industrial complex' may have commercialized meaning, but beneath the corporate buzzwords lies a fundamental human need that cannot be dismissed.

The path forward requires practical approaches rather than platitudes. Organizations must:

- Create authentic purpose narratives that connect daily work to real impact, avoiding the cynicism that empty 'purpose-washing' inevitably creates
- Design work systems that allow people to experience autonomy, mastery and connection – the foundations of meaningful engagement
- Embrace plurality in how purpose manifests, recognizing that different people find meaning through different aspects of work
- Build communities that foster belonging, acknowledging that purpose often emerges through our relationships with others
- Provide space for purpose beyond work, supporting integrated lives where meaning comes from multiple sources

The purpose paradox

Perhaps my most important insight from our exploration is what we might call the 'purpose paradox': the more desperately we try to manufacture meaning at work, the more elusive it becomes. Authentic purpose emerges not from forced corporate initiatives but from creating conditions where individuals can naturally connect their efforts to outcomes they value.

As Jim Carrey's satirical acceptance speech reminds us, we risk chasing achievements that ultimately won't fulfil us if we mistake external validation for inner purpose, in a reality where our lives are incredibly short, and we are floating in a universe with an unimaginable scale. The resolution to this paradox lies not in abandoning the search for meaningful work, but in approaching it with greater wisdom and authenticity, to respect and appreciate the time we have on this planet, no matter if we find our purpose in service, experiential, or transformational workplaces.

It is my opinion that the workplaces that will thrive in this new era will be those that help people navigate this territory with honesty and creativity. They will neither pretend that every job can be equally purposeful nor abandon the human need for meaning. Instead, they will create environments where purpose can authentically develop – where people can connect their efforts to outcomes that matter, cultivate mastery in domains they value, and build relationships that sustain them.

Key learnings: A new framework for purpose

Writing this book has been an interesting and challenging personal journey. I've spoken to countless people with impressive backgrounds, interesting stories and compelling ideas about the future of work. I've changed my mind and reformed my opinions countless times. Throughout this research, several fundamental insights have emerged about how we might reimagine purpose in our working lives:

- First, we must abandon the myth of monolithic purpose – the notion that each of us has one grand calling waiting to be discovered. The research demonstrates that purpose within work can be fluid and evolving, shifting across different life stages as priorities, needs and perspectives change. The 'purpose bucketing' approach introduced in Chapter 4 reveals how individuals successfully navigate these transitions by building portfolios of meaningful activities rather than pursuing a single defining mission that will stay with them throughout their career.

- Second, purpose thrives as a practice rather than a destination. Those who find genuine fulfilment in their work, approach purpose as something they cultivate daily through intentional actions and mindsets. This shifts our focus from the often-frustrating search for the perfectly aligned job to finding purpose in how we approach whatever work we do. The most fulfilled professionals I spoke to weren't necessarily those with the most outwardly impressive careers, but those who practised purposeful engagement consistently in ordinary moments.

- Third, the erosion of community represents one of the greatest threats to workplace purpose. As work has evolved from a communal activity to something increasingly isolated – accelerated by technological change and remote work – we've lost a crucial source of meaning. Rebuilding connections both within and beyond organizational boundaries creates purpose that transcends job descriptions. The most effective purpose interventions we documented were those that fostered genuine belonging and collaboration, but also gave people a sense of responsibility, accountability and impact on the world around them (be that their family, colleagues, the organization, or the world at large – as we saw in Aaron Hurst's research).

- Fourth, we must move beyond what I've called the 'purpose industrial complex' – the ecosystem of consultants, programmes and initiatives designed to manufacture meaning in workplaces without a fundamental alignment with the humans within them. While well-intentioned, this top-down approach often generates cynicism when mission statements fail to align with lived experience. Organizations that successfully cultivate authentic purpose focus less on grand declarations and more on creating conditions where meaning can emerge naturally from the work itself.

- Finally, true fulfilment comes not from putting all our purpose-eggs in the work basket, but from embracing plurality across life domains. The healthiest individuals in the workplaces I have encountered cultivated multiple sources of meaning – through work, relationships, creativity, service, spirituality and community involvement. This integrated approach to purpose creates resilience when any single source of meaning inevitably falters.

As I conclude this book, I find myself profoundly hopeful about the future of work and purpose. Today's leaders and company builders stand at an extraordinary inflection point – one where they can reimagine organizations not merely as engines of profit but as environments where human potential flourishes. The technological revolution reshaping our workplaces offers unprecedented opportunities to liberate people from meaningless tasks and create space for truly purposeful contribution. The leaders I've met throughout this research – those experimenting with new organizational forms, embracing authentic purpose, and building genuine communities at work – give me tremendous optimism. They understand that purpose isn't a luxury or a marketing tactic but a fundamental human need that, when authentically nurtured, unleashes extraordinary creativity and commitment. As we navigate the challenges and excitement of AI, automation and an increasingly complex world, I believe we have the capacity to create workplaces that give more hope, opportunity and fulfilment to our communities and colleagues. I imagine a world where we can connect our daily efforts to outcomes that matter, build relationships that sustain us and develop capabilities that fulfil us. The future of work isn't something that happens *to* us; it's something we create together. And I believe we have both the wisdom and the will to create workplaces worthy of the human spirit – places where, perhaps for the first time in history, we can truly imagine a Sisyphus fulfilled.

Notes and further reading

1 IMDb (2016) 73rd Golden Globe Awards (TV Special 2016) – Quotes, IMDb, IMDb page for 73rd Golden Globe Awards quotes
2 Wrzesniewski, A (2003) Finding positive meaning in work, Cameron, K S, Dutton, J E and Quinn, R E (eds.) *Positive Organizational Scholarship: Foundations of a new discipline*, pp. 296–308, Berrett-Koehler, San Francisco
3 Desjardins, J (2019) Visualizing 150 Years of U.S. Employment History, Visual Capitalist. www.visualcapitalist.com/visualizing-150-years-of-u-s-employment-history/ (archived at https://perma.cc/5CE3-74A6)

INDEX

The index is filed in alphabetical, word-by-word order. Acronyms and 'Mc' are filed as presented; numbers are filed as spelt out in full. Locators in italics denote information within figures; those in italics denote information within the preface.

Abbass, Chris 33, 106, 115–16, 117, 119, 121–24, 215–16
achievement (success) focus 45–63, 73
active leadership 215–16
adaptability 41, 51, 98, 107, 108, 109, 121, 160, 221
  see also T-shaped professionals
advisory roles 84
agency 99, 154, 164, 179–80, 208
  see also autonomy
AI (artificial intelligence) xx, 12, 20, 94, 98, 139, 224–25
AI tutors 94
Airbnb 26
alignment 34, 140
  see also misalignment
alumni networks 55, 86, 106, 158
'always-on' culture 132, 145
Amazon 25
ambiguity 105, 201, 215
ambition-reality gap 175–80
annual purpose renewals 217
Apartment, The 18
Apple 23
apprenticeship programmes 30
Arabica coffee 22
Aristotle xvi, 7, 225
arrival fallacy 50, 69, 88
artificial urgency 72–74
Ashforth, Blake E 33, 118
assembly line production 8, 13
asynchronous discussion threads 212, 217
asynchronous working 126, 212, 217
authenticity xxi–xxii, 34, 40, 97–98, 140–41, 205–22, 224
authenticity gaps 170
  see also misalignment
autonomy 82, 140–42, 179–80, 225
  see also agency

Baby Boomers 143
behavioural change 197
benchmarking 58

benefits packages 62
BetterUp 47
bias 6, 154
boomerang (returning) employees 106, 121–24
Borreltijd! 131
boundary setting 125, 136, 137, 184
budgets 36, 62, 79, 100, 101, 108, 194, 197
  budget reviews 195
burnout 118, 119, 128, 145, 157

CANVAS 99
capitalism 10, 18
card stacking method 61
career breaks 71
  see also sabbaticals
career change (crossroads) 88–94
career change (crossroads) indicators 90–92
career dialogues (conversations) 61, 81, 97–98
career ladders 58, 94–95, 97, 98
career lattices 97–99
career orientation 58, 60, 61–62
career paths (development) 61–62, 74, 75–76, 81, 86, 95, 107, 218
  ecosystem approach 108, 109, 219–20
career transparency 60, 61, 94–95, 97–102, 109, 121–22, 125, 182
Carrey, Jim 223, 226
centres of gravity 171–72
Chaos Monkey 71
ChatGPT 12
check-ins 78, 92–93, 97
checking-out 91
Chouinard, Yvon 29
climate tech startups 29, 30
co-creation 30, 182, 206, 208–22
coffee industry 22–23
collaboration 71, 79, 83–84, 119, 211, 217
collaborative documents 217
commodities 22
community building 214, 225, 227
community engagement programmes 126

compensation 26–27, 34, 61, 96, 98, 122, 127, 135, 146, 207
competency frameworks 61, 79
competition 119
concentric circles 171–72
consulting firms 4, 30, 164, 169, 189, 227
consumer behaviour 21
Corporate Bro 19
'corporate' culture 8–9, 18–21, 47
corporate social responsibility 142
#corporatetok 19
courage 21, 49, 184
Covid-19 pandemic impact xviii–xix, 11, 34, 119–20, 144–45
creativity 69, 128, 155, 157, 159, 160, 180
 see also innovation
'crisis' test 39
cross-functional projects 61, 79, 81, 94, 126
cross-functional skill mapping 100
cultural fit 48, 189
cultural stewardship 84–85
culture 6
 'always-on' 132, 145
 'corporate' 8–9, 18–21, 47
 organizational 27, 48, 75, 82, 84–85, 87, 89, 129, 154, 189, 217
 traditional 96, 98
curiosity 215
customer engagement 140
customer profiles 32, 34
customization 210
cynicism 17, 20, 33–34, 190

daily feedback 216
data collection 108
Dead Rabbit 67
DealMaker 104–05
'deathbed' perspective 69, 70
Deaton, Angus 45–46
decision filters 194–96
decision-making frameworks 184, 213
'departure story' test 38
Dickens, Charles 145
digital platforms 212–13, 217
discretionary effort 134–35, 141–42, 145
discussion threads 212, 217
disengagement 136, 144–45
diversity 81, 208, 210
 see also identity diversification
Dollar Tree 34
dynamic talent ecosystems 220

early purpose 72–74
economic spectrum assessment 35–40

economic value 22
ecosystem approach 75, 108, 109, 219–20
education policies 101–02
education sector 23
'elder statesperson' roles 84
emotional dissonance 138
emotional labour 9, 118–19, 138
emotional labour fatigue 138
emotional wellbeing 45–46, 47, 50, 62–63
 see also positive emotions
employee disengagement 136, 144–45
employee engagement 5–6, 34–35, 40–41, 52, 53–54, 55, 90, 93, 95, 139–40
 career dialogues 97
 and co-creation 30
 Genba AI 31, 141
 and happiness 145
 and retention 10
employee engagement surveys 218
employee experience 168–85
employee happiness 145
employee replacement costs 89
employee retention (turnover) 10, 89, 97, 128
employee value proposition (EVP) 29–30, 34, 171–72
employee wellbeing 45–46, 47, 50, 62–63
 see also mental health organizations
enclosure movement 7
Engels, Friedrich 8
Enron 189
environmental activism 101
ETHOS 212
eudaimonia xvi
Evernote 47
exit interviews 90
experience economy 21, 22, 23, 26–29, 34, 96, 160, 164, 166, 200
 co-creation metrics 218
 economic spectrum assessment 36, 37, 38–39
 identity diversification 127
 operating principles 192
 PERMA model 54–55
 and quiet quitting 142
 reality-ambition gap 179–80
 Shopify 71
 Talentful 116, 122
experimentation 79, 80
exploitation 119, 135, 139, 141
exploration 77, 80–82
external validation 223, 226

Facebook (Meta) 10, 26, 33

facilitation skills 215–16
failure 49
false urgency 72–74
family support 127
Faust syndrome 47
feedback loops 79, 196, 216–17
    implementation 'warning signs' 199–200
    see also check-ins
Feierabend 132
Finance Analyst Rotation programme (Spotify) 99
financial rewards 52, 62, 145–46
    see also compensation
financial services sector 25
fitness industry 23
flexible benefits packages 62
flexible working 61, 125–26, 126–27
    see also work schedules
flow state 52, 141
Fonda, Jane 23
Ford, Henry 8
foundership 157–58
fulfilment 45–63, 223–24, 226–27

Gallacher, Ben 69, 73, 74–76, 78–85, 86, 87, 116–17, 120
Gen X 143
Gen Z 143
Genba AI 31, 140–41
generative dialogue 215, 220
Gilmore, James 21
Give and Take (Grant) 27
Glassdoor 153–54
Goldman Sachs 46–47
goods economy 22, 24
Google 10, 26, 27, 33, 48
    20 per cent time policy 79
Great Resignation (Reflection) xviii, 11

Hagearty, Liz 47–48, 158–59, 163–64, 207–08
happiness, and engagement 145
Harvard Grant Study 50, 52
Hawthorne Studies xv
hedonic adaptation 51
hiring (recruitment) strategies 75, 76, 81, 83, 102, 104, 109, 123, 189
'honest purpose' 170
hospitality sector 25
HR function 10, 34
    see also People Operations function
Hubspot 27
human flourishing xvi
Human Half, The 169
Human Relations movement xv–xvi

humility 21, 215
hybrid roles 80
    see also cross-functional projects

ideal customer profiles 32, 34
identity 115–29, 157
identity diversification 120, 121, 124–29
'identity time' policies 124
identity-work fusion 118–24
ikigai 49
Incompass Labs 104
Industrial Revolution 7–8
innovation 82, 119
    see also creativity
InRehearsal 69, 70, 73, 75, 82, 87, 117
Instagram 19
integrity 188–89
internal forums 217
intrinsic motivation 139, 141
    see also autonomy; mastery
investment 122

job crafting 32, 62, 211
'job for life' mindset 8–9
job loss, impact of 120–21
job orientation 57, 60, 61, 62
Johnson, Olivia 52, 59–60

Kahneman, Daniel 45–46
Kaufman, Bruce 31
Kennedy, John F xiv
Kerr, Steven 161–62
Kerr test 165
Kets de Vries, Manfred F R 47
Khan, Zaid 131
knowledge transfer systems 84, 102, 182
knowledge workers 13, 26, 118
Kotler, Philip 24

language analysis 37–38
leadership (leadership modelling) 77, 82–84, 98, 125, 157, 198–99, 215–16
learning allocation trackers 93–94
learning management systems 93
learning objectives 100
    see also skills building; training courses
learning stipends 79, 124
Lee, Peggy 46
legacy projects 85
LEGO 155
leisure sector 25
life experiences (choices) 67–69
life satisfaction 45–46
life transitions 125
lifetime portfolio approach 74–87

listening 182
location flexibility 126–27

management 79, 135, 200, 218
    see also leadership (leadership modelling)
management consultants 4, 30, 164, 169, 189, 227
manufacturing sector 25
mapping exercises 77–78, 100, 219–220
mass customization 210
mastery 79, 80, 116, 119, 225
Mayo, Elton xv
McCann Group Worldgroup 99
McDonalds 34
meaning 52, 54, 55, 56
meaningful challenge perception 218
mental health organizations 29, 30, 155–56
    see also Olivia
mentoring 61, 62, 77–78, 81, 84–85, 100
Meta (Facebook) 10, 26, 33
metrics (measurement) 36, 107–09, 174, 182, 183–84, 200, 218–19, 220
middle managers 200
Millennials 143
mindset 226–27
misalignment 39, 92, 95, 181–82, 219
    see also authenticity gap; Kerr test
mission relevance ratings 219
mission statements 48, 169–70
mistakes, learning from 122–23
Modern Times 18
'Monday morning' test 38
monthly feedback 216
moral injury 139
motivation 4–5, 139, 141
mutual trust 140

narrative spaces 211–12
Nathwani, Genevieve 45, 46, 48, 91
negativity bias 154
network building 80–81
Neumann, Adam 168
newly developed interests 92
NGOs 30
Noom 22

observation 79
off-boarding 106–07, 121–22, 124–25
    see also exit interviews
Office, The 18
Office Space 18
older employees 144
Olivia 191, 199, 201, 205–06
operating principles 191–94, 198–200
operational metrics 36
operational stability 76, 80
optimal distinctiveness 27

organizational culture 27, 48, 75, 82, 84–85, 87, 89, 129, 154, 189, 217
    traditional 96, 98
    working hours 131–32
    see also 'corporate' culture
organizational identity 118–24
organizational structure 75–76, 98, 183, 208–11
    see also career ladders; career lattices; career paths (development)
outcome tracking 100
outside work interests 115, 124–25, 126–27

Parliamentary Enclosure period 7
Patagonia 29, 34, 35, 71, 101, 183–84
pattern recognition 77–78, 211, 212, 214
peer reviews 79, 104–05
'Peggy Lee' syndrome 46
People Operations function 4, 62
    see also HR function
performance 162–63
performance evaluation (management) systems 62, 104–05, 165, 193, 195
PERMA model 50, 51–57, 62–63
personal background, influence of 3–4, 8–9
personal impact frequency 219
personal orientation (construction) 32, 33, 34
personal projects 81
    see also 20 per cent time policy
personal qualities 75, 76, 81
    see also skills building
Pilates 23
pilot groups 102
Pine, Joe 21, 22, 209–10
planning horizons 91
playbooks 84, 196–97
pluralism 184, 225, 227
    see also outside work interests
Polman, Paul 181
portfolio approach 74–87
positioning triangle test 172–75
positive emotions 51, 53, 54, 55
positive psychology 50
'post wedding' blues 45
practice opportunities 79
present purpose 70–71, 72
process management 200
product mindset 5, 21, 24, 146, 206, 207, 208
productivity paradox 145
profitability 145, 161
project work 80, 81, 84, 85, 218
    approval templates 195
    cross-functional 61, 79, 81, 94, 126
    post-mortems 93
psychological distress 118

psychological safety 141, 181, 209
psychological vulnerability 120–21, 216
Pugh, Abbie 72
pulse surveys 199
purpose and profit paradox 161–62
purpose archaeology 212
purpose as a practice 226–27
purpose 'bucketing' 72, 226
'purpose industrial complex' 5, 227
purpose interpreters 200
purpose mapping exercise 77–78
purpose paradox 137–38, 225–26
purpose renewals 217
purpose 'show-and-tells' 212
purpose-washing 138–42

quarterly retrospectives 216–17
quiet quitting 88, 131–47

/r/antiwork 19, 40–41
reality-ambition gap 175–80
recognition 196, 200
recruitment (hiring) 75, 76, 81, 83, 102, 104, 109, 115, 123, 189
recruitment process outsourcing 115
Reddit 19, 40–41, 88, 169
reflection 77–78, 81, 100, 211
relationships 50, 52, 54–55, 127
research laboratories 30
resilience 49, 76, 120, 128, 221, 227
respect 173–74
restaurant sector 26
retrospectives 216–17
return on investment (ROI) 89–90, 100, 108
returning (boomerang) employees 106, 121–24
reward systems 52, 62, 145–46
    see also compensation
rightsizing 185
rituals 212–13
River, The (Springsteen) 158
Robichaux, Alexi 47
Robusta coffee 22
role definitions 126
role transitions 118
rotation programmes 80, 94, 99–100, 126
Rotational Product Management programme 99

sabbatical eligibility criteria 101
sabbatical funding frameworks 101
sabbatical planning processes 101
sabbaticals 56, 81, 101–02, 126
Salesforce 27
Sana 93, 94
scepticism 92, 199–200
Schönen Feierabend 132

Scientific Management (Taylorism) xv–xvi, 7–8
secondments 80
selective checking-out 91
self-discovery 77, 80–82
self-fulfilment 223–24
senior management observations 79
service economy 22, 23, 24–26, 34, 57, 96, 160, 164–65, 166, 200
    co-creation metrics 218
    economic spectrum assessment 36, 37, 38–39
    Genba AI 141
    identity diversification 127
    operating principles 192
    PERMA model 53–54
    and quiet quitting 142
    reality-ambition gap 178–79
shadowing programmes 79, 94
shame 73, 208
shared ownership 205–22
shareholder value xv, 118
Shopify 71
show-and-tells 212
Silicon Valley 5, 10, 47
Silicon Valley xiv–xv
simulation exercises 79
Sinek, Simon 4
Sisyphus, reimagination of myth 12–13
skill mapping 79, 100, 219–20
skills building 77, 78–80, 218
    see also personal qualities
Slack 17, 47, 90
Slater, Huw 51, 156–57, 191–93, 201, 205–06
Smith, Greg 46–47
social media 19, 131
    see also Meta (Facebook); Reddit; Slack; TikTok
social pressure 117, 120
social purpose 30, 33
Socrates 143
soldiering 8
Sophie 70
SoulCycle 23
specificity 214
spiritual bypass 169
Spotify 26, 99
stakeholder engagement 182–84
stakeholder mapping 184
start-ups 10, 29, 30, 34, 52, 193
status 46
stewardship 84–85
story gathering 211, 214
storytelling 84, 211–12, 213–14, 215–16
storytelling sessions 214
stretch assignments 61

subreddit 40–41
success (achievement) focus 45–63, 73
succession planning 129
Sullivan, Emory 31, 140–41, 147
Sumerian civilization 143
supervisor respect scores 218
surface acting (emotional labour) 9, 118–19, 138
surveys 199, 218
sustainability 31

T-shaped professionals 92, 98, 102–05
    see also cross-functional projects
talent ecosystems 35, 220
Talentful 106, 115, 116, 121–24
tangible experience 173
Taylor, Frederick xv–xvi, 7–8
Taylor, Nick 155
teaching sector 58
team development 82, 83
team meetings 214
team temperature maps 93
tech sector 23, 26–27, 28, 29, 30, 33–34, 52
    see also Genba AI
technology 10, 145, 227–28
    see also AI (artificial intelligence); digital platforms
telos xvi
TikTok 17, 19, 48, 131
Top Five Regrets of Dying, The 69
tracking systems 100, 102
    see also metrics (measurement)
'trade-off' test 38
traditional workplace culture 96, 98
training courses 30, 79
transferable skills 81
transformation economy 22–24, 29–32, 33, 34, 71, 96, 159–60, 164
    and co-creation 209–10, 219
    economic spectrum assessment 36–37, 37–39
    identity diversification 127
    operating principles 192
    PERMA model 55–56
    and quiet quitting 142
    reality-ambition gap 180
    see also work as a calling
transparency 60, 61, 94–95, 97–102, 109, 121–22, 125, 182
trust 123, 139, 140, 141, 182
20 per cent time policy 79
Twitter (X) 19, 26

UN agencies 29, 30

Unilever 181
Unmind 155
urgency 72–74

Vaillant, George 50
value, economic 22
value creation assessment 36–37
values 188, 194, 198–200
values alignment 83, 187–201
values delusion 188–90
Volkswagen 189
vulnerability 120–21, 216

Walmart 25–26
weekly feedback 216
'WEIRD' population 6
wellbeing 46, 47, 50, 62–63
    see also mental health organizations
Wells Fargo 189
WeWork 168, 169
Whereby 212
Whitlock, Andy 168–69, 185, 187, 210–11
'why' approach 4
Wonderbly 155
work xviii, 106, 124
    evolution of 7–12
work as a calling 23, 50, 58–59, 60–61, 62, 118–19, 206, 224
    see also transformation economy
work as a job 23, 25, 26, 57
    see also service economy
work as a product 5, 21, 24, 146, 206, 207, 208
Work for Humans (Lindsley) 21
work-identity fusion 118–24
work impact visibility 218
work orientation framework 50, 57–63
    see also experience economy; service economy; transformation economy
work schedules 218
work shadowing 79, 94
working hours 61, 131–32
WorkLife with Adam Grant (Grant) 95
workshops 210–11
Wrzesniewski, Amy 23, 26, 28, 30, 32, 50, 57–62, 206, 224
Wu, Howard 48–49

X (Twitter) 19, 26

younger employees 20, 143–46
    see also Gen Z; Millennials

Zitron, Ed 19–20, 133

Looking for another book?

Explore our award-winning books from global business experts in Human Resources, Learning and Development

Scan the code to browse

www.koganpage.com/hr-learning-development

Also from Kogan Page

Jessica Zwaan

BUILT FOR PEOPLE

Transform your employee experience using product management principles

ISBN: 9781398608023

www.koganpage.com

From 4 December 2025 the EU Responsible Person (GPSR) is:
eucomply oÜ, Pärnu mnt. 139b – 14, 11317 Tallinn, Estonia
www.eucompliancepartner.com